THE THEORY OF THE BUSINESS

HARVARD BUSINESS REVIEW
CLASSICS

THE THEORY OF THE BUSINESS

Peter F. Drucker

Harvard Business Review Press
Boston, Massachusetts

Copyright 2017 Harvard Business School Publishing Corporation
Originally published in *Harvard Business Review* in September–October 1994
Reprint #94506
All rights reserved

Printed in the United States of America

10 9 8 7 6 5 4 3 2 1

The web addresses referenced in this book were live and correct at the time of the book's publication but may be subject to change.

Cataloging-in-Publication data is forthcoming.

ISBN: 978-1-63369-252-7
eISBN: 978-1-63369-253-4

The paper used in this publication meets the requirements of the American National Standard for Permanence of Paper for Publications and Documents in Libraries and Archives Z39.48-1992.

THE HARVARD BUSINESS REVIEW CLASSICS SERIES

Since 1922, *Harvard Business Review* has been a leading source of breakthrough ideas in management practice—many of which still speak to and influence us today. The HBR Classics series now offers you the opportunity to make these seminal pieces a part of your permanent management library. Each volume contains a groundbreaking idea that has shaped best practices and inspired countless managers around the world—and will change how you think about the business world today.

THE THEORY OF THE BUSINESS

Not in a very long time—not, perhaps, since the late 1940s or early 1950s—have there been as many new major management techniques as there are today: downsizing, outsourcing, total quality management, economic value analysis, benchmarking, reengineering. Each is a powerful tool. But, with the exceptions of outsourcing and reengineering, these tools are designed primarily to do differently what is already being done. They are "how to do" tools.

Yet "what to do" is increasingly becoming the central challenge facing managements, especially those of big companies that have enjoyed long-term success. The story is a familiar one: a company that was a superstar only yesterday finds itself stagnating and frustrated, in trouble and, often, in a seemingly unmanageable crisis. This phenomenon is by no means confined to the United States. It has become common in Japan and Germany, the Netherlands and France, Italy and Sweden. And it occurs just as often outside business—in labor unions, government agencies, hospitals, museums, and churches. In fact, it seems even less tractable in those areas.

The root cause of nearly every one of these crises is not that things are being done poorly. It is not even that the wrong things are being done. Indeed, in most cases, the *right* things are being done—but fruitlessly. What accounts for this apparent paradox? The assumptions on which the organization has been built and is being run no longer fit reality. These are the assumptions that shape any organization's behavior, dictate its decisions about what to do and what not to do, and define what the organization considers meaningful results. These assumptions are about markets. They are about identifying customers and competitors, their values and behavior. They are about technology and its dynamics, about a company's strengths and weaknesses. These assumptions are about what a company gets paid for. They are what I call a company's *theory of the business*.

Every organization, whether a business or not, has a theory of the business. Indeed, a valid theory that is clear, consistent, and focused is extraordinarily powerful. In 1809, for instance, German statesman and scholar Wilhelm von Humboldt founded the University of Berlin on a radically new theory of the university. And for more than 100 years, until the rise of Hitler, his theory defined the German university, especially in scholarship and scientific research. In 1870, Georg Siemens, the architect and first CEO of Deutsche Bank, the first universal bank, had an equally clear theory of the business: to use entrepreneurial finance to unify a still rural and splintered Germany through industrial development. Within 20 years of its founding, Deutsche Bank had become Europe's premier financial institution, which it has remained to this day in spite of two world wars, inflation, and Hitler. And, in the 1870s, Mitsubishi was founded on a clear and completely new theory of the business, which within 10 years made it the leader in an emerging Japan and within another 20 years made it one of the first truly multinational businesses.

Similarly, the theory of the business explains both the success of companies like General Motors and IBM, which have dominated the U.S. economy for the latter half of the twentieth century, and the challenges they have faced. In fact, what underlies the current malaise of so many large and successful organizations worldwide is that their theory of the business no longer works.

Whenever a big organization gets into trouble–and especially if it has been successful for many years–people blame sluggishness, complacency, arrogance, mammoth bureaucracies. A plausible explanation? Yes. But rarely the relevant or correct one. Consider the two most visible and widely reviled "arrogant bureaucracies" among large U.S. companies that have recently been in trouble.

Since the earliest days of the computer, it had been an article of faith at IBM that the computer would go the way of electricity. The future, IBM knew, and could prove with scientific rigor, lay with the central station, the ever-more-powerful mainframe into which a huge number of users could plug. Everything—economics, the logic of information, technology—led to that conclusion. But then, suddenly, when it seemed as if such a central-station, main frame-based information system was actually coming into existence, two young men came up with the first personal computer. Every computer maker knew that the PC was absurd. It did not have the memory, the database, the speed, or the computing ability necessary to succeed. Indeed, every computer maker knew that the PC had to fail—the conclusion reached

by Xerox only a few years earlier, when its
research team had actually built the first PC.
But when that misbegotten monstrosity—
first the Apple, then the Macintosh—came
on the market, people not only loved it, they
bought it.

Every big, successful company throughout history, when confronted with such a
surprise, has refused to accept it. "It's a
stupid fad and will be gone in three years,"
said the CEO of Zeiss upon seeing the new
Kodak Brownie in 1888, when the German
company was as dominant in the world photographic market as IBM would be in the
computer market a century later. Most mainframe makers responded in the same way.
The list was long: Control Data, Univac,

Burroughs, and NCR in the United States; Siemens, Nixdorf, Machines Bull, and ICL in Europe; Hitachi and Fujitsu in Japan. IBM, the overlord of mainframes with as much in sales as all the other computer makers put together and with record profits, could have reacted in the same way. In fact, it *should* have. Instead, IBM immediately accepted the PC as the new reality. Almost overnight, it brushed aside all its proven and time-tested policies, rules, and regulations and set up not one but two competing teams to design an even simpler PC. A couple of years later, IBM had become the world's largest PC manufacturer and the industry standard setter.

There is absolutely no precedent for this achievement in all of business history; it hardly argues bureaucracy, sluggishness, or arrogance. Yet despite unprecedented flexibility, agility, and humility, IBM was floundering a few years later in both the mainframe and the PC business. It was suddenly unable to move, to take decisive action, to change.

The case of GM is equally perplexing. In the early 1980s—the very years in which GM's main business, passenger automobiles, seemed almost paralyzed—the company acquired two large businesses: Hughes Electronics and Ross Perot's Electronic Data Systems. Analysts generally considered both companies to be mature and chided GM for grossly overpaying for them. Yet, within a few short years, GM had more than tripled the revenues and profits of the allegedly mature EDS. And ten years later, in 1994, EDS had a market value six times the amount that GM had paid for it and ten times its original revenues and profits.

Similarly, GM bought Hughes Electronics —a huge but profitless company involved exclusively in defense—just before the defense industry collapsed. Under GM management, Hughes has actually increased its defense profits and has become the only big defense contractor to move successfully into large-scale nondefense work. Remarkably, the same bean counters who had been so ineffectual in the automobile business—30-year GM veterans who had never worked for any other company or, for that matter, outside of finance and accounting departments—were the ones who achieved those startling results. And in the two acquisitions, they simply applied policies, practices, and procedures that had already been used by GM.

This story is a familiar one at GM. Since the company's founding in a flurry of acquisitions 80 years ago, one of its core competencies has been to "overpay" for well-performing but mature businesses—as it did for Buick, AC Spark Plug, and Fisher Body in those early years—and then turn them into world-class champions. Very few companies have been able to match GM's performance in making successful acquisitions, and GM surely did not accomplish those feats by being bureaucratic, sluggish, or arrogant. Yet what worked so beautifully in those businesses that GM knew nothing about failed miserably in GM itself.

What can explain the fact that at both IBM and GM the policies, practices, and behaviors that worked for decades—and in the case of GM are still working well when applied to something new and different—no longer work for the organization in which and for which they were developed? The realities that each organization actually faces have changed quite dramatically from those that each still assumes it lives with. Put another way, reality has changed, but the theory of the business has not changed with it.

Before its agile response to the new reality of the PC, IBM had once before turned its basic strategy around overnight. In 1950, Univac, then the world's leading computer company, showed the prototype of the first machine designed to be a multipurpose computer. All earlier designs had been for single-purpose machines. IBM's own two earlier computers, built in the late 1930s and 1946, respectively, performed astronomical calculations only. And the machine that IBM had on the drawing board in 1950, intended for the SAGE air defense system in the Canadian Arctic, had only one purpose: early identification of enemy aircraft. IBM immediately scrapped its strategy of developing advanced single-purpose machines; it put its best engineers to work on perfecting the Univac architecture and, from it, designing the first multipurpose computer able to be manufactured (rather than handcrafted) and serviced. Three years later, IBM had become the world's dominant computer maker and standard-bearer. IBM did not create the computer. But in 1950, its flexibility, speed, and humility created the computer *industry*.

However, the same assumptions that had helped IBM prevail in 1950 proved to be its undoing 30 years later. In the 1970s, IBM assumed that there was such a thing as a "computer," just as it had in the 1950s. But the emergence of the PC invalidated that assumption. Mainframe computers and PCs are, in fact, no more one entity than are generating stations and electric toasters. The latter, while different, are interdependent and complementary. In contrast, mainframe computers and PCs are primarily competitors. And, in their basic definition of *information*, they actually contradict each other: for the mainframe, information means memory; for the brainless PC, it means software. Building generating stations and making toasters must be run as separate businesses, but they can be owned by the same corporate entity, as General Electric did for decades. In contrast, mainframe computers and PCs probably cannot coexist in the same corporate entity.

IBM tried to combine the two. But because the PC was the fastest growing part of the business, IBM could not subordinate it to the mainframe business. As a result, the company could not optimize the mainframe business. And because the mainframe was still the cash cow, IBM could not optimize the PC business. In the end, the assumption that a computer is a computer—or, more prosaically, that the industry is hardware driven—paralyzed IBM.

GM had an even more powerful, and successful, theory of the business than IBM had, one that made GM the world's largest and most profitable manufacturing organization. The company did not have one setback in 70 years—a record unmatched in business history. GM's theory combined in one seamless web assumptions about markets and customers with assumptions about core competencies and organizational structure.

Since the early 1920s, GM assumed that the U.S. automobile market was homogeneous in its values and segmented by extremely stable income groups. The resale value of the "good" used car was the only independent variable under management's control. High trade-in values enabled customers to upgrade their new-car purchases to the next category—in other words, to cars with higher profit margins. According to this theory, frequent or radical changes in models could only depress trade-in values.

Internally, these market assumptions went hand in hand with assumptions about how production should be organized to yield the biggest market share and the highest profit. In GM's case, the answer was long runs of mass-produced cars with a minimum of changes each model year, resulting in the largest number of uniform yearly models on the market at the lowest fixed cost per car.

GM's management then translated these assumptions about market and production into a structure of semiautonomous divisions, each focusing on one income segment and each arranged so that its highest priced model overlapped with the next division's lowest priced model, thus almost forcing people to trade up, provided that used-car prices were high.

For 70 years, this theory worked like a charm. Even in the depths of the Depression,

GM never suffered a loss while steadily gaining market share. But in the late 1970s, its assumptions about the market and about production became invalid. The market was fragmenting into highly volatile "lifestyle" segments. Income became one factor among many in the buying decision, not the only one. At the same time, lean manufacturing created an economics of small scale. It made short runs and variations in models less costly and more profitable than long runs of uniform products.

GM knew all this but simply could not believe it. (GM's union still doesn't.) Instead, the company tried to patch things over. It maintained the existing divisions based on income segmentation, but each division now offered a "car for every purse."

It tried to compete with lean manufacturing's economics of small scale by automating the large-scale, long-run mass production (losing some $30 billion in the process). Contrary to popular belief, GM patched things over with prodigious energy, hard work, and lavish investments of time and money. But patching only confused the customer, the dealer, and the employees and management of GM itself. In the meantime, GM neglected its *real* growth market, where it had leadership and would have been almost unbeatable: light trucks and minivans.

A theory of the business has three parts. First, there are assumptions about the environment of the organization: society and its structure, the market, the customer, and technology.

Second, there are assumptions about the specific mission of the organization. Sears, Roebuck and Company, in the years during and following World War I, defined its mission as being the informed buyer for the American family. A decade later, Marks and Spencer in Great Britain defined its mission as being the change agent in British society by becoming the first classless retailer. AT&T, again in the years during and immediately after World War I, defined its role as ensuring that every U.S. family and business have access to a telephone. An organization's mission need not be so ambitious. GM envisioned a far more modest role—as the leader in "terrestrial motorized transportation equipment," in the words of Alfred P. Sloan, Jr.

Third, there are assumptions about the core competencies needed to accomplish the organization's mission. For example, West Point, founded in 1802, defined its core competence as the ability to turn out leaders who deserve trust. Marks and Spencer, around 1930, defined its core competence as the ability to identify, design, and develop the merchandise it sold, instead of as the ability to buy. AT&T, around 1920, defined its core competence as technical leadership that would enable the company to improve service continuously while steadily lowering rates.

The assumptions about environment define what an organization is paid for. The assumptions about mission define what an organization considers to be meaningful results; in other words, they point to how it envisions itself making a difference in the economy and in the society at large. Finally, the assumptions about core competencies define where an organization must excel in order to maintain leadership.

Of course, all this sounds deceptively simple. It usually takes years of hard work, thinking, and experimenting to reach a clear, consistent, and valid theory of the business. Yet to be successful, every organization must work one out.

What are the specifications of a valid theory of the business? There are four.

1. *The assumptions about environment, mission, and core competencies must fit reality.* When four penniless young men from Manchester, England, Simon Marks and his three brothers-in-law, decided in the early 1920s that a humdrum penny bazaar should become an agent of social change, World War I had profoundly shaken their country's class structure. It had also created masses of new buyers for good-quality, stylish, but cheap merchandise like lingerie, blouses, and stockings—Marks and

Spencer's first successful product categories. Marks and Spencer then systematically set to work developing brand-new and unheard-of core competencies. Until then, the core competence of a merchant was the ability to buy well. Marks and Spencer decided that it was the merchant, rather than the manufacturer, who knew the customer. Therefore, the merchant, not the manufacturer, should design the products, develop them, and find producers to make the goods to his design, specifications, and costs. This new definition of the merchant took five to eight years to develop and make acceptable to traditional suppliers, who had always seen themselves as "manufacturers," not "subcontractors."

2. *The assumptions in all three areas have to fit one another.* This was perhaps GM's greatest strength in the long decades of its ascendancy. Its assumptions about the market and about the optimum manufacturing process were a perfect fit. GM decided in the mid-1920s that it also required new and as-yet-unheard-of core competencies: financial control of the manufacturing process and a theory of capital allocations. As a result, GM invented modern cost accounting and

the first rational capital-allocation process.

3. *The theory of the business must be known and understood throughout the organization.* That is easy in an organization's early days. But as it becomes successful, an organization tends increasingly to take its theory for granted, becoming less and less conscious of it. Then the organization becomes sloppy. It begins to cut corners. It begins to pursue what is expedient rather than what is right. It stops thinking. It stops questioning. It remembers the answers but has forgotten the questions. The theory of

the business becomes "culture." But culture is no substitute for discipline, and the theory of the business is a discipline.

4. *The theory of the business has to be tested constantly.* It is not graven on tablets of stone. It is a hypothesis. And it is a hypothesis about things that are in constant flux—society, markets, customers, technology. And so, built into the theory of the business must be the ability to change itself.

Some theories of the business are so powerful that they last for a long time. But being

human artifacts, they don't last forever,
and, indeed, today they rarely last for very
long at all. Eventually every theory of the
business becomes obsolete and then invalid.
That is precisely what happened to those
on which the great U.S. businesses of the
1920s were built. It happened to the GMs
and the AT&Ts. It has happened to IBM. It
is clearly happening today to Deutsche Bank
and its theory of the universal bank. It is also
clearly happening to the rapidly unraveling
Japanese *keiretsu*.

The first reaction of an organization
whose theory is becoming obsolete is almost
always a defensive one. The tendency is to
put one's head in the sand and pretend that
nothing is happening. The next reaction is

an attempt to patch, as GM did in the early
1980s or as Deutsche Bank is doing today.
Indeed, the sudden and completely unexpected crisis of one big German company
after another for which Deutsche Bank is
the "house bank" indicates that its theory
no longer works. That is, Deutsche Bank
no longer does what it was designed to do:
provide effective governance of the modern
corporation.

But patching never works. Instead, when
a theory shows the first signs of becoming
obsolete, it is time to start thinking again, to
ask again which assumptions about the environment, mission, and core competencies
reflect reality most accurately—with the clear
premise that our historically transmitted

assumptions, those with which all of us grew up, no longer suffice.

What, then, needs to be done? There is a need for preventive care—that is, for building into the organization systematic monitoring and testing of its theory of the business. There is a need for early diagnosis. Finally, there is a need to rethink a theory that is stagnating and to take effective action in order to change policies and practices, bringing the organization's behavior in line with the new realities of its environment, with a new definition of its mission, and with new core competencies to be developed and acquired.

PREVENTIVE CARE

There are only two preventive measures. But,
if used consistently, they should keep an organization alert and capable of rapidly changing
itself and its theory. The first measure is what
I call *abandonment*. Every three years, an
organization should challenge every product,
every service, every policy, every distribution
channel with the question, If we were not in
it already, would we be going into it now? By
questioning accepted policies and routines,
the organization forces itself to think about its
theory. It forces itself to test assumptions. It
forces itself to ask: Why didn't this work, even
though it looked so promising when we went
into it five years ago? Is it because we made a

mistake? Is it because we did the wrong things? Or is it because the right things didn't work?

Without systematic and purposeful abandonment, an organization will be overtaken by events. It will squander its best resources on things it should never have been doing or should no longer do. As a result, it will lack the resources, especially capable people, needed to exploit the opportunities that arise when markets, technologies, and core competencies change. In other words, it will be unable to respond constructively to the opportunities that are created when its theory of the business becomes obsolete.

The second preventive measure is to study what goes on outside the business, and especially to study *noncustomers*. Walk-around management became fashionable a few years back. It is important. And so is knowing as much as possible about one's customers—the area, perhaps, where information technology is making the most rapid advances. But the first signs of fundamental change rarely appear within one's own organization or among one's own customers. Almost always they show up first among one's noncustomers. Noncustomers always outnumber customers. Wal-Mart, today's retail giant, has 14% of the U.S. consumer-goods market. That means 86% of the market is noncustomers.

In fact, the best recent example of the importance of the noncustomer is U.S. department stores. At their peak some 20 years ago, department stores served 30% of the U.S. nonfood retail market. They questioned their customers constantly, studied them, surveyed them. But they paid no attention to the 70% of the market who were not their customers. They saw no reason why they should. Their theory of the business assumed that most people who could afford to shop in department stores did. Fifty years ago, that assumption fit reality. But when the baby boomers came of age, it ceased to be valid. For the dominant group among baby boomers—women in educated two-income families—it was not money that determined where to shop. Time was the primary factor, and this generation's women could not afford to spend their time shopping in department stores. Because department stores looked only at their own customers, they did not recognize this change until a few years ago. By then, business was already drying up. And it was too late to get the baby boomers back. The department stores learned the hard way that although being customer driven is vital, it is not enough. An organization must be market driven too.

EARLY DIAGNOSIS

To diagnose problems early, managers must pay attention to the warning signs. A theory of the business always becomes obsolete when an organization attains its original objectives. Attaining one's objectives, then, is not cause for celebration; it is cause for new thinking.

AT&T accomplished its mission to give every U.S. family and business access to the telephone by the mid-1950s. Some executives then said it was time to reassess the theory of the business and, for instance, separate local service—where the objectives had been reached—from growing and future businesses, beginning with long-distance service and extending into global telecommunications. Their arguments went unheeded, and a few years later AT&T began to flounder, only to be rescued by antitrust, which did by fiat what the company's management had refused to do voluntarily.

Rapid growth is another sure sign of crisis in an organization's theory. Any organization that doubles or triples in size within a fairly short period of time has necessarily outgrown its theory. Even Silicon Valley has learned that beer bashes are no longer adequate for communication once a company has grown so big that people have to wear name tags. But such growth challenges much deeper assumptions, policies, and habits. To continue in health, let alone grow, the organization has to ask itself again the questions about its environment, mission, and core competencies.

There are two more clear signals that an organization's theory of the business is no longer valid. One is unexpected success—whether one's own or a competitor's. The other is unexpected failure—again, whether one's own or a competitor's.

At the same time that Japanese automobile imports had Detroit's Big Three on the ropes, Chrysler registered a totally unexpected success. Its traditional passenger cars were losing market share even faster than GM's and Ford's were. But sales of its Jeep and its new minivans—an almost accidental development—skyrocketed. At the time, GM was the leader of the U.S. light-truck market and unchallenged in the design and quality of its products, but it wasn't paying any attention to its light-truck capacity. After all, minivans and light trucks had always been classified as commercial rather than passenger vehicles in traditional statistics, even though most of them are now being bought as passenger vehicles. However, had it paid attention to the success of its weaker competitor, Chrysler, GM might have realized much earlier that its assumptions about both its market and its core competencies were no longer valid. From the beginning, the minivan and light-truck market was not an income-class market and was little influenced by trade-in prices. And, paradoxically, light trucks were the one area in which GM, 15 years ago, had already moved quite far toward what we now call lean manufacturing.

Unexpected failure is as much a warning as unexpected success and should be taken as seriously as a 60-year-old man's first "minor" heart attack. Sixty years ago, in the midst of the Depression, Sears decided that automobile insurance had become an "accessory" rather than a financial product and that selling it would therefore fit its mission as being the informed buyer for the American family. Everyone thought Sears was crazy. But automobile insurance became Sears's most profitable business almost instantly. Twenty years later, in the 1950s, Sears decided that diamond rings had become a necessity rather than a luxury, and the company became the world's largest—and probably most profitable—diamond retailer. It was only logical for Sears to decide in 1981 that investment products had become consumer goods for the American family. It bought Dean Witter and moved its offices into Sears stores. The move was a total disaster. The U.S. public clearly did not consider its financial needs to be "consumer products." When Sears finally gave up and decided to run Dean Witter as a separate business outside Sears stores, Dean Witter at once began to blossom. In 1992, Sears sold it at a tidy profit.

Had Sears seen its failure to become the American family's supplier of investments as a failure of its theory and not as an isolated incident, it might have begun to restructure and reposition itself ten years earlier than it actually did, when it still had substantial market leadership. For Sears might then have seen, as several of its competitors like J.C. Penney immediately did, that the Dean Witter failure threw into doubt the entire concept of market homogeneity—the very concept on which Sears and other mass retailers had based their strategy for years.

CURE

Traditionally, we have searched for the miracle worker with a magic wand to turn an ailing organization around. To establish, maintain, and restore a theory, however, does not require a Genghis Khan or a Leonardo da Vinci in the executive suite. It is not genius; it is hard work. It is not being clever; it is being conscientious. It is what CEOs are paid for.

There are indeed quite a few CEOs who have successfully changed their theory of the business. The CEO who built Merck into the world's most successful pharmaceutical business by focusing solely on the research and development of patented, high-margin breakthrough drugs radically changed the company's theory by acquiring a large distributor of generic and nonprescription drugs. He did so without a "crisis," while Merck was ostensibly doing very well. Similarly, a few years ago, the new CEO of Sony, the world's best-known manufacturer of consumer electronic hardware, changed the company's theory of the business. He acquired a Hollywood movie production company and, with that acquisition, shifted the organization's center of gravity from being a hardware manufacturer in search of software to being a software producer that creates a market demand for hardware.

But for every one of these apparent miracle workers, there are scores of equally capable CEOs whose organizations stumble. We can't rely on miracle workers to rejuvenate an obsolete theory of the business any more than we can rely on them to cure other types of serious illness. And when one talks to these supposed miracle workers, they deny vehemently that they act by charisma, vision, or, for that matter, the laying on of hands. They start out with diagnosis and analysis. They accept that attaining objectives and rapid growth demand a serious rethinking of the theory of the business. They do not dismiss unexpected failure as the result of a subordinate's incompetence or as an accident but treat it as a symptom of "systems failure." They do not take credit for unexpected success but treat it as a challenge to their assumptions.

They accept that a theory's obsolescence is a degenerative and, indeed, life-threatening disease. And they know and accept the surgeon's time-tested principle, the oldest principle of effective decision making: A degenerative disease will not be cured by procrastination. It requires decisive action.

ABOUT THE AUTHOR

Peter F. Drucker was a writer, consultant, and professor of social science and management at Claremont Graduate University in California. His thirty-nine books have been published in more than seventy languages. He founded the Peter F. Drucker Foundation for Nonprofit Management, and counseled thirteen governments, public services institutions, and major corporations.

Article Summary

Idea in Brief

In his thirty-first article for HBR, Peter F. Drucker argues that what underlies the current malaise of so many large and successful organizations world-wide is that their theory of the business no longer works. The story is a familiar one: a company that was a superstar only yesterday finds itself stag-nating and frustrated, in trouble and, often, in a seemingly unmanageable crisis. The root cause of nearly every one of these crises is not that things are being done poorly. It is not even that the wrong things are being done. Indeed, in most cases, the right things are being done—but fruitlessly.

What accounts for this apparent paradox? The assumptions on which the organization has been built and is being run no longer fit reality. These are the assumptions that shape any organization's behavior, dictate its decisions about what to do and what not to do, and define what an organization considers meaningful results. These assumptions are what Drucker calls a company's theory of the business.

Every organization, whether a business or not, has a theory of the business. The theory of the business explains both the successes of companies like General Motors and IBM, which have dominated the U.S. economy for the latter half of the twentieth century, and the challenges they have faced.

Some theories of the business are so powerful that they last for a long time. But being human artifacts, they don't last forever, and today they rarely last for very long at all. Eventually, every theory of the business becomes obsolete and then invalid. When a theory shows the first signs of becoming obsolete, it is time to start rethinking the theory, with the clear premise that our historically transmitted assumptions no longer suffice.

The most important management ideas all in one place.

We hope you enjoyed this book from *Harvard Business Review*. For the best ideas HBR has to offer turn to HBR's 10 Must Reads Boxed Set. From books on leadership and strategy to managing yourself and others, this 6-book collection delivers articles on the most essential business topics to help you succeed.

HBR's 10 Must Reads Series

The definitive collection of ideas and best practices on our most sought-after topics from the best minds in business.

- Change Management
- Collaboration
- Communication
- Emotional Intelligence
- Innovation
- Leadership
- Making Smart Decisions

- Managing Across Cultures
- Managing People
- Managing Yourself
- Strategic Marketing
- Strategy
- Teams
- The Essentials

hbr.org/mustreads

Buy for your team, clients, or event.
Visit hbr.org/bulksales for quantity discount rates.

WHAT MAKES AN
EFFECTIVE EXECUTIVE

HARVARD BUSINESS REVIEW
CLASSICS

WHAT MAKES AN
EFFECTIVE EXECUTIVE

Peter F. Drucker

Harvard Business Review Press
Boston, Massachusetts

Copyright 2017 Harvard Business School Publishing Corporation
Originally published in *Harvard Business Review* in June 2004
Reprint #R0406C
All rights reserved

Printed in the United States of America

10 9 8 7 6 5 4 3 2

The web addresses referenced in this book were live and correct at the time of the book's publication but may be subject to change.

Cataloging-in-Publication data is forthcoming.

ISBN: 978-1-63369-254-1
eISBN: 978-1-63369-255-8

The paper used in this publication meets the requirements of the American National Standard for Permanence of Paper for Publications and Documents in Libraries and Archives Z39.48-1992.

THE HARVARD BUSINESS REVIEW CLASSICS SERIES

Since 1922, *Harvard Business Review* has been a leading source of breakthrough ideas in management practice—many of which still speak to and influence us today. The HBR Classics series now offers you the opportunity to make these seminal pieces a part of your permanent management library. Each volume contains a groundbreaking idea that has shaped best practices and inspired countless managers around the world—and will change how you think about the business world today.

WHAT MAKES AN
EFFECTIVE EXECUTIVE

An effective executive does not need to be a leader in the sense that the term is now most commonly used. Harry Truman did not have one ounce of charisma, for example, yet he was among the most effective chief executives in U.S. history. Similarly, some of the best business and nonprofit CEOs I've worked with over a 65-year consulting career were not stereotypical leaders. They were all over the map in terms of their personalities, attitudes, values, strengths, and weaknesses. They ranged from extroverted to nearly reclusive, from easygoing to controlling, from generous to parsimonious.

What made them all effective is that they followed the same eight practices:

- They asked, "What needs to be done?"

- They asked, "What is right for the enterprise?"

- They developed action plans.

- They took responsibility for decisions.

- They took responsibility for communicating.

- They were focused on opportunities rather than problems.

- They ran productive meetings.

- They thought and said "we" rather than "I."

The first two practices gave them the knowledge they needed. The next four helped them convert this knowledge into effective action. The last two ensured that the whole organization felt responsible and accountable.

GET THE KNOWLEDGE YOU NEED

The first practice is to ask what needs to be done. Note that the question is not "What do I want to do?" Asking what has to be done, and taking the question seriously, is crucial for managerial success. Failure to ask this question will render even the ablest executive ineffectual.

When Truman became president in 1945, he knew exactly what he wanted to do: complete the economic and social reforms of Roosevelt's New Deal, which had been deferred by World War II. As soon as he asked what needed to be done, though, Truman realized that foreign affairs had absolute priority. He organized his working day so that it began with tutorials on foreign policy by the secretaries of state and defense. As a result, he became the most effective president in foreign affairs the United States has ever known. He contained Communism in both Europe and Asia and, with the Marshall Plan, triggered 50 years of worldwide economic growth.

Similarly, Jack Welch realized that what needed to be done at General Electric when he took over as chief executive was not the overseas expansion he wanted to launch. It was getting rid of GE businesses that, no matter how profitable, could not be number one or number two in their industries.

The answer to the question "What needs to be done?" almost always contains more than one urgent task. But effective executives do not splinter themselves. They concentrate on one task if at all possible. If they are among those people—a sizable minority—who work best with a change of pace in their working day, they pick two tasks. I have never encountered an executive who remains effective while tackling more than two tasks at a time. Hence, after asking what needs to be done, the effective executive sets priorities and sticks to them. For a CEO, the priority task might be redefining the company's mission. For a unit head, it might be redefining the unit's relationship with headquarters. Other tasks, no matter how important or appealing, are postponed. However, after completing the original top-priority task, the executive resets priorities rather than moving on to number two from the original list. He asks, "What must be done now?" This generally results in new and different priorities.

To refer again to America's best-known CEO: Every five years, according to his autobiography, Jack Welch asked himself, "What needs to be done *now*?" And every time, he came up with a new and different priority.

But Welch also thought through another issue before deciding where to concentrate his efforts for the next five years. He asked himself which of the two or three tasks at the top of the list he himself was best suited to undertake. Then he concentrated on that task; the others he delegated. Effective executives try to focus on jobs they'll do especially well. They know that enterprises perform if top management performs—and don't if it doesn't.

Effective executives' second practice—fully as important as the first—is to ask, "Is this the right thing for the enterprise?" They do not ask if it's right for the owners, the stock price, the employees, or the executives. Of course they know that shareholders, employees, and executives are important constituencies who have to support a decision, or at least acquiesce in it, if the choice is to be effective. They know that the share price is important not only for the shareholders but also for the enterprise, since the price/earnings ratio sets the cost of capital. But they also know that a decision that isn't right for the enterprise will ultimately not be right for any of the stakeholders.

This second practice is especially important for executives at family owned or family run businesses—the majority of businesses in every country—particularly when they're making decisions about people. In the successful family company, a relative is promoted only if he or she is measurably superior to all nonrelatives on the same level. At DuPont, for instance, all top managers (except the controller and lawyer) were family members in the early years when the firm was run as a family business. All male descendants of the founders were entitled to entry-level jobs at the company. Beyond the entrance level, a family member got a promotion only if a panel composed primarily of nonfamily managers judged the person to be superior in ability and performance to all other employees at the same level. The same rule was observed for a century in the highly successful British family business J. Lyons & Company (now part of a major conglomerate) when it dominated the British food-service and hotel industries.

Asking "What is right for the enterprise?" does not guarantee that the right decision will be made. Even the most brilliant executive is human and thus prone to mistakes and prejudices. But failure to ask the question virtually guarantees the *wrong* decision.

WRITE AN ACTION PLAN

Executives are doers; they execute. Knowledge is useless to executives until it has been translated into deeds. But before springing into action, the executive needs to plan his course. He needs to think about desired results, probable restraints, future revisions, check-in points, and implications for how he'll spend his time.

First, the executive defines desired results by asking: "What contributions should the enterprise expect from me over the next 18 months to two years? What results will I commit to? With what deadlines?" Then he considers the restraints on action: "Is this course of action ethical? Is it acceptable within the organization? Is it legal? Is it compatible with the mission, values, and policies of the organization?" Affirmative answers don't guarantee that the action will be effective. But violating these restraints is certain to make it both wrong and ineffectual.

The action plan is a statement of intentions rather than a commitment. It must not become a straitjacket. It should be revised often, because every success creates new opportunities. So does every failure. The same is true for changes in the business environment, in the market, and especially in people within the enterprise—all these changes demand that the plan be revised. A written plan should anticipate the need for flexibility.

In addition, the action plan needs to create a system for checking the results against the expectations. Effective executives usually build two such checks into their action plans. The first check comes halfway through the plan's time period; for example, at nine months. The second occurs at the end, before the next action plan is drawn up.

Finally, the action plan has to become the basis for the executive's time management.

Time is an executive's scarcest and most precious resource. And organizations—whether government agencies, businesses, or nonprofits—are inherently time wasters. The action plan will prove useless unless it's allowed to determine how the executive spends his or her time.

Napoleon allegedly said that no successful battle ever followed its plan. Yet Napoleon also planned every one of his battles, far more meticulously than any earlier general had done. Without an action plan, the executive becomes a prisoner of events. And without check-ins to reexamine the plan as events unfold, the executive has no way of knowing which events really matter and which are only noise.

ACT

When they translate plans into action, executives need to pay particular attention to decision making, communication, opportunities (as opposed to problems), and meetings. I'll consider these one at a time.

Take Responsibility for Decisions

A decision has not been made until people know:

- the name of the person accountable for carrying it out;

- the deadline;

- the names of the people who will be affected by the decision and therefore have to know about, understand, and approve it—or at least not be strongly opposed to it—and

- the names of the people who have to be informed of the decision, even if they are not directly affected by it.

An extraordinary number of organizational decisions run into trouble because these bases aren't covered. One of my clients, 30 years ago, lost its leadership position in the fast-growing Japanese market because the company, after deciding to enter into a joint venture with a new Japanese partner, never made clear who was to inform the purchasing agents that the partner defined its specifications in meters and kilograms rather than feet and pounds—and nobody ever did relay that information.

It's just as important to review decisions periodically—at a time that's been agreed on in advance—as it is to make them carefully in the first place. That way, a poor decision can be corrected before it does real damage. These reviews can cover anything from the results to the assumptions underlying the decision.

Such a review is especially important for the most crucial and most difficult of all decisions, the ones about hiring or promoting people. Studies of decisions about people show that only one-third of such choices turn out to be truly successful. One-third are likely to be draws—neither successes nor outright failures. And one-third are failures, pure and simple. Effective executives know this and check-up (six to nine months later) on the results of their people decisions. If they find that a decision has not had the desired results, they don't conclude that the person has not performed. They conclude, instead, that they themselves made a mistake. In a well-managed enterprise, it is understood that people who fail in a new job, especially after a promotion, may not be the ones to blame.

Executives also owe it to the organization and to their fellow workers not to tolerate nonperforming individuals in important jobs. It may not be the employees' fault that they are underperforming, but even so, they have to be removed. People who have failed in a new job should be given the choice to go

back to a job at their former level and salary.
This option is rarely exercised; such people,
as a rule, leave voluntarily, at least when
their employers are U.S. firms. But the very
existence of the option can have a powerful
effect, encouraging people to leave safe,
comfortable jobs and take risky new assignments. The organization's performance
depends on employees' willingness to take
such chances.

A systematic decision review can be a
powerful tool for self-development, too.
Checking the results of a decision against
its expectations shows executives what their
strengths are, where they need to improve,
and where they lack knowledge or information. It shows them their biases. Very often

it shows them that their decisions didn't produce results because they didn't put the right people on the job. Allocating the best people to the right positions is a crucial, tough job that many executives slight, in part because the best people are already too busy. Systematic decision review also shows executives their own weaknesses, particularly the areas in which they are simply incompetent. In these areas, smart executives don't make decisions or take actions. They delegate. Everyone has such areas; there's no such thing as a universal executive genius.

Most discussions of decision making assume that only senior executives make decisions or that only senior

executives' decisions matter. This is
a dangerous mistake. Decisions are
made at every level of the organization,
beginning with individual professional
contributors and frontline supervisors.
These apparently low-level decisions
are extremely important in a knowledge-
based organization. Knowledge workers
are supposed to know more about their
areas of specialization—for example, tax
accounting—than anybody else, so their
decisions are likely to have an impact
throughout the company. Making good
decisions is a crucial skill at every level.
It needs to be taught explicitly to everyone
in organizations that are based on
knowledge.

Take Responsibility for Communicating

Effective executives make sure that both their action plans and their information needs are understood. Specifically, this means that they share their plans with and ask for comments from all their colleagues— superiors, subordinates, and peers. At the same time, they let each person know what information they'll need to get the job done. The information flow from subordinate to boss is usually what gets the most attention. But executives need to pay equal attention to peers' and superiors' information needs.

We all know, thanks to Chester Barnard's 1938 classic *The Functions of the Executive*, that organizations are held together by information rather than by ownership or command. Still, far too many executives behave as if information and its flow were the job of the information specialist—for example, the accountant. As a result, they get an enormous amount of data they do not need and cannot use, but little of the information they do need. The best way around this problem is for each executive to identify the information he needs, ask for it, and keep pushing until he gets it.

Focus on Opportunities

Good executives focus on opportunities rather than problems. Problems have to be taken care of, of course; they must not be swept under the rug. But problem solving, however necessary, does not produce results. It prevents damage. Exploiting opportunities produces results.

Above all, effective executives treat change as an opportunity rather than a threat. They systematically look at changes, inside and outside the corporation, and ask, "How can we exploit this change as an opportunity for our enterprise?" Specifically, executives scan these seven situations for opportunities:

- an unexpected success or failure in their own enterprise, in a competing enterprise, or in the industry;

- a gap between what is and what could be in a market, process, product, or service (for example, in the nineteenth century, the paper industry concentrated on the 10% of each tree that became wood pulp and totally neglected the possibilities in the remaining 90%, which became waste);

- innovation in a process, product, or service, whether inside or outside the enterprise or its industry;

- changes in industry structure and market structure;

- demographics;

- changes in mind-set, values, perception, mood, or meaning; and

- new knowledge or a new technology.

Effective executives also make sure that problems do not overwhelm opportunities.

In most companies, the first page of the monthly management report lists key problems. It's far wiser to list opportunities on the first page and leave problems for the second page. Unless there is a true catastrophe, problems are not discussed in management meetings until opportunities have been analyzed and properly dealt with.

Staffing is another important aspect of being opportunity focused. Effective executives put their best people on opportunities rather than on problems. One way to staff for opportunities is to ask each member of the management group to prepare two lists every six months—a list of opportunities for the entire enterprise and a list of the best-performing people throughout the enterprise. These are discussed, then melded into two master lists, and the best people are matched with the best opportunities. In Japan, by the way, this matchup is considered a major HR task in a big corporation or government department; that practice is one of the key strengths of Japanese business.

Make Meetings Productive

The most visible, powerful, and, arguably, effective nongovernmental executive in the America of World War II and the years thereafter was not a businessman. It was Francis Cardinal Spellman, the head of the Roman Catholic Archdiocese of New York and adviser to several U.S. presidents. When Spellman took over, the diocese was bankrupt and totally demoralized. His successor inherited the leadership position in the American Catholic church. Spellman often said that during his waking hours he was alone only twice each day, for 25 minutes each time: when he said Mass in his private chapel after getting up in the morning and when he said his evening prayers before going to bed. Otherwise he was always with people in a meeting, starting at breakfast with one Catholic organization and ending at dinner with another.

Top executives aren't quite as imprisoned as the archbishop of a major Catholic diocese. But every study of the executive workday has found that even junior executives and professionals are with other people—that is, in a meeting of some sort—more than half of every business day. The only exceptions are a few senior researchers. Even a conversation with only one other person is a meeting. Hence, if they are to be effective, executives must make meetings productive. They must make sure that meetings are work sessions rather than bull sessions.

The key to running an effective meeting is to decide in advance what kind of meeting it will be. Different kinds of meetings require different forms of preparation and different results:

- *A meeting to prepare a statement, an announcement, or a press release.* For this to be productive, one member has

to prepare a draft beforehand. At the
meeting's end, a preappointed member
has to take responsibility for disseminating the final text.

- *A meeting to make an announcement—
  for example, an organizational change.*
  This meeting should be confined to
  the announcement and a discussion
  about it.

- *A meeting in which one member
  reports.* Nothing but the report should
  be discussed.

- *A meeting in which several or all members report.* Either there should be
  no discussion at all or the discussion

should be limited to questions for clarification. Alternatively, for each report there could be a short discussion in which all participants may ask questions. If this is the format, the reports should be distributed to all participants well before the meeting. At this kind of meeting, each report should be limited to a preset time—for example, 15 minutes.

- *A meeting to inform the convening executive.* The executive should listen and ask questions. He or she should sum up but not make a presentation.

- *A meeting whose only function is to allow the participants to be in the executive's presence.* Cardinal Spellman's breakfast and dinner meetings were of that kind. There is no way to make these meetings productive. They are the penalties of rank. Senior executives are effective to the extent to which they can prevent such meetings from encroaching on their workdays. Spellman, for instance, was effective in large part because he confined such meetings to breakfast and dinner and kept the rest of his working day free of them.

Making a meeting productive takes a good deal of self-discipline. It requires that executives determine what kind of meeting is appropriate and then stick to that format. It's also necessary to terminate the meeting as soon as its specific purpose has been accomplished. Good executives don't raise another matter for discussion. They sum up and adjourn.

Good follow-up is just as important as the meeting itself. The great master of follow-up was Alfred Sloan, the most effective business executive I have ever known. Sloan, who headed General Motors from the 1920s until the 1950s, spent most of his six working days a week in meetings—three days a week in formal committee meetings with a set membership, the other three days in ad hoc meetings with individual GM executives or with a small group of executives. At the beginning of a formal meeting, Sloan announced the meeting's purpose. He then listened. He never took notes and he rarely spoke except to clarify a confusing point. At the end he summed up, thanked the participants, and left. Then he immediately wrote a short memo addressed to one attendee of the meeting. In that note, he summarized the discussion and its conclusions and spelled out any work assignment decided upon in the meeting (including a decision to hold another meeting on the subject or to study an issue). He specified the deadline and the executive who was to be accountable for the assignment. He sent a copy of the memo to everyone who'd been present at the meeting. It was through these memos—each a small masterpiece—that Sloan made himself into an outstandingly effective executive.

Effective executives know that any given meeting is either productive or a total waste of time.

THINK AND SAY "WE"

The final practice is this: Don't think or say "I." Think and say "we." Effective executives know that they have ultimate responsibility, which can be neither shared nor delegated. But they have authority only because they have the trust of the organization. This means that they think of the needs and the opportunities of the organization before they think of their own needs and opportunities. This one may sound simple; it isn't, but it needs to be strictly observed.

We've just reviewed eight practices of effective executives. I'm going to throw in one final, bonus practice. This one's so important that I'll elevate it to the level of a rule: Listen first, speak last.

Effective executives differ widely in their personalities, strengths, weaknesses, values, and beliefs. All they have in common is that they get the right things done. Some are born effective. But the demand is much too great to be satisfied by extraordinary talent. Effectiveness is a discipline. And, like every discipline, effectiveness can be learned and must be earned.

ABOUT THE AUTHOR

Peter F. Drucker was a writer, consultant, and professor of social science and management at Claremont Graduate University in California. His thirty-nine books have been published in more than seventy languages. He founded the Peter F. Drucker Foundation for Nonprofit Management, and counseled thirteen governments, public services institutions, and major corporations.

ALSO BY THIS AUTHOR

Harvard Business Review Press Books

The Changing World of the Executive

Classic Drucker: Essential Wisdom of Peter Drucker from the Pages of Harvard Business Review

The Frontiers of Management: Where Tomorrow's Ideas Are Being Shaped Today

Managing in a Time of Great Change

Men, Ideas, and Politics

Managing Oneself

People and Performance: The Best of Peter Drucker on Management

Peter Drucker on the Profession of Management

The Peter F. Drucker Reader

The Theory of the Business

Technology, Management, and Society

Toward the Next Economics, and Other Essays

Harvard Business Review Articles

"The Coming of the New Organization"

"The Discipline of Innovation"

"The Effective Decision"

"How to Make People Decisions"

"Managing for Business Effectiveness"

"Managing Oneself"

"New Templates for Today's Organizations"

"The Theory of the Business"

"They're Not Employees, They're People"

Article Summary

Idea in Brief

Worried that you're not a born leader? That you lack charisma, the right talents, or some other secret ingredient? No need: leadership isn't about personality or talent. In fact, the best leaders exhibit wildly different personalities, attitudes, values, and strengths—they're extroverted or reclusive, easygoing or controlling, generous or parsimonious, numbers or vision oriented.

So what do effective leaders have in common?
They get the right things done, in the right ways—
by following eight simple rules:

- Ask what needs to be done.

- Ask what's right for the enterprise.

- Develop action plans.

- Take responsibility for decisions.

- Take responsibility for communicating.

- Focus on opportunities, not problems.

- Run productive meetings.

- Think and say "We," not "I."

Using discipline to apply these rules, you
gain the knowledge you need to make smart
decisions, convert that knowledge into effective
action, and ensure accountability throughout your
organization.

Idea in Practice

Get the Knowledge You Need

- **Ask what needs to be done.** When Jack Welch asked this question while taking over as CEO at General Electric, he realized that dropping GE businesses that couldn't be first or second in their industries was essential— not the overseas expansion he had wanted to launch. Once you know what must be done, identify tasks you're best at, concentrating on one at a time. After completing a task, reset priorities based on new realities.

- **Ask what's right for the enterprise.** Don't agonize over what's best for owners, investors, employees, or customers. Decisions that are right for your enterprise are ultimately right for all stakeholders.

Convert Your Knowledge into Action

- **Develop action plans.** Devise plans that
  specify desired results and constraints (is
  the course of action legal and compatible
  with the company's mission, values, and
  policies?). Include check-in points and implications for how you'll spend your time. And
  revise plans to reflect new opportunities.

- **Take responsibility for decisions.** Ensure
  that each decision specifies who's accountable for carrying it out, when it must be
  implemented, who'll be affected by it, and
  who must be informed. Regularly review
  decisions, especially hires and promotions.
  This enables you to correct poor decisions
  before doing real damage.

Take Responsibility for Communicating

- **Get input from superiors, subordinates, and peers on your action plans.** Let each know what information you need to get the job done. Pay equal attention to peers' and superiors' information needs.

- **Focus on opportunities, not problems.** You get results by exploiting opportunities, not solving problems. Identify changes inside and outside your organization (new technologies, product innovations, new market structures), asking "How can we exploit this change to benefit our enterprise?" Then match your best people with the best opportunities.

Ensure Companywide Accountability

- **Run productive meetings.** Articulate each meeting's purpose (Making an announcement? Delivering a report?). Terminate the meeting once the purpose is accomplished. Follow up with short communications summarizing the discussion, spelling out new work assignments and deadlines for completing them. General Motors CEO Alfred Sloan's legendary mastery of meeting follow-up helped secure GM's industry dominance in the mid-twentieth century.

- **Think and say "We," not "I."** Your authority comes from your organization's trust in you. To get the best results, always consider your organization's needs and opportunities before your own.

The most important management ideas all in one place.

We hope you enjoyed this book from *Harvard Business Review*. For the best ideas HBR has to offer turn to HBR's 10 Must Reads Boxed Set. From books on leadership and strategy to managing yourself and others, this 6-book collection delivers articles on the most essential business topics to help you succeed.

HBR's 10 Must Reads Series

The definitive collection of ideas and best practices on our most sought-after topics from the best minds in business.

- Change Management
- Collaboration
- Communication
- Emotional Intelligence
- Innovation
- Leadership
- Making Smart Decisions

- Managing Across Cultures
- Managing People
- Managing Yourself
- Strategic Marketing
- Strategy
- Teams
- The Essentials

hbr.org/mustreads

THE DISCIPLINE
OF TEAMS

HARVARD BUSINESS REVIEW
CLASSICS

THE DISCIPLINE
OF TEAMS

Jon R. Katzenbach and
Douglas K. Smith

Harvard Business Review Press
Boston, Massachusetts

THE
HARVARD BUSINESS REVIEW
CLASSICS SERIES

Since 1922, *Harvard Business Review* has
been a leading source of breakthrough ideas
in management practice—many of which still
speak to and influence us today. The HBR
Classics series now offers you the opportunity
to make these seminal pieces a part of your
permanent management library. Each volume contains a groundbreaking idea that has
shaped best practices and inspired countless
managers around the world—and will change
how you think about the business world today.

THE DISCIPLINE
OF TEAMS

Early in the 1980s, Bill Greenwood and a small band of rebel railroaders took on most of the top management of Burlington Northern and created a multibillion-dollar business in "piggybacking" rail services despite widespread resistance, even resentment, within the company. The Medical Products Group at Hewlett-Packard owes most of its leading performance to the remarkable efforts of Dean Morton, Lew Platt, Ben Holmes, Dick Alberding, and a handful of their colleagues who revitalized a health care business that most others had written off. At Knight Ridder, Jim Batten's "customer obsession" vision took root at the *Tallahassee Democrat* when 14 frontline enthusiasts turned a charter to eliminate errors into a mission of major change and took the entire paper along with them.

Such are the stories and the work of teams—real teams that perform, not amorphous groups that we call teams because we think that the label is motivating and energizing. The difference between teams that perform and other groups that don't is a subject to which most of us pay far too little attention. Part of the problem is that "team" is a word and concept so familiar to everyone. (See the exhibit "Not All Groups Are Teams: How to Tell the Difference.")

Or at least that's what we thought when we set out to do research for our book *The Wisdom of Teams* (HarperBusiness, 1993). We wanted to discover what differentiates various levels of team performance, where and how teams work best, and what top management can do to enhance their effectiveness. We talked with hundreds of people on more than 50 different teams in 30 companies and beyond, from Motorola and Hewlett-Packard to Operation Desert Storm and the Girl Scouts.

We found that there is a basic discipline that makes teams work. We also found that teams and good performance are inseparable: You cannot have one without the other.

But people use the word "team" so loosely that it gets in the way of learning and applying the discipline that leads to good performance. For managers to make better decisions about whether, when, or how to encourage and use teams, it is important to be more precise about what a team is and what it isn't.

Most executives advocate teamwork. And they should. Teamwork represents a set of values that encourage listening and responding constructively to views expressed by others, giving others the benefit of the doubt, providing support, and recognizing the interests and achievements of others. Such values help teams perform, and they also promote individual performance as well as the performance of an entire organization.

But teamwork values by themselves are not exclusive to teams, nor are they enough to ensure team performance. (See "Building Team Performance" at the end of this article.)

Nor is a team just any group working together. Committees, councils, and task forces are not necessarily teams. Groups do not become teams simply because that is what someone calls them. The entire workforce of any large and complex organization is *never* a team, but think about how often that platitude is offered up.

To understand how teams deliver extra performance, we must distinguish between teams and other forms of working groups. That distinction turns on performance results. A working group's performance is a function of what its members do as individuals. A team's performance includes both individual results and what we call "collective work products." A collective work product is what two or more members must work on together, such as interviews, surveys, or experiments. Whatever it is, a collective work product reflects the joint, real contribution of team members.

Working groups are both prevalent and effective in large organizations where individual accountability is most important. The best working groups come together to share information, perspectives, and insights; to make decisions that help each person do his or her job better; and to reinforce individual performance standards. But the focus is always on individual goals and accountabilities. Working-group members don't take responsibility for results other than their own. Nor do they try to develop incremental performance contributions requiring the combined work of two or more members.

Teams differ fundamentally from working groups because they require both individual and mutual accountability. Teams rely on more than group discussion, debate, and decision, on more than sharing information and best-practice performance standards. Teams produce discrete work products through the joint contributions of their members. This is what makes possible performance levels greater than the sum of all the individual bests of team members.

Simply stated, a team is more than the sum of its parts.

The first step in developing a disciplined approach to team management is to think about teams as discrete units of performance and not just as positive sets of values. Having observed and worked with scores of teams in action, both successes and failures, we offer the following. Think of it as a working definition or, better still, an essential discipline that real teams share: *A team is a small number of people with complementary skills who are committed to a common purpose, set of performance goals, and approach for which they hold themselves mutually accountable*.

The essence of a team is common commitment. Without it, groups perform as individuals; with it, they become a powerful unit of collective performance. This kind of commitment requires a purpose in which team members can believe. Whether the purpose is to "transform the contributions of suppliers into the satisfaction of customers," to "make our company one we can be proud of again," or to "prove that all children can learn," credible team purposes have an element related to winning, being first, revolutionizing, or being on the cutting edge.

Teams develop direction, momentum, and commitment by working to shape a meaningful purpose. Building ownership and commitment to team purpose, however, is not incompatible with taking initial direction from outside the team. The often-asserted assumption that a team cannot "own" its purpose unless management leaves it alone actually confuses more potential teams than it helps. In fact, it is the exceptional case—for example, entrepreneurial situations—when a team creates a purpose entirely on its own.

Most successful teams shape their purposes in response to a demand or opportunity put in their path, usually by higher management. This helps teams get started by broadly framing the company's performance expectation. Management is responsible for clarifying the charter, rationale, and performance challenge for the team, but management must also leave enough flexibility for the team to develop commitment around its own spin on that purpose, set of specific goals, timing, and approach.

The best teams invest a tremendous amount of time and effort exploring, shaping, and agreeing on a purpose that belongs to them both collectively and individually. This "purposing" activity continues throughout the life of the team. By contrast, failed teams rarely develop a common purpose. For whatever reason—an insufficient focus on performance, lack of effort, poor leadership— they do not coalesce around a challenging aspiration.

The best teams also translate their common purpose into specific performance goals, such as reducing the reject rate from suppliers by 50% or increasing the math scores of graduates from 40% to 95%. Indeed, if a team fails to establish specific performance goals or if those goals do not relate directly to the team's overall purpose, team members become confused, pull apart, and revert to mediocre performance. By contrast, when purposes and goals build on one another and are combined with team commitment, they become a powerful engine of performance.

Transforming broad directives into specific and measurable performance goals is the surest first step for a team trying to shape a purpose meaningful to its members. Specific goals, such as getting a new product to market in less than half the normal time, responding to all customers within 24 hours, or achieving a zero-defect rate while simultaneously cutting costs by 40%, all provide firm footholds for teams. There are several reasons:

- Specific team-performance goals help define a set of work products that are different both from an organization-wide mission and from individual job objectives. As a result, such work products require the collective effort of team members to make something specific happen that, in and of itself, adds real value to results. By contrast, simply gathering from time to time to make decisions will not sustain team performance.

- The specificity of performance objectives facilitates clear communication and constructive conflict within the team. When a plant-level team, for example, sets a goal of reducing average machine changeover time to two hours, the clarity of the goal forces the team to concentrate on what it would take either to achieve or to reconsider the goal. When such goals are clear, discussions can focus on how to pursue them or whether to change them; when goals are ambiguous or nonexistent, such discussions are much less productive.

- The attainability of specific goals helps teams maintain their focus on getting results. A product-development team at Eli Lilly's Peripheral Systems Division set definite yardsticks for the market introduction of an ultrasonic probe to help doctors locate deep veins and arteries. The probe had to have an audible signal through a specified depth of tissue, be capable of being manufactured at a rate of 100 per day, and have a unit cost less than a preestablished amount. Because the team could measure its progress against each of these specific objectives, the team knew throughout the development process where it stood. Either it had achieved its goals or not.

- As Outward Bound and other team-building programs illustrate, specific objectives have a leveling effect conducive to team behavior. When a small group of people challenge themselves to get over a wall or to reduce cycle time by 50%, their respective titles, perks, and other stripes fade into the background. The teams that succeed evaluate what and how each individual can best contribute to the team's goal and, more important, do so in terms of the performance objective itself rather than a person's status or personality.

- Specific goals allow a team to achieve small wins as it pursues its broader purpose. These small wins are invaluable to building commitment and overcoming the inevitable obstacles that get in the way of a long-term purpose. For example, the Knight Ridder team mentioned at the outset turned a narrow goal to eliminate errors into a compelling customer service purpose.

- Performance goals are compelling. They are symbols of accomplishment that motivate and energize. They challenge the people on a team to commit themselves, as a team, to make a difference. Drama, urgency, and a healthy fear of failure combine to drive teams that have their collective eye on an attainable, but challenging, goal. Nobody but the team can make it happen. It's their challenge.

The combination of purpose and specific goals is essential to performance. Each depends on the other to remain relevant and vital. Clear performance goals help a team keep track of progress and hold itself accountable; the broader, even nobler, aspirations in a team's purpose supply both meaning and emotional energy.

Virtually all effective teams we have met, read or heard about, or been members of have ranged between two and 25 people. For example, the Burlington Northern piggy-backing team had seven members, and the Knight Ridder newspaper team had 14. The majority of them have numbered less than ten. Small size is admittedly more of a prag-matic guide than an absolute necessity for success. A large number of people, say 50 or more, can theoretically become a team. But groups of such size are more likely to break into subteams rather than function as a single unit.

Why? Large numbers of people have trou-ble interacting constructively as a group, much less doing real work together. Ten people are far more likely than 50 to work through their individual, functional, and hierarchical differences toward a common plan and to hold themselves jointly accountable for the results.

Large groups also face logistical issues, such as finding enough physical space and time to meet. And they confront more complex constraints, like crowd or herd behaviors, which prevent the intense sharing of viewpoints needed to build a team. As a result, when they try to develop a common purpose, they usually produce only superficial "missions" and well-meaning intentions that cannot be translated into concrete objectives. They tend fairly quickly to reach a point when meetings become a chore, a clear sign that most of the people in the group are un-certain why they have gathered, beyond some notion of getting along better. Anyone who has been through one of these exercises understands how frustrating it can be. This kind of failure tends to foster cynicism, which gets in the way of future team efforts.

In addition to finding the right size, teams must develop the right mix of skills; that is, each of the complementary skills necessary to do the team's job. As obvious as it sounds, it is a common failing in potential teams. Skill requirements fall into three fairly self-evident categories.

Technical or Functional Expertise

It would make little sense for a group of doctors to litigate an employment discrimination case in a court of law. Yet teams of doctors and lawyers often try medical malpractice or personal injury cases. Similarly, product development groups that include only marketers or engineers are less likely to succeed than those with the complementary skills of both.

Problem-Solving and Decision-Making Skills

Teams must be able to identify the problems and opportunities they face, evaluate the options they have for moving forward, and then make necessary trade-offs and decisions about how to proceed. Most teams need some members with these skills to begin with, although many will develop them best on the job.

Interpersonal Skills

Common understanding and purpose cannot arise without effective communication and constructive conflict, which in turn depend on interpersonal skills. These skills include risk taking, helpful criticism, objectivity, active listening, giving the benefit of the doubt, and recogniz-ing the interests and achievements of others.

Obviously, a team cannot get started without some minimum complement of skills, especially technical and functional ones. Still, think about how often you've been part of a team whose members were chosen primarily on the basis of personal compatibility or formal position in the organization, and in which the skill mix of its members wasn't given much thought.

It is equally common to overemphasize skills in team selection. Yet in all the successful teams we've encountered, not one had all the needed skills at the outset. The Burlington Northern team, for example, initially had no members who were skilled marketers despite the fact that their performance challenge was a marketing one. In fact, we discovered that teams are powerful vehicles for developing the skills needed to meet the team's performance challenge. Accordingly, team member selection ought to ride as much on skill potential as on skills already proven.

Effective teams develop strong commitment to a common approach; that is, to how they will work together to accomplish their purpose. Team members must agree on who will do particular jobs, how schedules will be set and adhered to, what skills need to be developed, how continuing membership in the team is to be earned, and how the group will make and modify decisions. This element of commitment is as important to team performance as the team's commitment to its purpose and goals.

Agreeing on the specifics of work and how they fit together to integrate individual skills and advance team performance lies at the heart of shaping a common approach. It is perhaps self-evident that an approach that delegates all the real work to a few members (or staff outsiders) and thus relies on reviews and meetings for its only "work together" aspects, cannot sustain a real team. Every member of a successful team does equivalent amounts of real work; all members, including the team leader, contribute in concrete ways to the team's work product. This is a very important element of the emotional logic that drives team performance.

When individuals approach a team situation, especially in a business setting, each has preexisting job assignments as well as strengths and weaknesses reflecting a variety of talents, backgrounds, personalities, and prejudices. Only through the mutual discovery and understanding of how to apply all its human resources to a common purpose can a team develop and agree on the best approach to achieve its goals. At the heart of such long and, at times, difficult interactions lies a commitment-building process in which the team candidly explores who is best suited to each task as well as how individual roles will come together. In effect, the team establishes a social contract among members that relates to their purpose and guides and obligates how they must work together.

No group ever becomes a team until it can hold itself accountable as a team. Like common purpose and approach, mutual accountability is a stiff test. Think, for example, about the subtle but critical difference between "the boss holds me accountable" and "we hold ourselves accountable." The first case can lead to the second, but without the second, there can be no team.

Companies like Hewlett-Packard and Motorola have an ingrained performance ethic that enables teams to form organically whenever there is a clear performance challenge requiring collective rather than individual effort. In these companies, the factor of mutual accountability is commonplace. "Being in the boat together" is how their performance game is played.

At its core, team accountability is about the sincere promises we make to ourselves and others, promises that underpin two critical aspects of effective teams: commitment and trust. Most of us enter a potential team situation cautiously because ingrained individualism and experience discourage us from putting our fates in the hands of others or accepting responsibility for others. Teams do not succeed by ignoring or wishing away such behavior.

Mutual accountability cannot be coerced any more than people can be made to trust one another. But when a team shares a common purpose, goals, and approach, mutual accountability grows as a natural counterpart. Accountability arises from and reinforces the time, energy, and action invested in figuring out what the team is trying to accomplish and how best to get it done.

When people work together toward a common objective, trust and commitment follow. Consequently, teams enjoying a strong common purpose and approach inevitably hold themselves responsible, both as individuals and as a team, for the team's performance. This sense of mutual accountability also produces the rich rewards of mutual achievement in which all members share. What we heard over and over from members of effective teams is that they found the experience energizing and motivating in ways that their "normal" jobs never could match.

On the other hand, groups established primarily for the sake of becoming a team or for job enhancement, communication, organizational effectiveness, or excellence rarely become effective teams, as demonstrated by the bad feelings left in many companies after experimenting with quality circles that never translated "quality" into specific goals. Only when appropriate performance goals are set does the process of discussing the goals and the approaches to them give team members a clearer and clearer choice: They can disagree with a goal and the path that the team selects and, in effect, opt out, or they can pitch in and become accountable with and to their teammates.

The discipline of teams we've outlined is critical to the success of all teams. Yet it is also useful to go one step further. Most teams can be classified in one of three ways: teams that recommend things, teams that make or do things, and teams that run things. In our experience, each type faces a characteristic set of challenges.

Teams That Recommend Things

These teams include task forces; project groups; and audit, quality, or safety groups asked to study and solve particular problems. Teams that recommend things almost always have predetermined completion dates. Two critical issues are unique to such teams: getting off to a fast and constructive start and dealing with the ultimate handoff that's required to get recommendations implemented.

The key to the first issue lies in the clarity of the team's charter and the composition of its membership. In addition to wanting to know why and how their efforts are important, task forces need a clear definition of whom management expects to participate and the time commitment required. Management can help by ensuring that the team includes people with the skills and influence necessary for crafting practical recommendations that will carry weight throughout the organization. Moreover, management can help the team get the necessary cooperation by opening doors and dealing with political obstacles.

Missing the handoff is almost always the problem that stymies teams that recommend things. To avoid this, the transfer of responsibility for recommendations to those who must implement them demands top management's time and attention. The more top managers assume that recommendations will "just happen," the less likely it is that they will. The more involvement task force members have in implementing their recommendations, the more likely they are to get implemented.

To the extent that people outside the task force will have to carry the ball, it is critical to involve them in the process early and often, certainly well before recommendations are finalized. Such involvement may take many forms, including participating in interviews, helping with analyses, contributing and critiquing ideas, and conducting experiments and trials. At a minimum, anyone responsible for implementation should receive a briefing on the task force's purpose, approach, and objectives at the beginning of the effort as well as regular reviews of progress.

Teams That Make or Do Things

These teams include people at or near the front lines who are responsible for doing the basic manufacturing, development, operations, marketing, sales, service, and other value-adding activities of a business. With

some exceptions, such as new-product development or process design teams, teams that
make or do things tend to have no set completion dates because their activities are
ongoing.

In deciding where team performance
might have the greatest impact, top management should concentrate on what we call the
company's "critical delivery points"—that is,
places in the organization where the cost and
value of the company's products and services
are most directly determined. Such critical
delivery points might include where accounts
get managed, customer service performed,
products designed, and productivity determined. If performance at critical delivery
points depends on combining multiple skills,

perspectives, and judgments in real time, then the team option is the smartest one.

When an organization does require a significant number of teams at these points, the sheer challenge of maximizing the performance of so many groups will demand a carefully constructed and performance-focused set of management processes. The issue here for top management is how to build the necessary systems and process supports without falling into the trap of appearing to promote teams for their own sake.

The imperative here, returning to our earlier discussion of the basic discipline of teams, is a relentless focus on performance. If management fails to pay persistent attention to the link between teams and performance, the organization becomes convinced that "this year, we are doing 'teams'." Top management can help by instituting processes like pay schemes and training for teams responsive to their real time needs, but more than anything else, top management must make clear and compelling demands on the teams themselves and then pay constant attention to their progress with respect to both team basics and performance results. This means focusing on specific teams and specific performance challenges. Otherwise "performance," like "team," will become a cliché.

Teams That Run Things

Despite the fact that many leaders refer to the group reporting to them as a team, few groups really are. And groups that become real teams seldom think of themselves as a team because they are so focused on performance results. Yet the opportunity for such teams includes groups from the top of the enterprise down through the divisional or functional level. Whether it is in charge of thousands of people or just a handful, as long as the group oversees some business, ongoing program, or significant functional activity, it is a team that runs things.

The main issue these teams face is determining whether a real team approach is the right one. Many groups that run things can be more effective as working groups than as teams. The key judgment is whether the sum of individual bests will suffice for the performance challenge at hand or whether the group must deliver substantial incremental performance requiring real joint work products. Although the team option promises greater performance, it also brings more risk, and managers must be brutally honest in assessing the trade-offs.

Members may have to overcome a natural reluctance to trust their fate to others. The price of faking the team approach is high: At best, members get diverted from their individual goals, costs outweigh benefits, and people resent the imposition on their time and priorities. At worst, serious animosities develop that undercut even the potential personal bests of the working-group approach.

Working groups present fewer risks. Effective working groups need little time to shape their purpose, since the leader usually establishes it. Meetings are run against well-prioritized agendas. And decisions are implemented through specific individual assignments and accountabilities. Most of the time, therefore, if performance aspirations can be met through individuals doing their respective jobs well, the working-group approach is more comfortable, less risky, and less disruptive than trying for more elusive team performance levels. Indeed, if there is no performance need for the team approach, efforts spent to improve the effectiveness of the working group make much more sense than floundering around trying to become a team.

Having said that, we believe the extra level of performance teams can achieve is becoming critical for a growing number of companies, especially as they move through major changes during which company performance depends on broad-based behavioral change. When top management uses teams to run things, it should make sure the team succeeds in identifying specific purposes and goals.

This is a second major issue for teams that run things. Too often, such teams confuse the broad mission of the total organization with the specific purpose of their small group at the top. The discipline of teams tells us that for a real team to form, there must be a team purpose that is distinctive and specific to the small group and that requires its members to roll up their sleeves and accomplish something beyond individual end products. If a group of managers looks only at the economic performance of the part of the organization it runs to assess overall effectiveness, the group will not have any team performance goals of its own.

While the basic discipline of teams does not differ for them, teams at the top are certainly the most difficult. The complexities of long-term challenges, heavy demands on executive time, and the deep-seated individualism of senior people conspire against teams at the top. At the same time, teams at the top are the most powerful. At first we thought such teams were nearly impossible. That is because we were looking at the teams as defined by the formal organizational structure; that is, the leader and all his or her direct reports equals the team. Then we discovered that real teams at the top were often smaller and less formalized: Whitehead and Weinberg at Goldman Sachs; Hewlett and Packard at HP; Krasnoff, Pall, and Hardy at Pall Corporation; Kendall, Pearson, and Calloway at Pepsi; Haas and Haas at Levi Strauss; Batten and Ridder at Knight Ridder. They were mostly twos and threes, with an occasional fourth.

Nonetheless, real teams at the top of large, complex organizations are still few and far between. Far too many groups at the top of large corporations needlessly constrain themselves from achieving real team levels of performance because they assume that all direct reports must be on the team, that team goals must be identical to corporate goals, that the team members' positions rather than skills determine their respective roles, that a team must be a team all the time, and that the team leader is above doing real work.

As understandable as these assumptions may be, most of them are unwarranted. They do not apply to the teams at the top we have observed, and when replaced with more realistic and flexible assumptions that permit the team discipline to be applied, real team performance at the top can and does occur. Moreover, as more and more companies are confronted with the need to manage major change across their organizations, we will see more real teams at the top.

We believe that teams will become the primary unit of performance in high-performance organizations. But that does not mean that teams will crowd out individual opportunity or formal hierarchy and process. Rather, teams will enhance existing structures without replacing them. A team opportunity exists anywhere hierarchy or organizational boundaries inhibit the skills and perspectives needed for optimal results. Thus, new-product innovation requires preserving functional excellence through structure while eradicating functional bias through teams. And frontline productivity requires preserving direction and guidance through hierarchy while drawing on energy and flexibility through self-managing teams.

We are convinced that every company faces specific performance challenges for which teams are the most practical and powerful vehicle at top management's disposal. The critical role for senior managers, therefore, is to worry about company performance and the kinds of teams that can deliver it. This means top management must recognize a team's unique potential to deliver results, deploy teams strategically when they are the best tool for the job, and foster the basic discipline of teams that will make them effective. By doing so, top management creates the kind of environment that enables team as well as individual and organizational performance.

Building Team Performance

Although there is no guaranteed how-to recipe for building team performance, we observed a number of approaches shared by many successful teams.

Establish urgency, demanding performance standards, and direction. All team members need to believe the team has urgent and worthwhile purposes, and they want to know what the expectations are. Indeed, the more urgent and meaningful the rationale, the more likely it is that the team will live up to its performance potential, as was the case for a customer-service team that was told that further growth for the entire company would be impossible without major improvements in that area. Teams work best in a compelling context. That is why companies with strong performance ethics usually form teams readily.

Select members for skill and skill potential, not personality. No team succeeds without all the skills needed to meet its purpose and performance goals. Yet most teams figure out the skills they will need after they are formed. The wise manager will choose people for their existing skills and their potential to improve existing skills and learn new ones.

Pay particular attention to first meetings and actions. Initial impressions always mean a great deal. When potential teams first gather, everyone monitors the signals given by others to confirm, suspend, or dispel assumptions and concerns. They pay particular attention to those in authority: the team leader and any executives who set up, oversee, or otherwise influence the team. And, as always, what such leaders do is more important than what they say. If a senior executive leaves the team kick-off to take a phone call ten minutes after the session has begun and he never returns, people get the message.

Set some clear rules of behavior. All effective teams develop rules of conduct at the outset to help them achieve their purpose and performance goals. The most critical initial rules pertain to attendance (for example, "no interruptions to take phone calls"), discussion ("no sacred cows"), confidentiality ("the only things to leave this room are what we agree on"), analytic approach ("facts are friendly"), end-product orientation ("everyone gets assignments and does them"), constructive confrontation ("no finger pointing"), and, often the most important, contributions ("everyone does real work").

Set and seize upon a few immediate performance-oriented tasks and goals.

Most effective teams trace their advancement to key performance-oriented events. Such events can be set in motion by immediately establishing a few challenging goals that can be reached early on. There is no such thing as a real team without performance results, so the sooner such results occur, the sooner the team congeals.

Challenge the group regularly with fresh facts and information. New information causes a team to redefine and enrich its understanding of the performance challenge, thereby helping the team shape a common purpose, set clearer goals, and improve its common approach. A plant quality improvement team knew the cost of poor quality was high, but it wasn't until they researched the different types of defects and put a price tag on each one that they knew where to go next. Conversely, teams err when they assume that all the information needed exists in the collective experience and knowledge of their members.

Spend lots of time together. Common sense tells us that team members must spend a lot of time together, scheduled and unscheduled, especially in the beginning. Indeed, creative insights as well as personal bonding require impromptu and casual interactions just as much as analyzing spreadsheets and interviewing customers. Busy executives and managers too often intentionally minimize the time they spend together. The successful teams we've observed all gave themselves the time to learn to be a team. This time need not always be spent together physically; electronic, fax, and phone time can also count as time spent together.

Exploit the power of positive feedback, recognition, and reward. Positive reinforcement works as well in a team context as elsewhere. Giving out "gold stars" helps shape new behaviors critical to team performance. If people in the group, for example, are alert to a shy person's initial efforts to speak up and contribute, they can give the honest positive reinforcement that encourages continued contributions. There are many ways to recognize and reward team performance beyond direct compensation, from having a senior executive speak directly to the team about the urgency of its mission to using awards to recognize contributions. Ultimately, however, the satisfaction shared by a team in its own performance becomes the most cherished reward.

EXHIBIT 1

Not all groups are teams: How to tell the difference

Working group	Team
Strong, clearly focused leader	Shared leadership roles
Individual accountability	Individual and mutual accountability
The group's purpose is the same as the broader organizational mission	Specific team purpose that the team itself delivers
Individual work products	Collective work products
Runs efficient meetings	Encourages open-ended discussion and active problem-solving meetings
Measures its effectiveness indirectly by its influence on others (such as financial performance of the business)	Measures performance directly by assessing collective work products
Discusses, decides, and delegates	Discusses, decides, and does real work together

ABOUT THE AUTHORS

Jon R. Katzenbach is a founder and senior partner of Katzenbach Partners, a strategic and organizational consulting firm, and a former director of McKinsey & Company.

Douglas K. Smith is an organizational consultant and a former partner at McKinsey & Company.

ALSO BY THESE AUTHORS

Jon R. Katzenbach

Harvard Business Press books

Peak Performance: Aligning the Hearts and Minds of Your Employees

Teams at the Top: Unleashing the Potential of Both Teams and Individual Leaders

The Wisdom of Teams: Creating the High-Performance Organization
with Douglas K. Smith

{ 55 }

Jon R. Katzenbach and Douglas K. Smith

The Work of Teams

***Harvard Business Review* articles**

"Firing Up the Front Line"
with Jason A. Santamaria

"The Myth of the Top Management Team"

Douglas K. Smith

Harvard Business Press books

The Wisdom of Teams: Creating the High-Performance Organization
with Jon R. Katzenbach

Article Summary

The Idea in Brief

The word *team* gets bandied about so loosely that many managers are oblivious to its real meaning—or its true potential. With a run-of-the-mill working group, performance is a function of what the members do as individuals. A team's performance, by contrast, calls for both individual and mutual accountability.

Though it may not seem like anything special, mutual accountability can lead to astonishing results. It enables a team to achieve performance levels that are far greater than the individual bests of the team's members. To achieve these benefits, team members must do more than listen, respond constructively, and provide support to one another. In addition to sharing these team-building values, they must share an *essential discipline*.

The Idea in Practice

A team's essential discipline comprises five characteristics:

1. *A meaningful common purpose that the team has helped shape.* Most teams are responding to an initial mandate from outside the team. But to be successful, the team must "own" this purpose, develop its own spin on it.

2. *Specific performance goals that flow from the common purpose.* For example, getting

a new product to market in less than half the
normal time. Compelling goals inspire and
challenge a team, give it a sense of urgency.
They also have a leveling effect, requiring
members to focus on the collective effort
necessary rather than any differences in title
or status.

3. *A mix of complementary skills.* These include technical or functional expertise, problem-solving and decision-making skills, and
   interpersonal skills. Successful teams rarely
   have all the needed skills at the outset — they
   develop them as they learn what the challenge requires.

4. *A strong commitment to how the work gets
   done.* Teams must agree on who will do
   what jobs, how schedules will be established
   and honored, and how decisions will be
   made and modified. On a genuine team,

each member does equivalent amounts of real work; all members, the leader included, contribute in concrete ways to the team's collective work-products.

5. *Mutual accountability.* Trust and commitment cannot be coerced. The process of agreeing upon appropriate goals serves as the crucible in which members forge their accountability to each other—not just to the leader.

Once the essential discipline has been established, a team is free to concentrate on the critical challenges it faces:

- For a team whose purpose is to make recommendations, that means making a fast and constructive start and providing a clean handoff to those who will implement the recommendations.

- For a team that makes or does things, it's keeping the specific performance goals in sharp focus.

- For a team that runs things, the primary task is distinguishing the challenges that require a real team approach from those that don't.

If a task doesn't demand joint work-products, a working group can be the more effective option. Team opportunities are usually those in which hierarchy or organizational boundaries inhibit the skills and perspectives needed for optimal results. Little wonder, then, that teams have become the primary units of productivity in high-performance organizations.

The most important management ideas all in one place.

We hope you enjoyed this book from *Harvard Business Review*. For the best ideas HBR has to offer turn to HBR's 10 Must Reads Boxed Set. From books on leadership and strategy to managing yourself and others, this 6-book collection delivers articles on the most essential business topics to help you succeed.

HBR's 10 Must Reads Series

The definitive collection of ideas and best practices on our most sought-after topics from the best minds in business.

- Change Management
- Collaboration
- Communication
- Emotional Intelligence
- Innovation
- Leadership
- Making Smart Decisions

- Managing Across Cultures
- Managing People
- Managing Yourself
- Strategic Marketing
- Strategy
- Teams
- The Essentials

hbr.org/mustreads

Buy for your team, clients, or event.
Visit hbr.org/bulksales for quantity discount rates.

MANAGING
ONESELF

HARVARD BUSINESS REVIEW
CLASSICS

MANAGING
ONESELF

Peter F. Drucker

Harvard Business Review Press
Boston, Massachusetts

25 24 23 22

Library of Congress Cataloging-in-Publication Data
Drucker, Peter F. (Peter Ferdinand), 1909-2005.
 Managing oneself / Peter F. Drucker.
    p. cm. – (Harvard Business review classics)
 Reprint of an article from the Harvard business review. Reprinted
earlier in 1999 as Reprint 99204.
  ISBN 978-1-4221-2312-6
 1. Career development. 2. Career changes. 3. Self-management
(Psychology) 4. Self-actualization (Psychology) 5. Success–
Psychological aspects. I. Harvard business review. II. Title.
  HF5381.D677 2008
  650.1–dc22

                                          2007037486

The paper used in this publication meets the requirements of the
American National Standard for Permanence of Paper for Publications and Documents in Libraries and Archives Z39.48-1992.

THE
HARVARD BUSINESS REVIEW
CLASSICS SERIES

Since 1922, *Harvard Business Review* has been a leading source of breakthrough ideas in management practice—many of which still speak to and influence us today. The HBR Classics series now offers you the opportunity to make these seminal pieces a part of your permanent management library. Each volume contains a groundbreaking idea that has shaped best practices and inspired countless managers around the world—and will change how you think about the business world today.

MANAGING
ONESELF

History's great achievers—a Napoléon, a da Vinci, a Mozart—have always managed themselves. That, in large measure, is what makes them great achievers. But they are rare exceptions, so unusual both in their talents and their accomplishments as to be considered outside the boundaries of ordinary human existence. Now, most of us, even those of us with modest endowments, will have to learn to manage ourselves. We will have to learn to develop ourselves. We will have to place ourselves where we can make the greatest contribution. And we will have to stay mentally alert and engaged during a 50-year working life, which means knowing how and when to change the work we do.

WHAT ARE MY STRENGTHS?

Most people think they know what they are good at. They are usually wrong. More often, people know what they are not good at—and even then more people are wrong than right. And yet, a person can perform only from strength. One cannot build performance on weaknesses, let alone on something one cannot do at all.

Throughout history, people had little need to know their strengths. A person was born into a position and a line of work: The peasant's son would also be a peasant; the artisan's daughter, an artisan's wife; and so on. But now people have choices. We need to know our strengths in order to know where we belong.

The only way to discover your strengths is through feedback analysis. Whenever you make a key decision or take a key action, write down what you expect will happen. Nine or 12 months later, compare the actual results with your expectations. I have been practicing this method for 15 to 20 years now, and every time I do it, I am surprised. The feedback analysis showed me, for instance—and to my great surprise—that I have an intuitive under-standing of technical people, whether they are engineers or accountants or market re-searchers. It also showed me that I don't really resonate with generalists.

Feedback analysis is by no means new. It was invented sometime in the fourteenth cen-tury by an otherwise totally obscure German theologian and picked up quite independently, some 150 years later, by John Calvin and Ig-natius of Loyola, each of whom incorporated it into the practice of his followers. In fact, the steadfast focus on performance and results that this habit produces explains why the insti-tutions these two men founded, the Calvinist church and the Jesuit order, came to dominate Europe within 30 years.

Practiced consistently, this simple method will show you within a fairly short period of time, maybe two or three years, where your strengths lie—and this is the most important thing to know. The method will show you what you are doing or failing to do that deprives you of the full benefits of your strengths. It will show you where you are not particularly competent. And finally, it will show you where you have no strengths and cannot perform.

Several implications for action follow from feedback analysis. First and foremost, concentrate on your strengths. Put yourself where your strengths can produce results.

Second, work on improving your strengths. Analysis will rapidly show where you need to improve skills or acquire new ones. It will also show the gaps in your knowledge—and those can usually be filled. Mathematicians are born, but everyone can learn trigonometry.

Third, discover where your intellectual arrogance is causing disabling ignorance and overcome it. Far too many people—especially people with great expertise in one area—are contemptuous of knowledge in other areas or believe that being bright is a substitute for knowledge. First-rate engineers, for instance, tend to take pride in not knowing anything about people. Human beings, they believe, are much too disorderly for the good engineering mind. Human resources professionals, by contrast, often pride themselves on their ignorance of elementary accounting or of quantitative methods alto-gether. But taking pride in such ignorance is self-defeating. Go to work on acquiring the skills and knowledge you need to fully realize your strengths.

It is equally essential to remedy your bad habits—the things you do or fail to do that in-hibit your effectiveness and performance. Such habits will quickly show up in the feed-back. For example, a planner may find that his beautiful plans fail because he does not follow through on them. Like so many bril-liant people, he believes that ideas move mountains. But bulldozers move mountains; ideas show where the bulldozers should go to work. This planner will have to learn that the work does not stop when the plan is com-pleted. He must find people to carry out the plan and explain it to them. He must adapt and change it as he puts it into action. And finally, he must decide when to stop pushing the plan.

At the same time, feedback will also reveal when the problem is a lack of manners. Manners are the lubricating oil of an organization. It is a law of nature that two moving bodies in contact with each other create friction. This is as true for human beings as it is for inanimate objects. Manners—simple things like saying "please" and "thank you" and knowing a person's name or asking after her family—enable two people to work together whether they like each other or not. Bright people, especially bright young people, often do not understand this. If analysis shows that someone's brilliant work fails again and again as soon as cooperation from others is required, it probably indicates a lack of courtesy—that is, a lack of manners.

Comparing your expectations with your results also indicates what not to do. We all have a vast number of areas in which we have no talent or skill and little chance of becoming even mediocre. In those areas a person— and especially a knowledge worker—should not take on work, jobs, and assignments. One should waste as little effort as possible on improving areas of low competence. It takes far more energy and work to improve from incompetence to mediocrity than it takes to improve from first-rate performance to excellence. And yet most people—

especially most teachers and most organizations—concentrate on making incompetent performers into mediocre ones. Energy, resources, and time should go instead to making a competent person into a star performer.

HOW DO I PERFORM?

Amazingly few people know how they get things done. Indeed, most of us do not even know that different people work and perform differently. Too many people work in ways that are not their ways, and that almost guarantees nonperformance. For knowledge workers, How do I perform? may be an even more important question than What are my strengths?

Like one's strengths, how one performs is unique. It is a matter of personality. Whether personality be a matter of nature or nurture, it surely is formed long before a person goes to work. And *how* a person performs is a given, just as *what* a person is good at or not good at is a given. A person's way of performing can be slightly modified, but it is unlikely to be completely changed—and certainly not easily. Just as people achieve results by doing what they are good at, they also achieve results by working in ways that they best perform. A few common personality traits usually determine how a person performs.

Am I a reader or a listener?

The first thing to know is whether you are a reader or a listener. Far too few people even know that there are readers and listeners and that people are rarely both. Even fewer know which of the two they themselves are. But some examples will show how damaging such ignorance can be.

When Dwight Eisenhower was Supreme Commander of the Allied forces in Europe, he was the darling of the press. His press conferences were famous for their style— General Eisenhower showed total command of whatever question he was asked, and he was able to describe a situation and explain a policy in two or three beautifully polished and elegant sentences. Ten years later, the same journalists who had been his admirers held President Eisenhower in open contempt. He never addressed the questions, they complained, but rambled on endlessly about something else. And they constantly ridiculed him for butchering the King's English in incoherent and ungrammatical answers.

Eisenhower apparently did not know that he was a reader, not a listener. When he was Supreme Commander in Europe, his aides made sure that every question from the press was presented in writing at least half an hour before a conference was to begin. And then Eisenhower was in total command. When he became president, he succeeded two listeners, Franklin D. Roosevelt and Harry Truman. Both men knew themselves to be listeners and both enjoyed free-for-all press conferences. Eisenhower may have felt that he had to do what his two predecessors had done. As a result, he never even heard the questions journalists asked. And Eisenhower is not even an extreme case of a nonlistener.

A few years later, Lyndon Johnson destroyed his presidency, in large measure, by not knowing that he was a listener. His predecessor, John Kennedy, was a reader who had assembled a brilliant group of writers as his assistants, making sure that they wrote to him before discussing their memos in person. Johnson kept these people on his staff—and they kept on writing. He never, apparently, understood one word of what they wrote. Yet as a senator, Johnson had been superb; for parliamentarians have to be, above all, listeners.

Few listeners can be made, or can make themselves, into competent readers—and vice versa. The listener who tries to be a reader will, therefore, suffer the fate of Lyndon Johnson, whereas the reader who tries to be a listener will suffer the fate of Dwight Eisenhower. They will not perform or achieve.

How do I learn?

The second thing to know about how one performs is to know how one learns. Many first-class writers—Winston Churchill is but one example—do poorly in school. They tend to remember their schooling as pure torture. Yet few of their classmates remember it the same way. They may not have enjoyed the school very much, but the worst they suffered was boredom. The explanation is that writers do not, as a rule, learn by listening and reading. They learn by writing. Because schools do not allow them to learn this way, they get poor grades.

Schools everywhere are organized on the assumption that there is only one right way to learn and that it is the same way for everybody. But to be forced to learn the way a school teaches is sheer hell for students who learn differently. Indeed, there are probably half a dozen different ways to learn.

There are people, like Churchill, who learn by writing. Some people learn by taking copious notes. Beethoven, for example, left behind an enormous number of sketchbooks, yet he said he never actually looked at them when he composed. Asked why he kept them, he is reported to have replied, "If I don't write it down immediately, I forget it right away. If I put it into a sketchbook, I never forget it and I never have to look it up again." Some people learn by doing. Others learn by hearing themselves talk.

A chief executive I know who converted a small and mediocre family business into the leading company in its industry was one of those people who learn by talking. He was in the habit of calling his entire senior staff into his office once a week and then talking at them for two or three hours. He would raise policy issues and argue three different positions on each one. He rarely asked his associates for comments or questions; he simply needed an audience to hear himself talk. That's how he learned. And although he is a fairly extreme case, learning through talking is by no means an unusual method. Successful trial lawyers learn the same way, as do many medical diagnosticians (and so do I).

Of all the important pieces of self-knowledge, understanding how you learn is the easiest to acquire. When I ask people, "How do you learn?" most of them know the answer. But when I ask, "Do you act on this knowledge?" few answer yes. And yet, acting on this knowledge is the key to performance; or rather, *not* acting on this knowledge condemns one to nonperformance.

Am I a reader or a listener? and How do I learn? are the first questions to ask. But they are by no means the only ones. To manage yourself effectively, you also have to ask, Do I work well with people, or am I a loner? And if you do work well with people, you then must ask, In what relationship?

Some people work best as subordinates. General George Patton, the great American military hero of World War II, is a prime example. Patton was America's top troop commander. Yet when he was proposed for an independent command, General George Marshall, the U.S. chief of staff— and probably the most successful picker of men in U.S. history—said, "Patton is the best subordinate the American army has ever produced, but he would be the worst commander."

Some people work best as team members. Others work best alone. Some are exceptionally talented as coaches and mentors; others are simply incompetent as mentors.

Another crucial question is, Do I produce results as a decision maker or as an adviser? A great many people perform best as advisers but cannot take the burden and pressure of making the decision. A good many other people, by contrast, need an adviser to force themselves to think; then they can make decisions and act on them with speed, self-confidence, and courage.

This is a reason, by the way, that the number two person in an organization often fails when promoted to the number one position. The top spot requires a decision maker.

Strong decision makers often put somebody they trust into the number two spot as their adviser—and in that position the person is outstanding. But in the number one spot, the same person fails. He or she knows what the decision should be but cannot accept the responsibility of actually making it.

Other important questions to ask include, Do I perform well under stress, or do I need a highly structured and predictable environment? Do I work best in a big organization or a small one? Few people work well in all kinds of environments. Again and again, I have seen people who were very successful in large organizations flounder miserably when they moved into smaller ones. And the reverse is equally true.

The conclusion bears repeating: Do not try to change yourself—you are unlikely to succeed. But work hard to improve the way you perform. And try not to take on work you cannot perform or will only perform poorly.

WHAT ARE MY VALUES?

To be able to manage yourself, you finally have to ask, What are my values? This is not a question of ethics. With respect to ethics, the rules are the same for everybody, and the test is a simple one. I call it the "mirror test."

In the early years of this century, the most highly respected diplomat of all the great powers was the German ambassador in London. He was clearly destined for great things—to become his country's foreign minister, at least, if not its federal chancellor. Yet in 1906 he abruptly resigned rather than preside over a dinner given by the diplomatic corps for Edward VII. The king was a notorious womanizer and made it clear what kind of dinner he wanted. The ambassador is reported to have said, "I refuse to see a pimp in the mirror in the morning when I shave."

That is the mirror test. Ethics requires that you ask yourself, What kind of person do I want to see in the mirror in the morning? What is ethical behavior in one kind of organization or situation is ethical behavior in another. But ethics is only part of a value system—especially of an organization's value system.

To work in an organization whose value system is unacceptable or incompatible with one's own condemns a person both to frustration and to nonperformance.

Consider the experience of a highly successful human resources executive whose company was acquired by a bigger organization. After the acquisition, she was promoted to do the kind of work she did best, which included selecting people for important positions. The executive deeply believed that a company should hire people for such positions from the outside only after exhausting all the inside possibilities. But her new company believed in first looking outside "to bring in fresh blood." There is something to be said for both approaches—in my experience, the proper one is to do some of both. They are, however, fundamentally incompatible—not as policies but as values. They bespeak different views of the relationship between organizations and people; different views of the responsibility of an organization to its people and their development; and different views of a person's most important contribution to an enterprise. After several years of frustration, the executive quit—at considerable financial loss. Her values and the values of the organization simply were not compatible.

Similarly, whether a pharmaceutical company tries to obtain results by making constant, small improvements or by achieving occasional, highly expensive, and risky "breakthroughs" is not primarily an economic question. The results of either strategy may be pretty much the same. At bottom, there is a conflict between a value system that sees the company's contribution in terms of helping physicians do better what they already do and a value system that is oriented toward making scientific discoveries.

Whether a business should be run for short-term results or with a focus on the long term is likewise a question of values. Financial analysts believe that businesses can be run for both simultaneously. Successful businesspeople know better. To be sure, every company has to produce short-term results. But in any conflict between short-term results and long-term growth, each company will determine its own priority. This is not primarily a disagreement about economics. It is fundamentally a value con-

flict regarding the function of a business and
the responsibility of management.

Value conflicts are not limited to business
organizations. One of the fastest-growing
pastoral churches in the United States measures success by the number of new parish-
ioners. Its leadership believes that what
matters is how many newcomers join the
congregation. The Good Lord will then minister to their spiritual needs or at least to the
needs of a sufficient percentage. Another
pastoral, evangelical church believes that
what matters is people's spiritual growth.
The church eases out newcomers who join
but do not enter into its spiritual life.

Again, this is not a matter of numbers.
At first glance, it appears that the second

church grows more slowly. But it retains a far larger proportion of newcomers than the first one does. Its growth, in other words, is more solid. This is also not a theological problem, or only secondarily so. It is a problem about values. In a public debate, one pastor argued, "Unless you first come to church, you will never find the gate to the Kingdom of Heaven."

"No," answered the other. "Until you first look for the gate to the Kingdom of Heaven, you don't belong in church."

Organizations, like people, have values. To be effective in an organization, a person's values must be compatible with the organization's values. They do not need to be the same, but they must be close enough to coexist. Otherwise, the person will not only be frustrated but also will not produce results.

A person's strengths and the way that person performs rarely conflict; the two are complementary. But there is sometimes a conflict between a person's values and his or her strengths. What one does well—even very well and successfully—may not fit with one's value system. In that case, the work may not appear to be worth devoting one's life to (or even a substantial portion thereof).

If I may, allow me to interject a personal note. Many years ago, I too had to decide between my values and what I was doing successfully. I was doing very well as a young investment banker in London in the mid-1930s,

{ 29 }

and the work clearly fit my strengths. Yet I did not see myself making a contribution as an asset manager. People, I realized, were what I valued, and I saw no point in being the richest man in the cemetery. I had no money and no other job prospects. Despite the continuing Depression, I quit—and it was the right thing to do. Values, in other words, are and should be the ultimate test.

WHERE DO I BELONG?

A small number of people know very early where they belong. Mathematicians, musicians, and cooks, for instance, are usually mathematicians, musicians, and cooks by the time they are four or five years old.

Physicians usually decide on their careers in their teens, if not earlier. But most people, especially highly gifted people, do not really know where they belong until they are well past their mid-twenties. By that time, however, they should know the answers to the three questions: What are my strengths? How do I perform? and, What are my values? And then they can and should decide where they belong.

Or rather, they should be able to decide where they do *not* belong. The person who has learned that he or she does not perform well in a big organization should have learned to say no to a position in one. The person who has learned that he or she is not a decision maker should have learned to say no to a decision-making assignment. A General Patton (who probably never learned this himself) should have learned to say no to an independent command.

Equally important, knowing the answer to these questions enables a person to say to an opportunity, an offer, or an assignment, "Yes, I will do that. But this is the way I should be doing it. This is the way it should be structured. This is the way the relationships should be. These are the kind of results you should expect from me, and in this time frame, because this is who I am."

Successful careers are not planned. They develop when people are prepared for opportunities because they know their strengths, their method of work, and their values. Knowing where one belongs can transform an ordinary person—hardworking and competent but otherwise mediocre—into an outstanding performer.

WHAT SHOULD I CONTRIBUTE?

Throughout history, the great majority of people never had to ask the question, What should I contribute? They were told what to contribute, and their tasks were dictated either by the work itself—as it was for the peasant or artisan—or by a master or a mistress—as it was for domestic servants. And until very recently, it was taken for granted that most people were subordinates who did as they were told. Even in the 1950s and 1960s, the new knowledge workers (the so-called organization men) looked to their company's personnel department to plan their careers.

Then in the late 1960s, no one wanted to be told what to do any longer. Young men and women began to ask, What do I want to do? And what they heard was that the way to contribute was to "do your own thing." But this solution was as wrong as the organization men's had been. Very few of the people who believed that doing one's own thing would lead to contribution, self-fulfillment, and success achieved any of the three.

But still, there is no return to the old answer of doing what you are told or assigned to do. Knowledge workers in particular have to learn to ask a question that has not been asked before: What *should* my contribution be? To answer it, they must address three distinct elements: What does the situation require? Given my strengths, my way of performing, and my values, how can I make the greatest contribution to what needs to be done? And finally, What results have to be achieved to make a difference?

Consider the experience of a newly appointed hospital administrator. The hospital was big and prestigious, but it had been coasting on its reputation for 30 years. The new administrator decided that his contribution should be to establish a standard of excellence in one important area within two years. He chose to focus on the emergency room, which was big, visible, and sloppy. He decided that every patient who came into the

ER had to be seen by a qualified nurse within 60 seconds. Within 12 months, the hospital's emergency room had become a model for all hospitals in the United States, and within another two years, the whole hospital had been transformed.

As this example suggests, it is rarely possible—or even particularly fruitful—to look too far ahead. A plan can usually cover no more than 18 months and still be reasonably clear and specific. So the question in most cases should be, Where and how can I achieve results that will make a difference within the next year and a half? The answer must balance several things. First, the results should be hard to achieve—they should require "stretching," to use the current buzzword.

But also, they should be within reach. To aim at results that cannot be achieved—or that can be only under the most unlikely circumstances—is not being ambitious; it is being foolish. Second, the results should be meaningful. They should make a difference. Finally, results should be visible and, if at all possible, measurable. From this will come a course of action: what to do, where and how to start, and what goals and deadlines to set.

RESPONSIBILITY FOR RELATIONSHIPS

Very few people work by themselves and achieve results by themselves—a few great artists, a few great scientists, a few great athletes. Most people work with others and are effective with other people. That is true whether they are members of an organization or independently employed. Managing yourself requires taking responsibility for relationships. This has two parts.

The first is to accept the fact that other people are as much individuals as you yourself are. They perversely insist on behaving like human beings. This means that they too have their strengths; they too have their ways of getting things done; they too have their values. To be effective, therefore, you have to know the strengths, the performance modes, and the values of your coworkers.

That sounds obvious, but few people pay attention to it. Typical is the person who was trained to write reports in his or her first assignment because that boss was a reader. Even if the next boss is a listener, the person goes on writing reports that, invariably, produce no results. Invariably the boss will think the employee is stupid, incompetent, and lazy, and he or she will fail. But that could have been avoided if the employee had only looked at the new boss and analyzed how *this* boss performs.

Bosses are neither a title on the organization chart nor a "function." They are individuals and are entitled to do their work in the way they do it best. It is incumbent on the people who work with them to observe them, to find out how they work, and to adapt themselves to what makes their bosses most effective. This, in fact, is the secret of "managing" the boss.

The same holds true for all your coworkers. Each works his or her way, not your way. And each is entitled to work in his or her way. What matters is whether they perform and what their values are. As for how they perform—each is likely to do it differently. The first secret of effectiveness is to understand the people you work with and depend on so that you can make use of their strengths, their ways of working, and their values. Working relationships are as much based on the people as they are on the work.

The second part of relationship responsibility is taking responsibility for communication. Whenever I, or any other consultant, start to work with an organization, the first thing I hear about are all the personality conflicts. Most of these arise from the fact that people do not know what other people are doing and how they do their work, or what contribution the other people are concentrating on and what results they expect. And the reason they do not know is that they have not asked and therefore have not been told.

This failure to ask reflects human stupidity less than it reflects human history. Until recently, it was unnecessary to tell any of these things to anybody. In the medieval city, everyone in a district plied the same trade. In the countryside, everyone in a valley planted the same crop as soon as the frost was out of the ground. Even those few people who did things that were not "common" worked alone, so they did not have to tell anyone what they were doing.

Today the great majority of people work with others who have different tasks and responsibilities. The marketing vice president may have come out of sales and know everything about sales, but she knows nothing about the things she has never done—pricing, advertising, packaging, and the like. So the people who do these things must make sure that the marketing vice president understands what they are trying to do, why they are trying to do it, how they are going to do it, and what results to expect.

If the marketing vice president does not understand what these high-grade knowledge specialists are doing, it is primarily their fault, not hers. They have not educated her. Conversely, it is the marketing vice president's responsibility to make sure that all of her coworkers understand how she looks at marketing: what her goals are, how she works, and what she expects of herself and of each one of them.

Even people who understand the importance of taking responsibility for relationships often do not communicate sufficiently with their associates. They are afraid of being thought presumptuous or inquisitive or stupid. They are wrong. Whenever someone goes to his or her associates and says, "This is what I am good at. This is how I work. These are my values. This is the contribution

I plan to concentrate on and the results I should be expected to deliver," the response is always, "This is most helpful. But why didn't you tell me earlier?"

And one gets the same reaction—without exception, in my experience—if one continues by asking, "And what do I need to know about your strengths, how you perform, your values, and your proposed contribution?" In fact, knowledge workers should request this of everyone with whom they work, whether as subordinate, superior, colleague, or team member. And again, whenever this is done, the reaction is always, "Thanks for asking me. But why didn't you ask me earlier?"

Organizations are no longer built on force but on trust. The existence of trust between people does not necessarily mean that they like one another. It means that they understand one another. Taking responsibility for relationships is therefore an absolute necessity. It is a duty. Whether one is a member of the organization, a consultant to it, a supplier, or a distributor, one owes that responsibility to all one's coworkers: those whose work one depends on as well as those who depend on one's own work.

THE SECOND HALF OF YOUR LIFE

When work for most people meant manual labor, there was no need to worry about the second half of your life. You simply kept on doing what you had always done. And if you were lucky enough to survive 40 years of hard work in the mill or on the railroad, you were quite happy to spend the rest of your life doing nothing. Today, however, most work is knowledge work, and knowledge workers are not "finished" after 40 years on the job, they are merely bored.

We hear a great deal of talk about the midlife crisis of the executive. It is mostly boredom. At 45, most executives have reached the peak of their business careers, and they know it. After 20 years of doing very much the same kind of work, they are very good at their jobs. But they are not learning or contributing or deriving challenge and satisfaction from the job. And yet they are still likely to face another 20 if not

25 years of work. That is why managing one-self increasingly leads one to begin a second career.

There are three ways to develop a second career. The first is actually to start one. Often this takes nothing more than moving from one kind of organization to another: the divisional controller in a large corporation, for instance, becomes the controller of a medium-sized hospital. But there are also growing numbers of people who move into different lines of work altogether: the business executive or government official who enters the ministry at 45, for instance; or the midlevel manager who leaves corporate life after 20 years to attend law school and become a small-town attorney.

We will see many more second careers undertaken by people who have achieved modest success in their first jobs. Such people have substantial skills, and they know how to work. They need a community—the house is empty with the children gone—and they need income as well. But above all, they need challenge.

The second way to prepare for the second half of your life is to develop a parallel career. Many people who are very successful in their first careers stay in the work they have been doing, either on a full-time or part-time or consulting basis. But in addition, they create a parallel job, usually in a nonprofit organization, that takes another ten hours of work a week. They might take over the administration of their church, for instance, or the presidency of the local Girl Scouts council. They might run the battered women's shelter, work as a children's librarian for the local public library, sit on the school board, and so on.

Finally, there are the social entrepreneurs. These are usually people who have been very successful in their first careers. They love their work, but it no longer challenges them. In many cases they keep on doing what they have been doing all along but spend less and less of their time on it. They also start another activity, usually a nonprofit. My friend Bob Buford, for example, built a very successful television company that he still runs. But he has also founded and built a successful nonprofit organization that works with Protestant churches, and he is building another to teach social entrepreneurs how to manage their own nonprofit ventures while still running their original businesses.

People who manage the second half of their lives may always be a minority. The majority may "retire on the job" and count the years until their actual retirement. But it is this minority, the men and women who see a long working-life expectancy as an opportunity both for themselves and for society, who will become leaders and models.

There is one prerequisite for managing the second half of your life: You must begin long before you enter it. When it first became clear 30 years ago that working-life expectancies were lengthening very fast, many observers (including myself) believed that retired people would increasingly become volunteers for nonprofit institutions. That has not happened. If one does not begin to volunteer before one is 40 or so, one will not volunteer once past 60.

Similarly, all the social entrepreneurs I know began to work in their chosen second enterprise long before they reached their peak in their original business. Consider the example of a successful lawyer, the legal counsel to a large corporation, who has started a venture to establish model schools in his state. He began to do volunteer legal work for the schools when he was around 35.

He was elected to the school board at age 40. At age 50, when he had amassed a fortune, he started his own enterprise to build and to run model schools. He is, however, still working nearly full-time as the lead counsel in the company he helped found as a young lawyer.

There is another reason to develop a second major interest, and to develop it early. No one can expect to live very long without experiencing a serious setback in his or her life or work. There is the competent engineer who is passed over for promotion at age 45. There is the competent college professor who realizes at age 42 that she will never get a professorship at a big university, even though she may be fully qualified for it. There are tragedies in one's family life: the breakup of one's marriage or the loss of a child. At such times, a second major interest—not just a hobby—may make all the difference. The engineer, for example, now knows that he has not been very successful in his job. But in his outside activity—as church treasurer, for example—he is a success. One's family may break up, but in that outside activity there is still a community.

In a society in which success has become so terribly important, having options will become increasingly vital. Historically, there was no such thing as "success." The overwhelming majority of people did not expect anything but to stay in their "proper station," as an old English prayer has it. The only mobility was downward mobility.

In a knowledge society, however, we expect everyone to be a success. This is clearly an impossibility. For a great many people, there is at best an absence of failure. Wherever there is success, there has to be failure. And then it is vitally important for the individual, and equally for the individual's family, to have an area in which he or she can contribute, make a difference, and be *somebody*. That means finding a second area—whether in a second career, a parallel career, or a social venture— that offers an opportunity for being a leader, for being respected, for being a success.

The challenges of managing oneself may seem obvious, if not elementary. And the answers may seem self-evident to the point of appearing naïve. But managing oneself requires new and unprecedented things from the individual, and especially from the knowledge worker. In effect, managing oneself demands that each knowledge worker think and behave like a chief executive officer. Further, the shift from manual workers who do as they are told to knowledge workers who have to manage themselves profoundly challenges social structure. Every existing society, even the most individualistic one, takes two things for granted, if only subconsciously: that organizations outlive workers, and that most people stay put.

But today the opposite is true. Knowledge workers outlive organizations, and they are mobile. The need to manage oneself is therefore creating a revolution in human affairs.

ABOUT THE AUTHOR

Peter F. Drucker was a writer, teacher, and consultant. His thirty-four books have been published in more than seventy languages. He founded the Peter F. Drucker Foundation for Nonprofit Management, and counseled thirteen governments, public services institutions, and major corporations.

—

ALSO BY THIS AUTHOR

Harvard Business School Press Books

People and Performance: The Best of Peter Drucker on Management

Classic Drucker: Essential Wisdom of Peter Drucker from the Pages of Harvard Business Review

Peter Drucker on the Profession of Management
Authors: Peter F. Drucker; Nan Stone ed.

Harvard Business Review Articles

"The Coming of the New Organization"

"The Discipline of Innovation"

Peter F. Drucker

"The Effective Decision"

"How to Make People Decisions"

"Managing for Business Effectiveness"

"New Templates for Today's Organizations"

"The Theory of the Business"

"They're Not Employees, They're People"

"What Makes an Effective Executive"

The most important management ideas all in one place.

We hope you enjoyed this book from *Harvard Business Review*. For the best ideas HBR has to offer turn to HBR's 10 Must Reads Boxed Set. From books on leadership and strategy to managing yourself and others, this 6-book collection delivers articles on the most essential business topics to help you succeed.

HBR's 10 Must Reads Series

The definitive collection of ideas and best practices on our most sought-after topics from the best minds in business.

- Change Management
- Collaboration
- Communication
- Emotional Intelligence
- Innovation
- Leadership
- Making Smart Decisions

- Managing Across Cultures
- Managing People
- Managing Yourself
- Strategic Marketing
- Strategy
- Teams
- The Essentials

hbr.org/mustreads

Buy for your team, clients, or event.
Visit hbr.org/bulksales for quantity discount rates.

TURNING GOALS INTO RESULTS

HARVARD BUSINESS REVIEW

CLASSICS

TURNING GOALS INTO RESULTS
The Power of Catalytic Mechanisms

Jim Collins

Harvard Business Review Press
Boston, Massachusetts

Library of Congress Cataloging-in-Publication Data

Names: Collins, James C. (James Charles), 1958– author.

Title: Turning goals into results : the power of catalytic mechanisms / Jim Collins.

Other titles: Harvard business review classics.

Description: Boston, Massachusetts : Harvard Business Review Press, [2017] | Series: Harvard Business Review classics

Identifiers: LCCN 2016041613 | ISBN 9781633692589 (pbk.)

Subjects: LCSH: Strategic planning. | Success in business. | Bureaucracy. | Organizational change.

Classification: LCC HD30.28 .C64317 2017 | DDC 658.4/012—dc23 LC record available at https://lccn.loc.gov/2016041613

ISBN: 978-1-63369-258-9
eISBN: 978-1-63369-259-6

THE HARVARD BUSINESS REVIEW CLASSICS SERIES

Since 1922, *Harvard Business Review* has been a leading source of breakthrough ideas in management practice—many of which still speak to and influence us today. The HBR Classics series now offers you the opportunity to make these seminal pieces a part of your permanent management library. Each volume contains a groundbreaking idea that has shaped best practices and inspired countless managers around the world—and will change how you think about the business world today.

TURNING GOALS INTO
RESULTS

Most executives have a big, hairy, audacious goal. One dreams of making his brand more popular than Coke; another aspires to create the most lucrative Web site in cyberspace; yet another longs to see her organization act with the guts necessary to depose its arch rival. So, too, most executives ardently hope that their outsized goals will become a reality. To that end, they write vision statements, deliver speeches, and launch change initiatives. They devise complicated incentive programs, formalize rules and checklists, and pen policies and procedures. In other words, with the best intentions, they create layer upon layer of stultifying bureaucracy. Is it any surprise that their wildly ambitious dreams are seldom realized?

But companies don't have to act that way. Over the past six years, I have observed and studied a simple yet extremely powerful managerial tool that helps organizations turn goals into results. I have recently codified it; I call it the *catalytic mechanism.* Catalytic mechanisms are the crucial link between objectives and performance; they are a galvanizing, nonbureaucratic means to turn one into the other. Put another way, catalytic mechanisms are to visions what the central elements of the U.S. Constitution are to the Declaration of Independence—devices that translate lofty aspirations into concrete reality. They make big, hairy, audacious goals reachable.

My research indicates that few companies—perhaps only 5% or 10%—currently employ catalytic mechanisms, and some of them aren't even aware that they do. I have also found that catalytic mechanisms are relatively easy to create and implement. Given their effectiveness, they are perhaps the most underutilized—and most promising—devices that executives can use to achieve their big, hairy, audacious goals, or BHAGs. (For more on BHAGs, see the box "Anatomy of a BHAG.")

Consider Granite Rock, a 99-year-old company in Watsonville, California, that sells crushed gravel, concrete, sand, and asphalt. Twelve years ago, when brothers Bruce and Steve Woolpert became copresidents, they gave their company a new BHAG. Granite Rock would provide total customer satisfaction and achieve a reputation for service that met or exceeded that of Nordstrom, the upscale department store that is world famous for delighting its customers. Not exactly a timid goal for a stodgy, family-owned company whose employees are mostly tough, sweaty people operating rock quarries and whose customers—mainly tough, sweaty construction workers and contractors—are not easily dazzled.

Now stop and think for a minute: What would it take to actually reach such an ambitious goal? Most people automatically think of galvanizing leadership. But that wasn't an option for Granite Rock, as the Woolperts are a quiet, thoughtful, and bookish clan. Nor did the answer lie in hosting hoopla events or launching grand customer service initiatives. The brothers had seen such efforts at other companies and believed they had little lasting effect.

They chose instead to implement a radical new policy called "short pay." The bottom of every Granite Rock invoice reads, "If you are not satisfied for any reason, don't pay us for it. Simply scratch out the line item, write a brief note about the problem, and return a copy of this invoice along with your check for the balance."

Let me be clear about short pay. It is not a refund policy. Customers do not need to return the product. They do not need to call and complain. They have complete discretionary power to decide whether and how much to pay based on their satisfaction level.

To put the radical nature of short pay in perspective, imagine paying for airline tickets after the flight and having the power to short pay depending on your travel experience—not just in the air, but during ticketing and deplaning as well. Or suppose universities issued tuition invoices at the end of the semester, along with the statement, "If you are not satisfied with the dedication of the professor in any course, simply scratch out that course and send us a tuition check for the balance." Or suppose your cell phone bill came with a statement that said, "If you are not satisfied with the quality of connection of any calls, simply identify and deduct those from the total and send a check for the balance."

In the years since it was instituted, short pay has had a profound and positive impact on Granite Rock. It serves as a warning system, providing hard-to-ignore feedback about the quality of service and products. It impels managers to relentlessly track down the root causes of problems in order to prevent repeated short payments. It signals to employees and customers alike that Granite

Rock is dead serious about customer satisfaction in a way that goes far beyond slogans. Finally, it keeps Granite Rock from basking in the glory of its remarkable success.

And it has had success, as has been widely reported. The little company—it has only 610 employees—has consistently gained market share in a commodity business dominated by behemoths, all the while charging a 6% price premium. It won the prestigious Malcolm Baldrige National Quality Award in 1992. And its financial performance has significantly improved—from razor-thin margins to profit ratios that rival companies like Hewlett-Packard, which has a pretax return of roughly 10%. No doubt, short pay was a critical device for turning the Woolpert brothers' BHAG into a reality.

FIVE PARTS OF A WHOLE

Obviously, not every company should institute short pay. Rather, companies should have catalytic mechanisms as powerful as short pay. What, then, is the difference between a catalytic mechanism and most traditional managerial devices, such as a company's hiring and compensation policies? Catalytic mechanisms share five distinct characteristics. (See the table "Catalytic mechanisms: Breaking from tradition.") Let's look at them in turn.

Characteristic 1: A catalytic mechanism produces desired results in unpredictable ways

When executives identify a bold organizational goal, the first thing they usually do is design a plethora of systems, controls, procedures, and practices that seem likely to make it happen. That process is called alignment, and it's wildly popular in the world of management, among business academics and executives alike. After all, alignment makes sense. If you want to make your brand more popular than Coke, you had better measure the effectiveness of advertising and reward successful marketing managers with big bonuses. But the problem, as I've said, is that the controls that undergird alignment also create bureaucracy, and it should be news to no one that bureaucracy does not breed extraordinary results.

Don't get me wrong. Bureaucracy may deliver results, but they will be mediocre because bureaucracy leads to predictability and conformity. History shows us that organizations achieve greatness when people are allowed to do unexpected things—to show initiative and creativity, to step outside the scripted path. That is when delightful, interesting, and amazing results occur.

Take 3M. For decades, its executives have dreamed of having a constant flow of terrific new products. To achieve that end, in 1956, the company instituted a catalytic mechanism that is by now well known: scientists are urged to spend 15% of their time experimenting and inventing in the area of their own choice. How very unbureaucratic! No one is told what products to work on, just how much to work. And that loosening of controls has led to a stream of profitable innovations, from the famous Post-it Notes to less well-known examples such as reflective license plates and machines that replace the functions of the human heart during surgery. 3M's sales and earnings have increased more than 40-fold since instituting the 15% rule. The mechanism has helped generate cumulative stock returns 36% in excess of the market and has earned the company a frequent ranking in the top ten of *Fortune*'s most-admired list.

In a happy coincidence, the variation sparked by catalytic mechanisms forces learning to occur. Suppose you set out to climb the 3,000-foot sheer rock face of El Capitan in Yosemite Valley. Once you pass pitch 15, you cannot possibly retreat from your particular route: you are, by dint of nature, 100% committed. Although you can't predict *how* you will overcome the remaining pitches—you have to improvise as you go—you can predict that you will invent a way to the top. Why? Because the reality of having no easy retreat forces you to reach the summit. Catalytic mechanisms have the same effect. Granite Rock's short pay commits the company to achieving complete customer satisfaction. Every time a customer exercises short pay, Granite Rock learns or invents a way to run its operations more effectively. Ultimately, such new knowledge leads to better results, making the catalytic mechanism part of a virtuous circle of variation, learning, improvement, and enhanced results.

My "red flag" device also illustrates that circle. When I first began teaching Stanford M.B.A. students by the case method in 1988, I noticed that a small number of them tended to dominate the discussion. I also noticed that there was no correlation between the degree of vocal aggressiveness and how much these students improved the class's overall learning experience. Some vocal students had much to contribute; others just liked to hear themselves talk. Worse, I noticed when chatting with students after class that some of the quieter individuals had significant contributions but were selective or shy about sharing them. Furthermore, seeing 15 to 20 hands raised at a time, I had no way of knowing which one represented a truly significant insight, and I sensed that I was frequently missing some students' one best contribution for the entire quarter.

I solved that problem by giving each student an 8.5 inch by 11 inch bright red sheet of paper at the beginning of every quarter. It had the following instructions: "This is your red flag for the quarter. If you raise your hand with your red flag, the classroom will stop for you. There are no restrictions on when and how to use your red flag; the decision rests entirely in your hands. You can use it to voice an observation, share a personal experience, present an analysis, disagree with the professor, challenge a CEO guest, respond to a fellow student, ask a question, make a suggestion, or whatever. There will be no penalty whatsoever for any use of a red flag. Your red flag can be used only once during the quarter. Your red flag is nontransferable; you cannot give or sell it to another student."

I had no idea precisely what would happen each day in class. And yet, the red flag device quickly created a better learning experience for everyone. In one case, it allowed a very thoughtful and quiet student from India to challenge Anita Roddick on the Body Shop's manufacturing practices in the Third World. Roddick, a charismatic CEO with ferociously held views, usually dominates any discussion. The red flag forced her to listen to a critic. The spirited interchange between these two passionate and well-informed people produced more learning than anything I could have scripted. Without the red flag, we would have just had another session of "I'm CEO and let me tell you how it is."

In another situation, a student used her red flag to state, "Professor Collins, I think you are doing a particularly ineffective job of running class today. You are leading too much with your questions and stifling our independent thinking. Let us think for ourselves." That was a tough moment for me. My BHAG as a professor was to create the most popular class at the business school while imposing the highest workload and the stiffest daily standards. The red flag system confronted me with the fact that my own questioning style stood in the way of my dream—but it also pointed the way to improvement, again, to everyone's benefit.

Interestingly, no other professors on campus adopted the red flag. One of them told me, "I can't imagine doing that. I mean, you never know what might happen. I could never give up that much control in my classroom." What he and others missed was a great paradox: by giving up control and decreasing predictability, you increase the probability of attaining extraordinary results.

Characteristic 2: A catalytic mechanism distributes power for the benefit of the overall system, often to the great discomfort of those who traditionally hold power

With enough power, executives can always get people to jump through hoops. If it is customer service they are after, for instance, they can threaten dismissal to coerce sales-people to smile and act friendly. If they seek higher profits per store, they can pay employees according to flowthrough. And if increased market share is the dream, they can promote only those managers who make it happen.

But consider how catalytic mechanisms work. Short pay distributes power to the customer, to the great discomfort of Granite Rock's executives, but toward the greater goal of continuous improvement for the benefit of customers and company alike. The red flag distributes power to the students, to the great discomfort of the teacher, but to the ultimate improvement of learning in general. The founders of the United States understood this point when they wrote the Constitution. After all, the Constitution is the set of catalytic mechanisms that reinforce and support the national vision. Voting, the system of checks and balances, the two-thirds vote to amend, the impeachment process—these disperse power away from one central source, to the great discomfort of those who seek power, but to the benefit of the overall nation.

Catalytic mechanisms force the right things to happen even though those in power often have a vested interest in the right things *not* happening. Or they have a vested interest in inertia—letting pointless, expensive practices stay in place. That's what happened for years, perhaps decades, at U.S. Marine recruit depots. All recruits are issued a uniform on their first day. Two weeks later, they need another—the pounds melt away when you run 12 miles every dawn. The military's rules required those two-week-old uniforms to be destroyed. Not washed and reissued, but destroyed.

In the early 1990s, Phil Archuleta, a materials manager at a recruiting depot in San Diego, suggested that they reuse the uniforms. His boss's response: "No. It's against regulations. Forget about it." So in a fabulous act of insubordination, Archuleta washed the uniforms, hid them in boxes, and bided his time until he finally got a supervisor willing to challenge the regulation.

In an effort to empower the Phil Archuletas of the world, the government launched a wide-ranging initiative in 1994 to fix its bureaucratic quagmire. A new rule regarding waivers was put in place, and it is a catalytic mechanism that exemplifies the beauty and power of redistributing power. It has two primary components:

- Waiver-of-regulation requests must be acted upon within 30 days. After 30 days, if no answer is forthcoming, the party asking for the waiver can *assume approval* and implement the waiver.

- Those officials who have the authority to change regulations can approve waiver requests, but *only the head of an agency* can deny a request.

Think for a minute about the impact of this catalytic mechanism. It subverts the default, knee-jerk tendency of bureaucracies to choose inaction over action, status quo over change, and idiotic rules over common sense. Supervisors can no longer say no or not respond. They would have to champion a no all the way to the head of their agency— the equivalent of the head commandant of the entire U.S. Marine Corps—within 30 days. Instead of having to go out of their way to demonstrate why it is a good idea, they would have to expend great energy to prove that it is a *bad* idea. The catalytic mechanism tilts the balance of power away from inertia and toward change.

Indeed, the primary effect of the new waiver rule—as with all catalytic mechanisms—is to give people the freedom to do the right thing. The waiver that allowed Archuleta to change the regulation on uniforms created a savings of half a million dollars in two years. Similar examples of people doing the right thing with the waiver rule abound throughout the federal government, from the FDA to NASA. Tort claims adjusters in the Department of Agriculture, for instance, waived regulations to reduce processing time of claims from 51 days to eight days—a manpower savings of 84%. When executives vest people with power and responsibility and step out of the way, vast reservoirs of energy and competence flow forth. Again we have a paradox: the more executives disperse power and responsibility, the more likely the organization is to reach its big, hairy, audacious goal.

Characteristic 3: A catalytic mechanism has teeth

Lots of companies dream of total customer satisfaction; few have a device for making it happen that has the teeth of short pay. Plenty of organizations state the lofty intention to empower people; few translate that into results with a mechanism that has the teeth of the red flag. Many companies state that they intend to "become number one or number two in every competitive arena"; few have added an effective means of enforcement by saying, "and if the business is not number one or number two, or on a clear trajectory to get there, *we will exit within three months.*"

The fact is, executives spend hours drafting, redrafting, and redrafting yet again statements of core values, missions, and visions. This is often a very useful process, but a statement by itself will not accomplish anything. By contrast, a catalytic mechanism puts a process in place that all but guarantees that the vision will be fulfilled. A catalytic mechanism has a sharp set of teeth.

Consider the case of Nucor Corporation, the most successful U.S. steel company of the last three decades. It has a unique vision for a Rust Belt company: to be an organization whose workers and management share the common goal of being the most efficient, high-quality steel operation in the world, thereby creating job security and corporate prosperity in an industry ravaged by foreign competition. Behind that vision lies the belief held deeply by Nucor's senior leaders that decent, hard-working people should be well paid for their efforts and, so long as they are highly productive, that they need not worry about job security. On the surface, Nucor's vision may sound warm and fuzzy. Dig deeper, and you'll see that it actually leaves no room for unproductive employees. Nucor has created a culture of intense productivity whereby five people do the work that ten do at other steel companies, and get paid like eight. The vision came to life through a series of powerful catalytic mechanisms with teeth, such as the way frontline workers get paid:

- Base hourly pay is 25% to 33% below the industry average.

- People work in teams of 20 to 40; team-productivity rankings are posted daily.

- A bonus of 80% to 200% of base pay, based on *team* productivity, is paid weekly to all teams that meet or exceed productivity goals.

- If you are five minutes late, you lose your bonus for the day.

- If you are 30 minutes late, you lose your bonus for the week.

- If a machine breaks down, thereby stopping production, there is no compensating adjustment in the bonus calculation.

- If a product is returned for poor quality, bonus pay declines accordingly.

You might be thinking that the Nucor system concentrates power in the hands of management, which would seem to contradict the idea of distributing power for the sake of the system. But in fact, the catalytic mechanism actually takes the power out of the hands of individual managers and their whims. Nucor has no discretionary bonuses. It's more like a sports bonus system: if you score so many points or win a certain number of races, you get a bonus based on a predetermined formula. Period. That formula gives workers more power over their own destiny than bonus programs that give large discretionary power to management. If your team scores the points, your team gets the bonus, and no manager can take it away, citing, "We're just not having a very good year" or "I don't like your attitude."

Nucor's catalytic mechanisms for managers, incidentally, have even sharper teeth. Its executive compensation system works very much like its worker compensation system, except that the "team" is the entire plant (for plant managers) or the entire company (for corporate officers). And, unlike most companies, when times are bad, Nucor's executives assume greater pain than front-line workers: workers' pay drops about 25%, plant managers' pay drops about 40%, and corporate officers' pay drops about 60%. In the 1982 recession, CEO Ken Iverson's pay dropped 75%.

Characteristic 4: A catalytic mechanism ejects viruses

A lot of traditional controls are designed to get employees to act the "right" way and do the "right" things, even if they are not so inclined. Catalytic mechanisms, by contrast, help organizations to get the right people in the first place, keep them, and eject those who do not share the company's core values.

Great organizations have figured something out. The old adage "People are your most important asset" is wrong; the *right* people are your most important asset. The right people are those who would exhibit the desired behaviors anyway, as a natural extension of their character and attitude, regardless of any control and incentive system. The challenge is not to train all people to share your core values. The real challenge is to find people who already share your core values and to create catalytic mechanisms that so strongly reinforce those values that the people who don't share them either never get hired or, if they do, they self-eject.

Let's return to the Nucor example. Nucor doesn't try to make lazy people productive. Its catalytic mechanisms create a high-performance environment in which those with an innate work ethic thrive and free riders get out in a hurry. Management usually doesn't fire unproductive workers; *workers* do. In one case, team members chased a lazy coworker out of the plant. And one reporter writing a story on Nucor described showing up for a shift on time but thinking he was late because all the workers had been there for 30 minutes arranging their tools and getting ready to fire off the starting line precisely at 7:00 a.m.

Interestingly, Nucor sets up its mills not in traditional steel towns, but primarily in rural, agricultural areas. The thinking is simple: you can't teach the work ethic—either a person has it or he doesn't. But you can teach steel making. That's why Nucor hires farmers and trains them. The company's catalytic mechanisms wouldn't have it any other way.

Another example of a catalytic mechanism ejecting viruses comes from W.L. Gore & Associates, a fabric company worth nearly $2 billion. Bill Gore founded the company in 1958 with the vision of creating a culture of natural leadership. Leadership, in Gore's view, could not be assigned or bestowed by hierarchical position. You are a leader if and only if people choose to follow you. Gore's theory sprang not just from his personal values but also from his business sense: he thought that the most creative and productive work came when people freely made commitments to one another, not when bosses told them what to do.

To turn his vision into reality, Gore invented a catalytic mechanism that attracted the right people like a magnet and scared away the others. At W.L. Gore & Associates, employees have the authority to fire their bosses. Now, they can't fire the person from the company but, if they feel their boss isn't leading them effectively, they can simply bypass him or her and follow a different leader.

Who would want to work at such a company? Exactly the people who belong there—people who know they can lead without the crutch of a formal position or title and who believe in the philosophy of nonhierarchical leadership. Who would avoid it like the plague? Anyone who gets giddy pulling the levers of position and power just for the pulling's sake. And if you're a hierarchical leader who happens to make it through the company's door but can't quickly shake the notion that "the boss has to be the boss," it won't take you long to find the exit.

Characteristic 5: A catalytic mechanism produces an ongoing effect

Catalytic mechanisms differ fundamentally from catalytic events. A rousing speech to the troops, an electrifying off-site meeting, a euphoria-producing new buzzword, a new initiative or strategic imperative, an impending crisis—all of these are catalytic events, and some are useful. But they do not produce the persistent, ongoing effect of catalytic mechanisms. In fact, a good catalytic mechanism, as long as it evolves, can last for decades, as the 15% rule at 3M and the impeachment mechanism in the Constitution illustrate.

The lack of catalytic mechanisms is one reason many organizations rally in a crisis but languish once the crisis has passed. Leaders who feign a crisis—those who create a burning platform without simultaneously building catalytic mechanisms—do more long-term harm than good by creating a syndrome of crisis addiction. Executives who rely only on catalytic events are left wondering why the momentum stalls after the first phase of euphoria, excitement, or fear has passed. To produce lasting results, they must shift from orchestrating a series of events to building catalytic mechanisms.

Take, for example, the decades of ineffectual attempts to reform public education in the United States. Part of the failure lies in the approach to reform; too often it is based on onetime events and fashionable buzzwords rather than on catalytic mechanisms that produce sustained effects. As Roger Briggs, a high school teacher in Boulder, Colorado, wrote in an essay on school reform: "Every year we get a new program or fad. And they never really work. And we teachers eventually just learn to ignore them, smile, and go about our business of teaching." Now take a look at what happened when the state of Texas started using a catalytic mechanism in 1995: comparison-band ranking of schools, which is directly tied to resource allocation and, in some cases, school closures. The ongoing effect of this device forced the momentum of reform forward. Why? Well, if you rank fifth out of 40 schools but you just sit still, you'll drop in the ratings. Sit still long enough, and you'll eventually rank 35th rather than fifth, and you may face closure. Because every school is ranked on the same criteria, the bar for performance keeps rising. Within four years of installing the mechanism, student achievement in Texas improved across the board. The percentage of students who passed the Texas math skill exam, for example, rose from roughly half to 80%, and the share of black and Hispanic students who passed doubled to 64% and 72%, respectively.

And consider the ongoing impact of a good catalytic mechanism in a more corporate setting. Darwin Smith, former CEO of Kimberly-Clark, created in 1971 the BHAG to transform Kimberly-Clark from a mediocre forest- and paper-products company into a world-class consumer goods company. At the time, Wall Street analysts scoffed at the idea, as did most of Kimberly-Clark's competitors. Smith was undeterred. He created one catalytic event and one equally important catalytic mechanism. For the first, he sold a big chunk of the company's traditional paper-production mills, thus leaving no easy escape route from the dream. For the second, he committed the company to head-to-head competition with the best consumer-products company in the world: Procter & Gamble. With its entry into disposable diapers, Kimberly-Clark would henceforth be a direct rival of P&G. Kimberly-Clark would either become excellent at consumer products or get crushed. The beauty of this catalytic mechanism is that, unlike the "change or die" ranting all too common among modern executives, its ongoing effect is as powerful today as when it was first put in place nearly 30 years ago.

GETTING STARTED

This is not intended to be a how-to article; my main objective has been to introduce the concept of catalytic mechanisms and demonstrate how they have helped some companies—and individuals—turn their BHAGs into reality. (For more on the personal use of catalytic mechanisms, see the insert "Not for Companies Only.") Nonetheless, my research suggests that there are a few general principles that support the process of building catalytic mechanisms effectively.

Don't just add, remove

When pursuing BHAGs, our natural inclination is to add—new initiatives, new systems, new strategies, new priorities, and now, new catalytic mechanisms. But in doing so, we overwhelm ourselves. Isn't it frightening that the new version of the Palm Pilot has space for 1,500 items on its to-do list? Sadly, few of us have a "stop doing" list. We should, because to take something away—to unplug it—can be as catalytic as adding something new.

Take the case of a circuit division at Hewlett-Packard. It had tried countless programs and initiatives to reach its BHAG of becoming "a place where people would walk on the balls of their feet, feel exhilarated about their work, and search for imaginative ways to improve and innovate everything we do." The events produced short-term results—a moment of sparkle and excitement—but within a month or two, the division always drifted back into its sleepy, humdrum mode.

Then its executives considered the question, "What policies should we remove?" For most of its history, the division had comfortably lived off a captive internal market. What if HP's divisions were allowed to buy their components from outside competitors? Never again would the circuit division have fat internal orders just handed to it. Never again could it just sit still. Two months, four months, a year, five years, and ten years down the road—fierce competitors would still be there, constantly upping the ante. The prospect was both terrifying and exhilarating. Managers decided to unplug the "buy internal" requirement and open the doors to free-market competition.

Within weeks, the circuit division was well on its way to realizing its BHAG. You could sense a completely different environment the moment you walked in the door. The place hummed with activity, and its performance showed it.

Create, don't copy

Creating mechanisms is exactly that: a creative act. You can, of course, get good ideas by looking at what other organizations do, but the best catalytic mechanisms are idiosyncratic adaptations, if not wholesale creations, for a unique situation.

Because catalytic mechanisms require fresh ideas, it makes sense to invite all members of an organization to participate in their creation. Everyone. Certainly, some mechanisms require input from senior executives, like short pay at Granite Rock. Yet many of the best catalytic mechanisms were not created by top management. The idea for the federal government's waiver rule, for example, originated with two staff members—Lance Cope and Jeff Goldstein. They were working in the national reinvention labs, and neither had direct authority over any federal agency.

Allow me also to use a personal example. Part of my professional vision is to contribute through teaching and to harness my curiosity and passion for learning in ways that make a positive impact on the world. From that goal flows the imperative that I allocate time primarily to research, writing, and teaching and limit consulting work only to those situations in which I can contribute as a teacher.

To reinforce that imperative, I have created two catalytic mechanisms: the "come to Boulder rule" and the "four day rule." The first rule states that I will not engage in a direct advisory relationship with any organization unless the chief executive agrees to travel to my Boulder research laboratory. Executives spend huge sums of money on consultants, but money doesn't equal commitment—if you have a big enough budget, invoices just don't hurt. Yet all chief executives, no matter how large their budgets, have only 24 hours in a day. If a CEO flies all the way to Boulder, he or she has demonstrated commitment to serious discussions and hard work, and the likelihood that I will make a significant impact as a teacher increases exponentially. Most important, those not committed to real (and perhaps uncomfortable) change eject right up front.

The second mechanism—my four-day rule—states that any given organization has an upper limit of four days of my advisory time in a year. The most lasting impact comes by teaching people how to fish, not by fishing for them. Organizations that want an adviser to fish for them self-eject through this catalytic mechanism. Admittedly, these are highly unusual devices, and they would be disastrous for most consulting firms that depend on continuous growth to feed their machine. Yet they are perfectly designed for a strategy aimed at explicitly *not* building a large consulting business. They are unique to me, as all catalytic mechanisms should be to their creators.

Use money, but not only money

The examples in this article may lead you to believe that most catalytic mechanisms use money. But, in fact, when my research colleague Lane Hornung cataloged my database of catalytic mechanisms, he found that only half do. That might surprise some people—in particular those who ascribe to the old saw that money is the best motivator. I'm not going to claim that money doesn't impel people toward desired results; money can add teeth to any catalytic mechanism. But to rely entirely on money reflects a shallow understanding of human behavior.

The U.S. Marine Corps illustrates my point precisely. The Corps builds extraordinary commitment through a set of catalytic mechanisms that create intense psychological bonds among its members. By isolating recruits at boot camps and creating an environment where recruits survive only by relying upon one another, the Corps triggers the deep human drive, hardwired into most of us, to support and protect those we consider family. Most people will not risk their lives for a year-end bonus, but they will go to great lengths to earn the respect and protect the well-being of their comrades.

William Manchester, who returned to his unit on Okinawa after receiving a wound that earned him a Purple Heart, eloquently describes the psychology of commitment in his book *Goodbye Darkness*:

And then, in one of those great thundering jolts in which a man's real motives are revealed to him in an electrifying vision, I understand, at last, why I jumped hospital that Sunday thirty-five years ago, and, in violation of orders, returned to the front and almost certain death. It was an act of love. Those men on the line were my family, my home. . . . They had never let me down, and I couldn't do it to them. I had to be with them rather than to let them die and me live with the knowledge that I might have saved them. Men, I now knew, do not fight for flag or country, for the Marine Corps or glory or any other abstraction. They fight for one another.[1]

Yes, catalytic mechanisms sometimes use money to add bite, but the best ones also tap deeper wells of human motivation. Even at Nucor, the effectiveness of its catalytic mechanisms lies as much in the peer pressure and the desire to not let teammates down as in the number of dollars in the weekly bonus envelope. The best people *never* work solely for money. And catalytic mechanisms should reflect that fact.

Allow your mechanisms to evolve

New catalytic mechanisms sometimes produce unintended negative consequences and need correction. For instance, the first version of the red flag failed because certain students continued to dominate class discussion, thinking that every comment of theirs was worth a red flag. So I added the stipulation: "Your red flag can be used only once during the quarter. Your red flag is nontransferable; you cannot give or sell it to another student."

All catalytic mechanisms, in fact, even if they work perfectly at first, should evolve. 3M's 15% rule is a case in point. In 1956, executives urged 3M scientists to use 3M labs during their lunch break to work on anything they wanted. In the 1960s, that catalytic mechanism became formalized as the "15% rule," whereby scientists could use *any* 15% of their time. In the 1980s, the 15% rule became widely available to 3Mers other than scientists, to be used for manufacturing and marketing innovations, for example. In the 1990s, 3M's executives worried that fewer people were using the mechanism than in previous decades. It put together a task force to reinvent the 15% rule, bolstering it with special recognition rewards for those who used their "bootleg time"—as it has come to be called—to create profitable innovations.

The 15% rule has been a catalytic mechanism at 3M for more than 40 years, but it has continually evolved in order to remain relevant and effective. That's the right approach; no catalytic mechanism should be viewed as sacred. In a great company, only the core values and purpose are sacred; everything else, including a catalytic mechanism, should be open for change.

Build an integrated set

One catalytic mechanism is good; several that reinforce one another as a set is even better. That's not to say a company needs hundreds of catalytic mechanisms—a handful will do. Consider Granite Rock again. It certainly doesn't rely just on short pay. It also has a catalytic mechanism that requires an employee and manager to create a focused development plan for the employee during the performance evaluation process. Indeed, every employee and manager must together complete a form that reads: "Learn _____ so that I can contribute _____." Two sets of teeth make this form effective. First, employees and their managers must both sign off on the final development plan, which forces a continual dialogue until they reach agreement. Second, compensation ties directly to learning and improvement, not just job performance: people who do not go out of their way to improve their skills receive lower than midpoint pay. Only those who do a good job *and* improve their skills *and* make a contribution to improving the overall Granite Rock system receive higher than midpoint pay. So people who merely do a good job self-eject out of Granite Rock. This catalytic mechanism has produced delightful surprises: one previously illiterate employee used it to get the company to send him to a reading program. When Granite Rock won the Baldrige Award, he read an acceptance speech.

Granite Rock also uses catalytic mechanisms to guide hiring, encourage risk taking, and stimulate new capabilities. The point here is not so much in the details as it is in the big picture: Granite Rock does not rely solely on short pay to pursue its BHAG of attaining a reputation for customer satisfaction that exceeds Nordstrom's. It has about a dozen catalytic mechanisms that support and reinforce one another.

That said, however, it would be a mistake to take this article and launch a grand catalytic mechanism initiative. Developing a set of catalytic mechanisms should be an organic process, an ongoing discipline, a habit of mind and action. The dozen or so catalytic mechanisms at Granite Rock came into being over a ten-year period. You certainly don't want to use the idea to create another layer of bureaucracy. Catalytic mechanisms should be catalysts, not inhibitors.

CASTLES IN THE AIR

I recently worked with a large retail chain to define its BHAG for the twenty-first century. The company is doing well, but it wants its performance to be outrageously great. And so its executives came up with a wildly ambitious goal: to make its brand more popular than Coke.

That company's challenge now is to invent the catalytic mechanisms that will make the dream a reality. I've advised its executives against investing heavily in hoopla events to fire up thousands of frontline employees about the new BHAG. Instead, they should create and implement a set of catalytic mechanisms—specific, concrete, and powerful devices to lend discipline to their vision.

After all, catalytic mechanisms alone will not create greatness; they need a dream to guide them. But if you can blend huge, intangible aspirations with simple, tangible catalytic mechanisms, then you'll have the magic combination from which sustained excellence grows.

At the conclusion of *Walden,* Henry David Thoreau wrote: "If you have built castles in the air, your work need not be lost; that is where they should be. Now put the foundations under them." BHAGs are a company's wildest dreams. Catalytic mechanisms are their foundations. Build them both.

TABLE 1

Catalytic mechanisms: Breaking from tradition

Catalytic mechanisms share five distinct characteristics that distinguish them from traditional controls

A traditional managerial device, control, or mechanism:	A catalytic mechanism:	Examples of catalytic mechanisms:
Reduces variation as it enlarges the organization's bureaucracy.	Produces desired results in unpredictable ways.	The red flag made a ferociously opinionated CEO listen to the challenge of an M.B.A. student—improving the knowledge of the whole class, despite the unexpected nature of the exchange.
Concentrates power in the hands of authorities who can force people to obey their commands.	Distributes power for the benefit of the overall system, often to the great discomfort of those who traditionally hold power.	A new government rule allowed a low-level manager to expunge an immensely wasteful regulation that required nearly new uniforms to be burned.

(Continued)

TABLE 1 (CONTINUED)

A traditional managerial device, control, or mechanism:	A catalytic mechanism:	Examples of catalytic mechanisms:
Is understood by employees and executives alike as merely an intention.	Has a sharp set of teeth.	Short pay at Granite Rock allows customers to pay only for the products that satisfy them.
Attempts to stimulate the right behaviors from the wrong people.	Attracts the right people and ejects viruses.	At W.L. Gore & Associates, employees can, in effect, fire their bosses, ensuring nonhierarchical leadership.
Has the short-lived impact of a single event or a fad.	Produces an ongoing effect.	Kimberly-Clark knowingly put itself into head-to-head competition with Procter & Gamble to impel better performance in the consumer goods marketplace. Such a strategy is still working 30 years later.

Anatomy of a BHAG

In our research for *Built to Last,* Jerry Porras and I discovered that most enduring great companies set and pursue BHAGs (pronounced BEE-hags and shorthand for big, hairy, audacious goals). There are three key characteristics of a good BHAG:

1. **It has a long time frame—ten to 30 years or more.** The whole point of a BHAG is to stimulate your organization to make changes that dramatically improve its fundamental capabilities over the long run. Citicorp's first BHAG, set in 1915— to become the most powerful, the most serviceable, the most far-reaching world financial institution ever—took more than

five decades to achieve. Its new BHAG, set in the early 1990s—to attain 1 billion customers worldwide—will require at least two decades to achieve. (Today it has less than 100 million.) BHAGs with short time frames can lead executives to sacrifice long-term results for the sake of achieving a short-term goal.

2. **It is clear, compelling, and easy to grasp.** The goal in a good BHAG is obvious, no matter how you phrase it. For example, Philip Morris's BHAG, set in the 1950s—to knock off R.J. Reynolds as the number one tobacco company in the world—didn't leave much room for confusion. I call this the "Mount Everest

standard." The goal to climb Mount
Everest can be said as "Climb the most
famous mountain in the world" or "Climb
the biggest mountain in the world" or
"Climb the mountain at 87 degrees east,
28 degrees north" or "Climb the mountain
in Nepal that measures 29,028 feet" or
hundreds of other ways. If you find yourself
spending countless hours tinkering with a
statement, you don't yet have a BHAG.

3. **It connects to the core values and
   purpose of the organization.** The best
   BHAGs aren't random; they fit with the
   fundamental core values and reason
   for being of the company. For example,
   Nike's BHAG in the 1960s—to crush

Adidas—fit perfectly with Nike's core purpose "to experience the emotion of competition, winning, and crushing competitors." Sony's BHAG in the 1950s—to become the company most known for changing the worldwide poor-quality image of Japanese products—flowed directly from its stated core value of elevating the Japanese culture and national status.

This last criterion connects back to the reason for having a BHAG in the first place. It is a powerful way to stimulate progress—change, improvement, innovation, renewal—while simultaneously preserving your core values and purpose. It is this remarkable ability to blend continuity with change that separates enduring great companies from merely successful ones. The trick, of course, is not just to set a BHAG but to achieve it, and therein lies the power of catalytic mechanisms.

Not for Companies Only

My research has focused on the impact of catalytic mechanisms in organizational settings—on how they can turn a company's most ambitious goals into reality. But catalytic mechanisms can also have a powerful impact on individuals. Indeed, I have made catalytic mechanisms a fundamental part of how I manage my time, with my "come to Boulder rule" and "four day rule."

I am not alone. Several of my former students at Stanford Business School have applied a catalytic mechanism to reach their goals. In one case, a student emerged from his courses on entrepreneurship fired up by the idea of forgoing the traditional path and striking out on his own. But as time passed and he felt the crushing burden of school debt as well as the lure of lucrative job offers, his personal vision waned. He took a job at a large, established disc drive manufacturer and promised himself, "I'm going to launch out on my own in five years when I've paid off all my school debts."

In most cases, such dreams fade as the years go by—with the advent of cars, houses, children, and all the rest. My former student, however, implemented an interesting catalytic mechanism to keep his vision alive. He drafted a resignation letter and dated it five years out. Then he gave copies of the letter to a handful of reliable people, along with the following instructions, "If I don't leave my job and launch out on my own by the specified date, then send the letter in for me." His plan worked. In 1996, I received an e-mail from him that described how he saved his money and spent his off-hours developing his entrepreneurial options. Then, right on schedule, he quit his secure job and launched a fund to buy and run his own company.

In another case, a former student created a personal board of directors composed of people he admires and would not want to disappoint, and he made a personal commitment to follow the board's guidance—it has power in his life. In 1996, he wrote me: "I recently used my personal board in deciding whether to leave Morgan Stanley and go to work with a friend in his two-year-old business. 'Yes' was the unanimous vote." So despite the risk of leaving a lucrative and prestigious position, he leapt into the small company, which has since grown fourfold to employ more than 80 people.

Consider also the highly effective catalytic mechanism that a colleague of mine has been using for the past three years to attain her BHAG: to lead a full and active life as a mother, wife, professional writer, and church volunteer, without going crazy. That part about maintaining sanity is important because before her catalytic mechanism was in place, my colleague constantly found herself overextended and miserable. The main culprit was her work as a freelance writer: she accepted too many jobs. "Even if we didn't need the money, I would still take on every project that came my way," she recalls. "Maybe because my family was so poor when I was growing up, I just found it impossible to leave money on the table." Not surprisingly, the woman's children paid the price of her constant working, as did her husband and close-knit extended family. "Either I was too exhausted to see people or else I was calling them for a baby-sitting favor," she says.

One day, my colleague was lamenting her situation to her sister, who came up with an effective catalytic mechanism. Every time the woman took on work beyond a certain level of revenue—a comfortable annual salary, in essence—she would pay her sister a $200-a-day penalty fee. My colleague, instantly seeing the wonderful impact of the plan, immediately agreed.

Since she redistributed power to her sister, my colleague has gained new control over her life. Now she happily accepts jobs up to a certain level of income, but she assesses each additional offer with newly critical eyes. (She has taken on extra work on only two occasions; both projects were too lucrative to pass up.) Indeed, the catalytic mechanism has so freed my colleague from overwork that she has taken on a new role as a volunteer at her children's school. With its undeniable bite, my colleague's catalytic mechanism will have an ongoing effect as long as she honors it. And given its results, she plans to do so for a long time.

Would any of these people have changed their lives without catalytic mechanisms? Perhaps, but I think it less likely. Personal catalytic mechanisms have all the benefits of organizational mechanisms: they put bite into good intentions, dramatically increasing the odds of actually being true to your personal vision instead of letting your dreams remain unrealized.

NOTE

1. William Manchester, *Goodbye Darkness* (Boston: Little, Brown and Company, 1979).

ABOUT THE AUTHOR

Jim Collins operates a management research laboratory in Boulder, Colorado. He is the coauthor, with Jerry I. Porras, of *Built to Last: Successful Habits of Visionary Companies* (HarperBusiness, 1994) and of "Building Your Company's Vision" (*HBR* September–October 1996).

Article Summary

Idea in Brief

Many change programs trumpet their arrival with well-known Big Hairy Audacious Goals (BHAGs). But just as many get stuck at the first hurdle to meeting those goals—mobilizing the organization away from the status quo. Catalytic mechanisms help catapult organizations over this hurdle. This simple yet powerful tool enables companies to propel commitment levels past the point of no return. They are galvanizing, nonbureaucratic means of turning visions into reality, usually involving a redistribution of power. Short pay is a

defining example of a catalytic mechanism. Granite
Rock mobilized its employees to feverish levels
of performance improvement with this simple
but radical policy that invites customers who are
not completely satisfied to reduce their invoice
payment—without returning product. Of course,
short pay is not appropriate for every company,
but other catalytic mechanisms wielding that much
power definitely are.

The most important management ideas all in one place.

We hope you enjoyed this book from *Harvard Business Review*. For the best ideas HBR has to offer turn to HBR's 10 Must Reads Boxed Set. From books on leadership and strategy to managing yourself and others, this 6-book collection delivers articles on the most essential business topics to help you succeed.

HBR's 10 Must Reads Series

The definitive collection of ideas and best practices on our most sought-after topics from the best minds in business.

- Change Management
- Collaboration
- Communication
- Emotional Intelligence
- Innovation
- Leadership
- Making Smart Decisions

- Managing Across Cultures
- Managing People
- Managing Yourself
- Strategic Marketing
- Strategy
- Teams
- The Essentials

hbr.org/mustreads

Buy for your team, clients, or event.
Visit hbr.org/bulksales for quantity discount rates.

RED OCEAN TRAPS

HARVARD BUSINESS REVIEW
CLASSICS

RED OCEAN TRAPS
*The Mental Models That Undermine
Market-Creating Strategies*

W. Chan Kim and
Renée Mauborgne

Harvard Business Review Press
Boston, Massachusetts

Copyright 2017 Harvard Business School Publishing Corporation
Originally published in *Harvard Business Review* in March 2015
Reprint #R1503D

Printed in the United States of America

10 9 8 7 6 5 4 3 2

The web addresses referenced in this book were live and correct at the time of the book's publication but may be subject to change.

Cataloging-in-Publication data is forthcoming.

ISBN: 978-1-63369-266-4
eISBN: 978-1-63369-267-1

The paper used in this publication meets the requirements of the American National Standard for Permanence of Paper for Publications and Documents in Libraries and Archives Z39.48-1992.

THE HARVARD BUSINESS REVIEW CLASSICS SERIES

Since 1922, *Harvard Business Review* has
been a leading source of breakthrough ideas
in management practice—many of which still
speak to and influence us today. The HBR
Classics series now offers you the opportunity
to make these seminal pieces a part of your
permanent management library. Each volume contains a groundbreaking idea that has
shaped best practices and inspired countless
managers around the world—and will change
how you think about the business world today.

RED OCEAN TRAPS

I n America, corporate performance has been deteriorating for decades. According to Deloitte's landmark study "The Shift Index," the aggregate return on assets of U.S. public companies has fallen below 1%, to about a quarter of its 1965 level. As market power has moved from companies to consumers, and global competition has intensified, managers in almost all industries have come to face steep performance challenges. To turn things around, they need to be more creative in developing and executing their competitive strategies. But long-term success will not be achieved through competitiveness alone. Increasingly, it will depend on the ability to generate new demand and create and capture new markets.

The payoffs of market creation are huge. Just compare the experiences of Apple and Microsoft. Over the past 15 years, Apple has made a series of successful market-creating moves, introducing the iPod, iTunes, the iPhone, the App Store, and the iPad. From the launch of the iPod in 2001 to the end of its 2014 fiscal year, Apple's market cap surged more than 75-fold as its sales and profits exploded. Over the same period,

Microsoft's market cap crept up by a mere 3% while its revenue went from nearly five times larger than Apple's to nearly half of Apple's. With close to 80% of profits coming from two old businesses—Windows and Office—and no compelling market-creating move, Microsoft has paid a steep price.

Of course, it's not that companies don't recognize the value of new market spaces. To the contrary, their leaders increasingly are committed to creating them and dedicate significant amounts of money to efforts to do so. But despite this, few companies seem to crack the code. What, exactly, is getting in their way?

In the decade since the publication of the first edition of our book, *Blue Ocean*

Strategy, we've had conversations with many managers involved in executing market-creating strategies. As they shared their successes and failures with us, we identified a common factor that seemed to consistently undermine their efforts: their mental models—ingrained assumptions and theories about the way the world works. Though mental models lie below people's cognitive awareness, they're so powerful a determinant of choices and behaviors that many neuroscientists think of them almost as automated algorithms that dictate how people respond to changes and events.

Mental models have their merits. In dangerous times, a robust mental model can help you quickly make decisions that are critical to survival. And we have no issue with the soundness of the mental models that we saw managers apply. They were grounded in knowledge acquired in classrooms and from years of business experience. They help managers respond better to competitive challenges. But our conversations suggest that the mental models managers rely on to negotiate existing market spaces also undermine their ability to create new markets.

In our research and discussions, we've encountered six especially salient assumptions built into managers' mental models. We have come to think of them as red ocean traps, because they effectively anchor managers in red oceans—crowded market spaces where companies engage in bloody competition for market share—and prevent them from entering blue oceans, previously unknown and uncontested market spaces with ample potential.

The first two traps stem from assumptions about marketing, in particular an emphasis on customer orientation and niches; the next two from economic lessons on technology innovation and creative destruction; and the final two from principles of competitive strategy that regard differentiation and low cost as mutually exclusive choices. In the following pages, we'll look at each trap in detail and see how it thwarts companies' attempts to create markets.

TRAP ONE: SEEING MARKET-CREATING STRATEGIES AS CUSTOMER-ORIENTED APPROACHES

Generating new demand is at the heart of market-creating strategies. It hinges on converting noncustomers into customers, as Salesforce.com did with its on-demand CRM software, which opened up a new market space by winning over small and midsize firms that had previously rejected CRM enterprise software.

The trouble is that managers, especially those in marketing, have been quite reasonably brought up to believe that the customer is king. It's all too easy for them to assume, therefore, that market-creating strategies are customer led, which causes them to reflexively stick to their focus on existing customers and how to make them happier.

This approach, however, is unlikely to create new markets. To do that, an organization needs to turn its focus to noncustomers and why they refuse to patronize an industry's offering. Noncustomers, not customers, hold the greatest insight into the points of pain and intimidation that limit the boundary of an industry. A focus on existing customers, by contrast, tends to drive organizations to come up with better solutions for them than what competitors currently offer—but keeps companies moored in red oceans.

Consider Sony's launch of the Portable Reader System (PRS) in 2006. The company's aim was to unlock a new market space in books by opening the e-reader market to a wide customer base. To figure out how to realize that goal, it looked to the experience of existing e-reader customers, who were dissatisfied with the size and poor display quality of current products. Sony's response was a thin, lightweight device with an easy-to-read screen. Despite the media's praise and happier customers, the PRS lost out to Amazon's Kindle because it failed to attract the mass of noncustomers whose main reason for rejecting e-readers was the shortage of worthwhile books, not the size and the display of the devices. Without a rich choice of titles and an easy way to download them, the noncustomers stuck to print books.

Amazon understood this when it launched the Kindle in 2007, offering more than four times the number of e-titles available from the PRS and making them easily downloadable over Wi-Fi. Within six hours of their release, Kindles sold out, as print book customers rapidly became e-reader customers as well. Though Sony has since exited e-readers, the Kindle grew the industry from around a mere 2% of total book buyers in 2008 to 28% in 2014. It now offers more than 2.5 million e-titles.

TRAP TWO: TREATING MARKET-CREATING STRATEGIES AS NICHE STRATEGIES

The field of marketing has placed great emphasis on using ever finer market segmentation to identify and capture niche markets. Though niche strategies can often be very effective, uncovering a niche in an existing space is not the same thing as identifying a new market space.

Consider Song, an airline launched in 2003 by Delta. Delta's aim was to create a new market space in low-cost carriers by targeting a distinct segment of fliers. It decided to focus on stylish professional women travelers, a segment it figured had needs and preferences different from those of the businessmen and other passengers most airlines targeted. No airline had ever been built around this group. After many focus group discussions with upwardly mobile and professional women, Delta came up with a plan to cater to them with organic food, custom cocktails, a variety of entertainment choices, free in-flight workouts with complementary exercise bands, and crew members dressed in Kate Spade. The strategy was intended to fill a gap in the market. It may well have done that successfully, but the segment proved too small to be sustainable despite competitive pricing. Song flew its last flight in April 2006, just 36 months after its launch.

Successful market-creating strategies don't focus on finer segmentation. More often, they "desegment" markets by identifying key commonalities across buyer groups that could help generate broader demand. Pret A Manger, a British food chain, looked across three different prepared-lunch buyer groups: restaurant-going professionals, fast food customers, and the brown bag set. Although there were plenty of differences across these groups, there were three key commonalities: All of them wanted a lunch that was fresh and healthful, wanted it fast, and wanted it at a reasonable price. That insight helped Pret A Manger see how it could unlock and aggregate untapped demand across those groups to create a commercially compelling new market.

Its concept was to offer restaurant-quality sandwiches made fresh every day from high-end ingredients, preparing them at a speed even greater than that of fast food, and delivering that experience in a sleek setting at reasonable prices. Today, nearly 30 years on, Pret A Manger continues to enjoy robust profitable growth in the new market space it established.

TRAP THREE: CONFUSING TECHNOLOGY INNOVATION WITH MARKET-CREATING STRATEGIES

R&D and technology innovation are widely recognized as key drivers of market development and industry growth. It's

understandable, therefore, that managers
might assume that they are also key drivers in
the discovery of new markets. But the reality
is that market creation is not inevitably
about technological innovation. Yellow Tail
opened a new market (in its case, for a fun
and simple wine for everyone) without any
bleeding-edge technologies. So did the
coffee chain Starbucks and the performing
arts company Cirque du Soleil. Even when
technology is heavily involved, as it was with
market creators Salesforce.com, Intuit's
Quicken, or Uber, it is not the reason that
new offerings are successful. Such products
and services succeed because they are so
simple to use, fun, and productive that people fall in love with them. The technology

that enables them essentially disappears from buyers' minds.

Consider the Segway Personal Transporter, which was launched in 2001. Was it a technology innovation? Sure. It was the world's first self-balancing human transporter, and it worked well. Lean forward and you go forward; lean back and you go back. This engineering marvel was one of the most-talked-about technology innovations of its time. But most people were unwilling to pay up to $5,000 for a product that posed difficulties in use and convenience: Where could you park it? How would you take it with you in a car? Where could you use it—sidewalks or roads? Could you take it on a bus or a train? Although the Segway was expected to reach breakeven just six months after its launch, sales fell way below initial predictions, and the company was sold in 2009. Not everyone was surprised. At the time of the product's release, a prescient *Time* magazine article about Dean Kamen, Segway's inventor, struck a cautionary note: "One of the hardest truths for any technologist to hear is that success or failure in business is rarely determined by the quality of the technology."

Value innovation, not technology innovation, is what launches commercially compelling new markets. Successful new products or services open market spaces by offering a leap in productivity, simplicity, ease of use, convenience, fun, or environmental friendliness. But when companies mistakenly assume that market creation hinges on breakthrough technologies, their organizations tend to push for products or services that are too "out there," too complicated, or, like the Segway, lacking a necessary ecosystem. In fact, many technology innovations fail to create new markets even if they win the company accolades and their developers scientific prizes.

TRAP FOUR: EQUATING CREATIVE DESTRUCTION WITH MARKET CREATION

Joseph Schumpeter's theory of creative destruction lies at the heart of innovation economics. Creative destruction occurs when an invention disrupts a market by displacing an earlier technology or existing product or service. Digital photography, for example, wiped out the photographic film industry, becoming the new norm. In Schumpeter's framework, the old is incessantly destroyed and replaced by the new.

But does market creation always involve destruction? The answer is no. It also involves nondestructive creation, wherein new demand is created without displacing existing products or services. Take Viagra, which established a new market in lifestyle drugs. Did Viagra make any earlier technology or existing product or service obsolete? No. It unlocked new demand by offering for the first time a real solution to a major problem experienced by many men in their personal relationships. Grameen Bank's creation of the microfinance industry is another example. Many market-creating moves are nondestructive, because they offer solutions where none previously existed. We've also seen this happen with the social networking and crowdfunding industries. And even when a certain amount of destruction is involved in market creation, nondestructive creation is often a larger element than you might think. Nintendo's Wii game player, for example, complemented more than replaced existing game systems, because it attracted younger children and older adults who hadn't previously played video games.

Conflating market creation with creative destruction not only limits an organization's set of opportunities but also sets off resistance to market-creating strategies. People in established companies typically don't like the notion of creative destruction or disruption because it may threaten their current status and jobs. As a result, managers often undermine their company's market-creating efforts by starving them of resources, allocating undue overhead costs to the initiatives, or not cooperating with the people working on them. It's critical for market creators to head this danger off early by clarifying that their project is at least as much about nondestructive creation as it is about disruption.

TRAP FIVE: EQUATING MARKET-CREATING STRATEGIES WITH DIFFERENTIATION

In a competitive industry companies tend to choose their position on what economists call the "productivity frontier," the range of value-cost trade-offs that are available given the structure and norms of the industry. Differentiation is the strategic position on this frontier in which a company stands out from competitors by providing premium value; the trade-off is usually higher costs to the company and higher prices for customers. We've found that many managers assume that market creation is the same thing.

In reality, a market-creating move breaks the value-cost trade-off. It is about pursuing differentiation and low cost simultaneously. Are Yellow Tail and Salesforce.com differentiated from other players? You bet. But are Yellow Tail and Salesforce.com also low cost? Yes again. A market-creating move is a "both-and," not an "either-or," strategy. It's important to realize this difference, because when companies mistakenly assume that market creation is synonymous with differentiation, they often focus on what to improve or create to stand apart and pay scant heed to what they can eliminate or reduce to simultaneously achieve low cost. As a result, they may inadvertently become premium competitors in an existing industry space rather than discover a new market space of their own.

Take BMW, which set out to establish a new market in urban transport with its launch of the C1 in 2000. Traffic problems in European cities are severe, and people waste many hours commuting by car there, so BMW wanted to develop a vehicle people could use to beat rush-hour congestion. The C1 was a two-wheeled scooter targeting the premium end of the market. Unlike other scooters, it had a roof and a full windshield with wipers. BMW also invested heavily in safety. The C1 held drivers in place with a four-point seat-belt system and protected them with an aluminum roll cage, two shoulder-height roll bars, and a crumple zone around the front wheel.

With all these extra features, the C1 was expensive to build, and its price ranged from

$7,000 to $10,000—far more than the $3,000 to $5,000 that typical scooters fetched. Although the C1 succeeded in differentiating itself within the scooter industry, it did not create the new market space in transportation BMW had hoped for. In the summer of 2003, BMW announced it was stopping production because the C1 hadn't met sales expectations.

TRAP SIX: EQUATING MARKET-CREATING STRATEGIES WITH LOW-COST STRATEGIES

This trap, in which managers assume that they can create a new market solely by driving down costs, is the obvious flip side of trap five. When organizations see market-creating strategies as synonymous with low-cost strategies alone, they focus on what to eliminate and reduce in current offerings and largely ignore what they should improve or create to increase the offerings' value.

Ouya is a video-game console maker that fell into this trap. When the company began selling its products, in June 2013, big players like Sony, Microsoft, and Nintendo were offering consoles connected to TV screens and controllers that provided a high-quality gaming experience, for prices ranging from $199 to $419. With no low-cost console available, many people would play video games either on handheld devices or on TV screens connected to mobile devices via inexpensive cables.

An attempt to create a market space between high-end consoles and mobile handhelds, the $99 Ouya was introduced as a low-cost open-source "microconsole" offering reasonable quality on TV screens and most games free to try. Although people admired the inexpensive, simple device, Ouya didn't have the rich catalog of quality games, 3-D intensity, great graphics, and processing speed that traditional gamers prized but the company had to some extent sacrificed to drop cost and price. At the same time, Ouya lacked the distinctive advantage of mobile handheld devices— namely, their play-on-the-go functionality. In the absence of those features, potential gamers had no compelling reason to buy

Ouyas. The company is now shopping itself to acquirers—on the basis of its staff's talent more than the strength of its console business—but as yet hasn't found one.

Our point, again, is that a market-creating strategy takes a "both-and" approach: It pursues both differentiation and low cost. In this framework, new market space is created not by pricing against the competition within an industry but by pricing against substitutes and alternatives that noncustomers are currently using. Accordingly, a new market does not have to be created at the low end of an industry. Instead it can be created at the high end, as Cirque du Soleil did in circus entertainment, Starbucks did in coffee, and Dyson did in vacuum cleaners.

Even when companies create new markets at the low end, the offerings also are clearly differentiated in the eyes of buyers. Consider Southwest Airlines and Swatch. Southwest stands out for its friendly, fast, ground-transportation-in-the-air feel, while stylish, fun designs make Swatches a fashion statement. Both companies' offerings are perceived as both differentiated and low cost.

The approaches or strategies presented as the red ocean traps are not wrong or bad. They all serve important purposes. A customer focus, for example, can improve products and services, and technology innovation is a key input for market development and economic growth. Likewise, differentiation or low cost is an effective competitive strategy. What these approaches are not, however, is the path to successful market-creating strategies. And when they drive market-creating efforts that involve big investments, they may result in new businesses that don't earn back those investments and that ultimately fail, as we have seen here. That's why it's key to surface and check the mental models and assumptions of the people who are central to executing market-creating strategies. If those models and assumptions are misaligned with the intended strategic purpose of new market creation, you need to challenge, question, and reframe them. Otherwise, you may fall into the red ocean traps.

W. Chan Kim and *Renée Mauborgne* are professors at INSEAD, the world's second-largest business school, and codirectors of the INSEAD Blue Ocean Strategy Institute. They are the authors of *Blue Ocean Strategy*, which is recognized as one of the most iconic and impactful strategy books ever written. The theory of blue ocean strategy has been actively embraced by companies, governments, and nonprofits across the globe and is currently being taught in more than eighteen hundred universities around the world. *Blue Ocean Strategy* is a bestseller across five continents. It has sold over 3.6 million copies and has been published in a record-breaking 44 languages. Kim and Mauborgne are ranked in the top three of the Thinkers50 global list of top management thinkers and were named among the world's top five best business school professors by MBA Rankings. They have received numerous academic and management awards around the globe, including the Nobels Colloquia Prize for Leadership on Business and Economic Thinking, the Carl S. Sloane Award by the Association of Management Consulting Firms, the Leadership Hall of Fame by *Fast Company* magazine, and the

Eldridge Haynes Prize by the Academy of International Business, among others. Kim and Mauborgne are Fellows of the World Economic Forum in Davos. Mauborgne is a member of President Barack Obama's Board of Advisors on Historically Black Colleges and Universities (HBCUs). Kim is an advisory member for the European Union and is an advisor for several countries.

ALSO BY THESE AUTHORS

Harvard Business Review Press Books

Blue Ocean Strategy, Expanded Edition: How to Create Uncontested Market Space and Make the Competition Irrelevant

The W. Chan Kim and Renée Mauborgne Blue Ocean Strategy Reader

***Harvard Business Review* Articles**

"Blue Ocean Leadership"

"Blue Ocean Strategy"

"Charting Your Company's Future"

"Creating New Market Space"

"Fair Process: Managing in the
Knowledge Economy"

"How Strategy Shapes Structure"

"Knowing a Winning Business Idea
When You See One"

"Tipping Point Leadership"

"Value Innovation: The Strategic Logic of
High Growth"

Article Summary

Idea in Brief

The Problem

To succeed in the long term, companies must find ways to create new markets. Competing in existing markets is growing less profitable. But despite much investment and commitment, companies find it extraordinarily difficult to establish new market spaces.

Why It Happens

Managers' mental models are based on their experiences in existing markets. Though these assumptions and beliefs have worked in the past, they undermine efforts to create new spaces.

The Solution

To avoid being trapped in old markets, managers need to:

- focus on attracting new customers

- worry less about segmentation

- understand that market creation is not synonymous with either technological innovation or creative destruction

- stop focusing on premium versus low-cost strategies

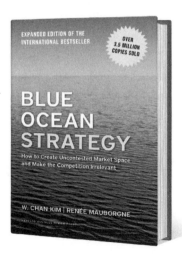

The most important management ideas all in one place.

We hope you enjoyed this book from *Harvard Business Review*. For the best ideas HBR has to offer turn to HBR's 10 Must Reads Boxed Set. From books on leadership and strategy to managing yourself and others, this 6-book collection delivers articles on the most essential business topics to help you succeed.

HBR's 10 Must Reads Series

The definitive collection of ideas and best practices on our most sought-after topics from the best minds in business.

- Change Management
- Collaboration
- Communication
- Emotional Intelligence
- Innovation
- Leadership
- Making Smart Decisions

- Managing Across Cultures
- Managing People
- Managing Yourself
- Strategic Marketing
- Strategy
- Teams
- The Essentials

hbr.org/mustreads

Buy for your team, clients, or event.
Visit hbr.org/bulksales for quantity discount rates.

Harvard Business Review Press

HOW WILL YOU
MEASURE YOUR LIFE?

HARVARD BUSINESS REVIEW
CLASSICS

HOW WILL YOU
MEASURE YOUR LIFE?

Clayton M. Christensen

Harvard Business Review Press
Boston, Massachusetts

Copyright 2017 Harvard Business School Publishing Corporation
Originally published in *Harvard Business Review* in July 2010
Reprint #R1007B
All rights reserved

Printed in the United States of America

10 9 8 7 6 5 4 3 2

The web addresses referenced in this book were live and correct at the time of the book's publication but may be subject to change.

Names: Christensen, Clayton M., author.
Title: How will you measure your life? / Clayton M. Christensen.
Other titles: Harvard business review classics.
Description: Boston, Massachusetts : Harvard Business Review Press, [2017]
  | Series: Harvard business review classics
Identifiers: LCCN 2016042146 | ISBN 9781633692565 (pbk. : alk. paper)
Subjects: LCSH: Quality of life. | Integrity. | Management.
  | Business ethics. | Self-perception.
Classification: LCC HN25 .C48 2017 | DDC 306—dc23 LC record available
  at https://lccn.loc.gov/2016042146

ISBN: 978-1-63369-256-5
eISBN: 978-1-63369-257-2

THE HARVARD BUSINESS
REVIEW CLASSICS SERIES

Since 1922, *Harvard Business Review* has
been a leading source of breakthrough ideas
in management practice—many of which still
speak to and influence us today. The HBR
Classics series now offers you the opportunity
to make these seminal pieces a part of your
permanent management library. Each volume contains a groundbreaking idea that has
shaped best practices and inspired countless
managers around the world—and will change
how you think about the business world today.

HOW WILL YOU
MEASURE YOUR LIFE?

B efore I published *The Innovator's Dilemma,* I got a call from Andrew Grove, then the chairman of Intel. He had read one of my early papers about disruptive technology, and he asked if I could talk to his direct reports and explain my research and what it implied for Intel. Excited, I flew to Silicon Valley and showed up at the appointed time, only to have Grove say, "Look, stuff has happened. We have only 10 minutes for you. Tell us what your model of disruption means for Intel." I said that I couldn't—that I needed a full 30 minutes to explain the model, because only with it as context would any comments about Intel make sense. Ten minutes into my explanation, Grove interrupted: "Look, I've got your model. Just tell us what it means for Intel."

I insisted that I needed 10 more minutes to describe how the process of disruption had worked its way through a very different industry, steel, so that he and his team could understand how disruption worked. I told the story of how Nucor and other steel minimills had begun by attacking the lowest end of the market—steel reinforcing bars, or rebar—and later moved up toward the high end, undercutting the traditional steel mills.

When I finished the minimill story, Grove said, "OK, I get it. What it means for Intel is . . ." and then went on to articulate what would become the company's strategy for going to the bottom of the market to launch the Celeron processor.

I've thought about that a million times since. If I had been suckered into telling Andy Grove what he should think about the microprocessor business, I'd have been killed. But instead of telling him what to think, I taught him how to think—and then he reached what I felt was the correct decision on his own.

That experience had a profound influence on me. When people ask what I think they should do, I rarely answer their question directly.

Instead, I run the question aloud through one of my models. I'll describe how the process in the model worked its way through an industry quite different from their own. And then, more often than not, they'll say, "OK, I get it." And they'll answer their own question more insightfully than I could have.

My class at Harvard Business School is structured to help my students understand what good management theory is and how it is built. To that backbone I attach different models or theories that help students think about the various dimensions of a general manager's job in stimulating innovation and growth. In each session we look at one company through the lenses of those theories—using them to explain how the company got into its situation and to examine what managerial actions will yield the needed results.

On the last day of class, I ask my students to turn those theoretical lenses on themselves, to find cogent answers to three questions: First, how can I be sure that I'll be happy in my career? Second, how can I be sure that my relationships with my spouse and my family become an enduring source of happiness? Third, how can I be sure I'll stay out of jail? Though the last question sounds lighthearted, it's not. Two of the 32 people in my Rhodes scholar class spent time in jail. Jeff Skilling of Enron fame was a classmate of mine at HBS. These were good guys—but something in their lives sent them off in the wrong direction.

As the students discuss the answers to these questions, I open my own life to them as a case study of sorts, to illustrate how they can use the theories from our course to guide their life decisions.

One of the theories that gives great insight on the first question—how to be sure we find happiness in our careers—is from Frederick Herzberg, who asserts that the powerful motivator in our lives isn't money; it's the opportunity to learn, grow in responsibilities, contribute to others, and be recognized for achievements. I tell the students about a vision of sorts I had while I was running the company I founded before becoming an academic. In my mind's eye I saw one of my managers leave for work one morning with a relatively strong level of self-esteem. Then I pictured her driving home to her family 10 hours later, feeling unappreciated, frustrated, underutilized, and demeaned. I imagined how profoundly her lowered self-esteem affected the way she interacted with her children. The vision in my mind then fast-forwarded to another day, when she drove home with greater self-esteem—feeling that she had learned a lot, been recognized for achieving valuable things, and played a significant role in the success of some important initiatives. I then imagined how positively that affected her as a spouse and a parent. My conclusion: Management is the most noble of professions if it's practiced well. No other occupation offers as many ways to help others learn and grow, take responsibility and be recognized for achievement, and contribute to the success of a team. More and more MBA students come to school thinking that a career in business means buying, selling, and investing in companies. That's unfortunate. Doing deals doesn't yield the deep rewards that come from building up people.

I want students to leave my classroom knowing that.

CREATE A STRATEGY FOR YOUR LIFE

A theory that is helpful in answering the second question—How can I ensure that my relationship with my family proves to be an enduring source of happiness?—concerns how strategy is defined and implemented. Its primary insight is that a company's strategy is determined by the types of initiatives that management invests in. If a company's resource allocation process is not managed masterfully, what emerges from it can be very different from what management intended. Because companies' decision-making systems are designed to steer investments to initiatives that offer the most tangible and immediate returns, companies shortchange investments in initiatives that are crucial to their long-term strategies.

Over the years I've watched the fates of my HBS classmates from 1979 unfold; I've seen more and more of them come to reunions unhappy, divorced, and alienated from their children. I can guarantee you that not a single one of them graduated with the deliberate strategy of getting divorced and raising children who would become estranged from them. And yet a shocking number of them implemented that strategy. The reason? They didn't keep the purpose of their lives front and center as they decided how to spend their time, talents, and energy.

It's quite startling that a significant fraction of the 900 students that HBS draws each year from the world's best have given little thought to the purpose of their lives. I tell the students that HBS might be one of their last chances to reflect deeply on that question. If they think that they'll have more time and energy to reflect later, they're nuts, because life only gets more demanding: You take on a mortgage; you're working 70 hours a week; you have a spouse and children.

For me, having a clear purpose in my life has been essential. But it was something I had to think long and hard about before I understood it. When I was a Rhodes scholar, I was in a very demanding academic program, trying to cram an extra year's worth of work into my time at Oxford. I decided to spend an hour every night reading, thinking, and praying about why God put me on this earth. That was a very challenging commitment to keep, because every hour I spent doing that, I wasn't studying applied econometrics. I was conflicted about whether I could really afford to take that time away from my studies, but I stuck with it—and ultimately figured out the purpose of my life.

Had I instead spent that hour each day learning the latest techniques for mastering the problems of autocorrelation in regression analysis, I would have badly misspent my life. I apply the tools of econometrics a few times a year, but I apply my knowledge of the purpose of my life every day. It's the single most useful thing I've ever learned. I promise my students that if they take the time to figure out their life purpose, they'll look back on it as the most important thing they discovered at HBS. If they don't figure it out, they will just sail off without a rudder and get buffeted in the very rough seas of life. Clarity about their purpose will trump knowledge of activity-based costing, balanced scorecards, core competence, disruptive innovation, the four Ps, and the five forces.

My purpose grew out of my religious faith, but faith isn't the only thing that gives people direction. For example, one of my former students decided that his purpose was to bring honesty and economic prosperity to his country and to raise children who were as capably committed to this cause, and to each other, as he was. His purpose is focused on family and others—as mine is.

The choice and successful pursuit of a profession is but one tool for achieving your purpose. But without a purpose, life can become hollow.

ALLOCATE YOUR RESOURCES

Your decisions about allocating your personal time, energy, and talent ultimately shape your life's strategy.

I have a bunch of "businesses" that compete for these resources: I'm trying to have a rewarding relationship with my wife, raise great kids, contribute to my community, succeed in my career, contribute to my church, and so on. And I have exactly the same problem that a corporation does. I have a limited amount of time and energy and talent. How much do I devote to each of these pursuits?

Allocation choices can make your life turn out to be very different from what you intended. Sometimes that's good:

Opportunities that you never planned for emerge. But if you misinvest your resources, the outcome can be bad. As I think about my former classmates who inadvertently invested for lives of hollow unhappiness, I can't help believing that their troubles relate right back to a short-term perspective.

When people who have a high need for achievement—and that includes all HBS graduates—have an extra half hour of time or an extra ounce of energy, they'll unconsciously allocate it to activities that yield the most tangible accomplishments. And our careers provide the most concrete evidence that we're moving forward. You ship a product, finish a design, complete a presentation, close a sale, teach a class, publish a paper, get paid, get promoted. In contrast, investing time and energy in your relationship with your spouse and children typically doesn't offer that same immediate sense of achievement. Kids misbehave every day. It's really not until 20 years down the road that you can put your hands on your hips and say, "I raised a good son or a good daughter." You can neglect your relationship with your spouse, and on a day-to-day basis, it doesn't seem as if things are deteriorating. People who are driven to excel have this unconscious propensity to underinvest in their families and overinvest in their careers—even though intimate and loving relationships with their families are the most powerful and enduring source of happiness.

If you study the root causes of business disasters, over and over you'll find this predisposition toward endeavors that offer immediate gratification. If you look at personal lives through that lens, you'll see the same stunning and sobering pattern: people allocating fewer and fewer resources to the things they would have once said mattered most.

CREATE A CULTURE

There's an important model in our class called the Tools of Cooperation, which basically says that being a visionary manager isn't all it's cracked up to be. It's one thing to see into the foggy future with acuity and chart the course corrections that the company must make. But it's quite another to persuade employees who might not see the changes ahead to line up and work cooperatively to take the company in that new direction. Knowing what tools to wield to elicit the needed cooperation is a critical managerial skill.

The theory arrays these tools along two dimensions—the extent to which members of the organization agree on what they want from their participation in the enterprise, and the extent to which they agree on what actions will produce the desired results. When there is little agreement on both axes, you have to use "power tools"—coercion, threats, punishment, and so on—to secure cooperation. Many companies start in this quadrant, which is why the founding executive team must play such an assertive role in defining what must be done and how. If employees' ways of working together to address those tasks succeed over and over, consensus begins to form. MIT's Edgar Schein has described this process as the mechanism by which a culture is built. Ultimately, people don't even think about whether their way of doing things yields success. They embrace priorities and follow procedures by instinct and assumption rather than by explicit decision—which means that they've created a culture. Culture, in compelling but unspoken ways, dictates the proven, acceptable methods by which members of the group address recurrent problems. And culture defines the priority given to different types of problems. It can be a powerful management tool.

In using this model to address the question, How can I be sure that my family becomes an enduring source of happiness?, my students quickly see that the simplest tools that parents can wield to elicit cooperation from children are power tools. But there comes a point during the teen years when power tools no longer work. At that point parents start wishing that they had begun working with their children at a very young age to build a culture at home in which children instinctively behave respectfully toward one another, obey their parents, and choose the right thing to do. Families have cultures, just as companies do. Those cultures can be built consciously or evolve inadvertently.

If you want your kids to have strong self-esteem and confidence that they can solve hard problems, those qualities won't magically materialize in high school. You have to design them into your family's culture—and you have to think about this very early on. Like employees, children build self-esteem by doing things that are hard and learning what works.

AVOID THE "MARGINAL COSTS" MISTAKE

We're taught in finance and economics that in evaluating alternative investments, we should ignore sunk and fixed costs, and instead base decisions on the marginal costs and marginal revenues that each alternative entails. We learn in our course that this doctrine biases companies to leverage what they have put in place to succeed in the past, instead of guiding them to create the capabilities they'll need in the future. If we knew the future would be exactly the same as the past, that approach would be fine. But if the future's different—and it almost always is— then it's the wrong thing to do.

This theory addresses the third question I discuss with my students—how to live a life of integrity (stay out of jail). Unconsciously, we often employ the marginal cost doctrine in our personal lives when we choose between right and wrong. A voice in our head says,

"Look, I know that as a general rule, most people shouldn't do this. But in this particular extenuating circumstance, just this once, it's OK." The marginal cost of doing something wrong "just this once" always seems alluringly low. It suckers you in, and you don't ever look at where that path ultimately is headed and at the full costs that the choice entails. Justification for infidelity and dishonesty in all their manifestations lies in the marginal cost economics of "just this once."

I'd like to share a story about how I came to understand the potential damage of "just this once" in my own life. I played on the Oxford University varsity basketball team. We worked our tails off and finished the season undefeated. The guys on the team were the best friends I've ever had in my life. We got to the British equivalent of the NCAA tournament—and made it to the final four. It turned out the championship game was scheduled to be played on a Sunday. I had made a personal commitment to God at age 16 that I would never play ball on Sunday. So I went to the coach and explained my problem. He was incredulous. My teammates were, too, because I was the starting center. Every one of the guys on the team came to me and said, "You've got to play. Can't you break the rule just this one time?"

I'm a deeply religious man, so I went away and prayed about what I should do. I got a very clear feeling that I shouldn't break my commitment—so I didn't play in the championship game.

In many ways that was a small decision—involving one of several thousand Sundays in my life. In theory, surely I could have crossed over the line just that one time and then not done it again. But looking back on it, resisting the temptation whose logic was "In this extenuating circumstance, just this once, it's OK" has proven to be one of the most important decisions of my life. Why? My life has been one unending stream of extenuating circumstances. Had I crossed the line that one time, I would have done it over and over in the years that followed.

The lesson I learned from this is that it's easier to hold to your principles 100% of the time than it is to hold to them 98% of the time. If you give in to "just this once," based on a marginal cost analysis, as some of my former classmates have done, you'll regret where you end up. You've got to define for yourself what you stand for and draw the line in a safe place.

REMEMBER THE IMPORTANCE OF HUMILITY

I got this insight when I was asked to teach a class on humility at Harvard College. I asked all the students to describe the most humble person they knew. One characteristic of these humble people stood out: They had a high level of self-esteem. They knew who they were, and they felt good about who they were. We also decided that humility was defined not by self-deprecating behavior or attitudes but by the esteem with which you regard others. Good behavior flows naturally from that kind of humility. For example, you would never steal from someone, because you respect that person too much. You'd never lie to someone, either.

It's crucial to take a sense of humility into the world. By the time you make it to a top graduate school, almost all your learning has come from people who are smarter and more experienced than you: parents, teachers, bosses. But once you've finished at Harvard Business School or any other top academic institution, the vast majority of people you'll interact with on a day-to-day basis may not be smarter than you. And if your attitude is that only smarter people have something to teach you, your learning opportunities will be very limited. But if you have a humble eagerness to learn something from everybody, your learning opportunities will be unlimited. Generally, you can be humble only if you feel really good about yourself— and you want to help those around you feel really good about themselves, too. When we see people acting in an abusive, arrogant, or demeaning manner toward others, their behavior almost always is a symptom of their lack of self-esteem. They need to put someone else down to feel good about themselves.

CHOOSE THE RIGHT YARDSTICK

This past year I was diagnosed with cancer and faced the possibility that my life would end sooner than I'd planned. Thankfully, it now looks as if I'll be spared. But the experience has given me important insight into my life.

I have a pretty clear idea of how my ideas have generated enormous revenue for companies that have used my research; I know I've had a substantial impact. But as I've confronted this disease, it's been interesting to see how unimportant that impact is to me now. I've concluded that the metric by which God will assess my life isn't dollars but the individual people whose lives I've touched.

I think that's the way it will work for us all. Don't worry about the level of individual prominence you have achieved; worry about the individuals you have helped become better people. This is my final recommendation: Think about the metric by which your life will be judged, and make a resolution to live every day so that in the end, your life will be judged a success.

ABOUT THE AUTHOR

Clayton M. Christensen is the Kim B. Clark Professor of Business Administration at Harvard Business School. He has authored several critically acclaimed books, including *New York Times* bestsellers *The Innovator's Dilemma*, *The Innovator's Solution*, and *Disrupting Class*. Christensen is the cofounder of Innosight, a global strategy and innovation consultancy; Rose Park Advisors, an investment firm; and the Clayton Christensen Institute for Disruptive

Innovation, a nonprofit think tank. In 2011 and 2013, Christensen was named the world's most influential business thinker by Thinkers50.

Harvard Business Review Press Books

The Clayton M. Christensen Reader

The Innovator's Dilemma: When New Technologies Cause Great Firms to Fail

The Innovator's DNA: Mastering the Five Skills of Disruptive Innovators
with Jeffrey H. Dyer and Hal B. Gregersen

The Innovator's Solution: Creating and Sustaining Successful Growth
with Michael E. Raynor

Harvard Business Review Articles

"The Capitalist's Dilemma"
with Derek van Bever

"Consulting on the Cusp of Disruption"
with Dina Wang and Derek van Bever

"Disruptive Innovation for Social Change"
with Heiner Baumann, Rudy Ruggles, and
Thomas M. Sadtler

"Disruptive Technologies: Catching the
Wave"
with Joseph L. Bower

"The Future of Commerce"
with Adrian Slywotzky, Richard S.
Tedlow, and Nicholas G. Carr

"Innovation Killers: How Financial Tools Destroy Your Capacity to Do New Things"
with Stephen P. Kaufman and Willy Shih

"The Innovator's DNA"
with Jeffrey H. Dyer and Hal B. Gregersen

"Know Your Customers' 'Jobs to Be Done'"
with Taddy Hall, Karen Dillon, and David Duncan

"Making Strategy: Learning by Doing"

"Marketing Malpractice: The Cause and the Cure"
with Scott Cook and Taddy Hall

"Meeting the Challenge of Disruptive Innovation"
with Michael Overdorf

"The New M&A Playbook"
with Richard Alton, Curtis Rising, and Andrew Waldeck

"Reinventing Your Business Model"
with Henning Kagermann and Mark W. Johnson

"Skate to Where the Money Will Be"
with Michael E. Raynor and Matthew C. Verlinden

"Surviving Disruption"
with Max Wessel

"The Tools of Cooperation and Change"
with Howard H. Stevenson and Matt Marx

"What is Disruptive Innovation?"
with Michael E. Raynor and Rory
McDonald

"Why Hard-Nosed Executives Should
Care About Executive Theory"
with Michael E. Raynor

"Will Disruptive Innovations Cure Health
Care?"
with Richard Bohmer and John Kenagy

Article Summary

Idea in Brief

Harvard Business School's Christensen teaches aspiring MBAs how to apply management and innovation theories to build stronger companies. But he also believes that these models can help people lead better lives. In this article, he explains how, exploring questions everyone needs to ask. How can I be happy in my career? How can I be sure that my relationship with my family is an enduring source of happiness? And how can I live my life with integrity? The answer to the first

question comes from Frederick Herzberg's assertion that the most powerful motivator isn't money;
it's the opportunity to learn, grow in responsibilities, contribute, and be recognized. That's why
management, if practiced well, can be the noblest
of occupations; no others offer as many ways to
help people find those opportunities.

It isn't about buying, selling, and investing
in companies, as many think. The principles of
resource allocation can help people attain happiness at home. If not managed masterfully, what
emerges from a firm's resource allocation process
can be very different from the strategy management intended to follow. That's true in life too: If
you're not guided by a clear sense of purpose,
you're likely to fritter away your time and energy
on obtaining the most tangible, short-term signs
of achievement, not what's really important to you.
And just as a focus on marginal costs can cause
bad corporate decisions, it can lead people astray.

The marginal cost of doing something wrong "just this once" always seems alluringly low. You don't see the end result to which that path leads. The key is to define what you stand for and draw the line in a safe place.

The most important management ideas all in one place.

We hope you enjoyed this book from *Harvard Business Review*. For the best ideas HBR has to offer turn to HBR's 10 Must Reads Boxed Set. From books on leadership and strategy to managing yourself and others, this 6-book collection delivers articles on the most essential business topics to help you succeed.

HBR's 10 Must Reads Series

The definitive collection of ideas and best practices on our most sought-after topics from the best minds in business.

- Change Management
- Collaboration
- Communication
- Emotional Intelligence
- Innovation
- Leadership
- Making Smart Decisions

- Managing Across Cultures
- Managing People
- Managing Yourself
- Strategic Marketing
- Strategy
- Teams
- The Essentials

hbr.org/mustreads

Buy for your team, clients, or event.
Visit hbr.org/bulksales for quantity discount rates.

Harvard
Business
Review
Press

TEACHING
SMART PEOPLE
HOW TO LEARN

HARVARD BUSINESS REVIEW
CLASSICS

TEACHING
SMART PEOPLE
HOW TO LEARN

Chris Argyris

Harvard Business Review Press
Boston, Massachusetts

Library of Congress Cataloging-in-Publication Data
Argyris, Chris, 1923-
  Teaching smart people how to learn / Chris Argyris.
     p. cm. — (The Harvard business review classics series)
  "Reprint 4304"—T.P. verso.
  Reprint of an article previously published in the Harvard business
review.
  ISBN 978-1-4221-2600-4 (pbk. : alk. paper) 1. Organizational
learning--Psychological aspects. 2. Defensiveness (Psychology)
3. Self-evaluation. 4. Active learning. 5. Organizational effective-
ness. I. Harvard business review. II. Title.
  HD58.82.A739 2008
  658.3'124—dc22

                                                        2008005632

THE
HARVARD BUSINESS REVIEW
CLASSICS SERIES

Since 1922, *Harvard Business Review* has
been a leading source of breakthrough ideas
in management practice—many of which still
speak to and influence us today. The HBR
Classics series now offers you the opportunity
to make these seminal pieces a part of your
permanent management library. Each volume contains a groundbreaking idea that has
shaped best practices and inspired countless
managers around the world—and will change
how you think about the business world today.

{ v }

TEACHING
SMART PEOPLE
HOW TO LEARN

Any company that aspires to succeed in the tougher business environment of the 1990s must first resolve a basic dilemma: success in the marketplace increasingly depends on learning, yet most people don't know how to learn. What's more, those members of the organization that many assume to be the best at learning are, in fact, not very good at it. I am talking about the well-educated, high-powered, high-commitment professionals who occupy key leadership positions in the modern corporation.

Most companies not only have tremendous difficulty addressing this learning dilemma; they aren't even aware that it exists. The reason: they misunderstand what learning is and how to bring it about. As a result, they tend to make two mistakes in their efforts to become a learning organization.

First, most people define learning too narrowly as mere "problem solving," so they focus on identifying and correcting errors in the external environment. Solving problems is important. But if learning is to persist, managers and employees must also look inward. They need to reflect critically on their own behavior, identify the ways they often inadvertently contribute to the organization's problems, and then change how they act. In particular, they must learn how the very way they go about defining and solving problems can be a source of problems in its own right.

I have coined the terms "single loop" and "double loop" learning to capture this crucial distinction. To give a simple analogy: a thermostat that automatically turns on the heat whenever the temperature in a room drops below 68 degrees is a good example of single-loop learning. A thermostat that could ask, "Why am I set at 68 degrees?" and then explore whether or not some other temperature might more economically achieve the goal of heating the room would be engaging in double-loop learning.

Highly skilled professionals are frequently very good at single-loop learning. After all, they have spent much of their lives acquiring academic credentials, mastering one or a number of intellectual disciplines, and applying those disciplines to solve real-world problems. But ironically, this very fact helps explain why professionals are often so bad at double-loop learning.

Put simply, because many professionals are almost always successful at what they do, they rarely experience failure. And because they have rarely failed, they have never learned how to learn from failure. So whenever their single-loop learning strategies go wrong, they become defensive, screen out criticism, and put the "blame" on anyone and everyone but themselves. In short, their ability to learn shuts down precisely at the moment they need it the most.

The propensity among professionals to behave defensively helps shed light on the second mistake that companies make about learning. The common assumption is that getting people to learn is largely a matter of motivation. When people have the right attitudes and commitment, learning automatically follows. So companies focus on creating new organizational structures—compensation programs, performance reviews, corporate cultures, and the like—that are designed to create motivated and committed employees.

But effective double-loop learning is not simply a function of how people feel. It is a reflection of how they think—that is, the cognitive rules or reasoning they use to design and implement their actions. Think of these rules as a kind of "master program" stored in the brain, governing all behavior. Defensive reasoning can block learning even when the individual commitment to it is high, just as a computer program with hidden bugs can produce results exactly the opposite of what its designers had planned.

Companies can learn how to resolve the learning dilemma. What it takes is to make the ways managers and employees reason about their behavior a focus of organizational learning and continuous improvement programs. Teaching people how to reason about their behavior in new and more effective ways breaks down the defenses that block learning.

All of the examples that follow involve a particular kind of professional: fast-track consultants at major management consulting companies. But the implications of my argument go far beyond this specific occupational group. The fact is, more and more jobs—no matter what the title—are taking on the contours of "knowledge work." People at all levels of the organization must combine the mastery of some highly specialized technical expertise with the ability to work effectively in teams, form productive relationships with clients and customers, and critically reflect on and then change their own organizational practices. And the nuts and bolts of management—whether of high-powered consultants or service representatives, senior managers or factory technicians—increasingly consists of guiding and integrating the autonomous but interconnected work of highly skilled people.

HOW PROFESSIONALS AVOID LEARNING

For 15 years, I have been conducting in-depth studies of management consultants. I decided to study consultants for a few simple reasons. First, they are the epitome of the highly educated professionals who play an increasingly central role in all organizations. Almost all of the consultants I've studied have MBAs from the top three or four U.S. business schools. They are also highly committed to their work. For instance, at one company, more than 90% of the consultants responded in a survey that they were "highly satisfied" with their jobs and with the company.

I also assumed that such professional consultants would be good at learning. After all, the essence of their job is to teach others how to do things differently. I found, however, that these consultants embodied the learning dilemma. The most enthusiastic about continuous improvement in their own organizations, they were also often the biggest obstacle to its complete success.

As long as efforts at learning and change focused on external organizational factors—job redesign, compensation programs, performance reviews, and leadership training—the professionals were enthusiastic participants. Indeed, creating new systems and structures was precisely the kind of challenge that well-educated, highly motivated professionals thrived on.

And yet the moment the quest for continuous improvement turned to the professionals' *own* performance, something went wrong. It wasn't a matter of bad attitude. The professionals' commitment to excellence was genuine, and the vision of the company was clear. Nevertheless, continuous improvement did not persist. And the longer the continuous improvement efforts continued, the greater the likelihood that they would produce ever-diminishing returns.

What happened? The professionals began to feel embarrassed. They were threatened by the prospect of critically examining their own role in the organization. Indeed, because they were so well paid (and generally believed that their employers were supportive and fair), the idea that their performance might not be at its best made them feel guilty.

Far from being a catalyst for real change, such feelings caused most to react defensively. They projected the blame for any problems away from themselves and onto what they said were unclear goals, insensitive and unfair leaders, and stupid clients.

Consider this example. At a premier management consulting company, the manager of a case team called a meeting to examine the team's performance on a recent consulting project. The client was largely satisfied and had given the team relatively high marks, but the manager believed the team had not created the value added that it was capable of and that the consulting company had promised. In the spirit of continuous improvement, he felt that the team could do better. Indeed, so did some of the team members.

The manager knew how difficult it was for people to reflect critically on their own work performance, especially in the presence of their manager, so he took a number of steps to make possible a frank and open discussion. He invited to the meeting an outside consultant whom team members knew and trusted—"just to keep me honest," he said. He also agreed to have the entire meeting tape-recorded. That way, any subsequent confusions or disagreements about what went on at the meeting could be checked against the transcript. Finally, the manager opened the meeting by emphasizing that no subject was off limits—including his own behavior.

"I realize that you may believe you cannot confront me," the manager said. "But I encourage you to challenge me. You have a responsibility to tell me where you think the leadership made mistakes, just as I have the responsibility to identify any I believe you made. And all of us must acknowledge our own mistakes. If we do not have an open dialogue, we will not learn."

The professionals took the manager up on the first half of his invitation but quietly ignored the second. When asked to pinpoint the key problems in the experience with the client, they looked entirely outside themselves. The clients were uncooperative and arrogant. "They didn't think we could help them." The team's own managers were unavailable and poorly prepared. "At times, our managers were not up to speed before they walked into the client meetings." In effect, the professionals asserted that they were helpless to act differently—not because of any limitations of their own but because of the limitations of others.

The manager listened carefully to the team members and tried to respond to their criticisms. He talked about the mistakes that he had made during the consulting process. For example, one professional objected to the way the manager had run the project meetings. "I see that the way I asked questions closed down discussions," responded the manager. "I didn't mean to do that, but I can see how you might have believed that I had already made up my mind." Another team member complained that the manager had caved in to pressure from his superior to produce the project report far too quickly, considering the team's heavy work load. "I think that it was my responsibility to have said no," admitted the manager. "It was clear that we all had an immense amount of work."

Finally, after some three hours of discussion about his own behavior, the manager began to ask the team members if there were any errors *they* might have made. "After all," he said, "this client was not different from many others. How can we be more effective in the future?"

The professionals repeated that it was really the clients' and their own managers' fault. As one put it, "They have to be open to change and want to learn." The more the manager tried to get the team to examine its own responsibility for the outcome, the more the professionals bypassed his concerns. The best one team member could suggest was for the case team to "promise less"— implying that there was really no way for the group to improve its performance.

The case team members were reacting defensively to protect themselves, even though their manager was not acting in ways that an outsider would consider threatening. Even if there were some truth to their charges—the clients may well have been arrogant and closed, their own managers distant—the way they presented these claims was guaranteed to stop learning. With few exceptions, the professionals made attributions about the behavior of the clients and the managers but never publicly tested their claims. For instance, they said that the clients weren't motivated to learn but never really presented any evidence supporting that assertion. When their lack of concrete evidence was pointed out to them, they simply repeated their criticisms more vehemently.

If the professionals had felt so strongly about these issues, why had they never mentioned them during the project? According to the professionals, even this was the fault of others. "We didn't want to alienate the client," argued one. "We didn't want to be seen as whining," said another.

The professionals were using their criticisms of others to protect themselves from the potential embarrassment of having to admit that perhaps they too had contributed to the team's less-than-perfect performance. What's more, the fact that they kept repeating their defensive actions in the face of the manager's efforts to turn the group's attention to its own role shows that this defensiveness had become a reflexive routine. From the professionals' perspective, they weren't resisting; they were focusing on the "real" causes. Indeed, they were to be respected, if not congratulated, for working as well as they did under such difficult conditions.

The end result was an unproductive parallel conversation. Both the manager and the professionals were candid; they expressed their views forcefully. But they talked past each other, never finding a common language to describe what had happened with the client. The professionals kept insisting that the fault lay with others. The manager kept trying, unsuccessfully, to get the professionals to see how they contributed to the state of affairs they were criticizing. The dialogue of this parallel conversation looks like this:

Professionals: "The clients have to be open. They must want to change."

Manager: "It's our task to help them see that change is in their interest."

Professionals: "But the clients didn't agree with our analyses."

Manager: "If they didn't think our ideas were right, how might we have convinced them?"

Professionals: "Maybe we need to have more meetings with the client."

Manager: "If we aren't adequately prepared and if the clients don't think we're credible, how will more meetings help?"

Professionals: "There should be better communication between case team members and management."

Manager: "I agree. But professionals should take the initiative to educate the manager about the problems they are experiencing."

Professionals: "Our leaders are unavailable and distant."

Manager: "How do you expect us to know that if you don't tell us?"

Conversations such as this one dramatically illustrate the learning dilemma. The problem with the professionals' claims is not that they are wrong but that they aren't useful. By constantly turning the focus away from their own behavior to that of others, the professionals bring learning to a grinding halt. The manager understands the trap but does not know how to get out of it. To learn how to do that requires going deeper into the dynamics of defensive reasoning—and into the special causes that make professionals so prone to it.

DEFENSIVE REASONING AND THE DOOM LOOP

What explains the professionals' defensiveness? Not their attitudes about change or commitment to continuous improvement; they really wanted to work more effectively. Rather, the key factor is the way they reasoned about their behavior and that of others.

It is impossible to reason anew in every situation. If we had to think through all the possible responses every time someone asked, "How are you?" the world would pass us by. Therefore, everyone develops a theory of action—a set of rules that individuals use to design and implement their own behavior as well as to understand the behavior of others. Usually, these theories of actions become so taken for granted that people don't even realize they are using them.

One of the paradoxes of human behavior, however, is that the master program people actually use is rarely the one they think they use. Ask people in an interview or questionnaire to articulate the rules they use to govern their actions, and they will give you what I call their "espoused" theory of action. But observe these same people's behavior, and you will quickly see that this espoused theory has very little to do with how they actually behave. For example, the professionals on the case team said they believed in continuous improvement, and yet they consistently acted in ways that made improvement impossible.

When you observe people's behavior and try to come up with rules that would make sense of it, you discover a very different theory of action—what I call the individual's "theory-in-use." Put simply, people consistently act inconsistently, unaware of the contradiction between their espoused theory and their theory-in-use, between the way they think they are acting and the way they really act.

What's more, most theories-in-use rest on the same set of governing values. There seems to be a universal human tendency to design one's actions consistently according to four basic values:

1. To remain in unilateral control;

2. To maximize "winning" and minimize "losing";

3. To suppress negative feelings; and

4. To be as "rational" as possible—by which people mean defining clear objectives and evaluating their behavior in terms of whether or not they have achieved them.

The purpose of all these values is to avoid embarrassment or threat, feeling vulnerable or incompetent. In this respect, the master program that most people use is profoundly defensive. Defensive reasoning encourages individuals to keep private the premises, inferences, and conclusions that shape their behavior and to avoid testing them in a truly independent, objective fashion.

Because the attributions that go into defensive reasoning are never really tested, it is a closed loop, remarkably impervious to conflicting points of view. The inevitable response to the observation that somebody is reasoning defensively is yet more defensive reasoning. With the case team, for example, whenever anyone pointed out the professionals' defensive behavior to them, their initial reaction was to look for the cause in somebody else—clients who were so sensitive that they would have been alienated if the consultants had criticized them or a manager so weak that he couldn't have taken it had the consultants raised their concerns with him. In other words, the case team members once again denied their own responsibility by externalizing the problem and putting it on someone else.

In such situations, the simple act of encouraging more open inquiry is often attacked by others as "intimidating." Those who do the attacking deal with their feelings about possibly being wrong by blaming the more open individual for arousing these feelings and upsetting them.

Needless to say, such a master program inevitably short-circuits learning. And for a number of reasons unique to their psychology, well-educated professionals are especially susceptible to this.

Nearly all the consultants I have studied have stellar academic records. Ironically, their very success at education helps explain the problems they have with learning. Before they enter the world of work, their lives are primarily full of successes, so they have rarely experienced the embarrassment and sense of threat that comes with failure. As a result, their defensive reasoning has rarely been activated. People who rarely experience failure, however, end up not knowing how to deal with it effectively. And this serves to reinforce the normal human tendency to reason defensively.

In a survey of several hundred young consultants at the organizations I have been studying, these professionals describe themselves as driven internally by an unrealistically high ideal of performance: "Pressure on the job is self-imposed." "I must not only do a good job; I must also be the best." "People around here are very bright and hardworking; they are highly motivated to do an outstanding job." "Most of us want not only to succeed but also to do so at maximum speed."

These consultants are always comparing themselves with the best around them and constantly trying to better their own performance. And yet they do not appreciate being required to compete openly with each other. They feel it is somehow inhumane.

They prefer to be the individual contributor—what might be termed a "productive loner."

Behind this high aspiration for success is an equally high fear of failure and a propensity to feel shame and guilt when they do fail to meet their high standards. "You must avoid mistakes," said one. "I hate making them. Many of us fear failure, whether we admit it or not."

To the extent that these consultants have experienced success in their lives, they have not had to be concerned about failure and the attendant feelings of shame and guilt. But to exactly the same extent, they also have never developed the tolerance for feelings of failure or the skills to deal with these feelings. This in turn has led them not only to fear failure but also to fear the fear of failure itself. For they know that they will not cope with it superlatively—their usual level of aspiration.

The consultants use two intriguing metaphors to describe this phenomenon. They talk about the "doom loop" and "doom zoom." Often, consultants will perform well on the case team, but because they don't do the jobs perfectly or receive accolades from their managers, they go into a doom loop of despair. And they don't ease into the doom loop, they zoom into it.

As a result, many professionals have extremely "brittle" personalities. When suddenly faced with a situation they cannot immediately handle, they tend to fall apart. They cover up their distress in front of the client. They talk about it constantly with their fellow case team members. Interestingly, these conversations commonly take the form of bad-mouthing clients.

Such brittleness leads to an inappropriately high sense of despondency or even despair when people don't achieve the high levels of performance they aspire to. Such despondency is rarely psychologically devastating, but when combined with defensive reasoning, it can result in a formidable predisposition against learning.

There is no better example of how this brittleness can disrupt an organization than performance evaluations. Because it represents the one moment when a professional must measure his or her own behavior against some formal standard, a performance evaluation is almost tailor-made to push a professional into the doom loop. Indeed, a poor evaluation can reverberate far beyond the particular individual involved to spark defensive reasoning throughout an entire organization.

At one consulting company, management established a new performance-evaluation process that was designed to make evaluations both more objective and more useful to those being evaluated. The consultants participated in the design of the new system and in general were enthusiastic because it corresponded to their espoused values of objectivity and fairness. A brief two years into the new process, however, it had become the object of dissatisfaction. The catalyst for this about-face was the first unsatisfactory rating.

Senior managers had identified six consultants whose performance they considered below standard. In keeping with the new evaluation process, they did all they could to communicate their concerns to the six and to help them improve. Managers met with each individual separately for as long and as often as the professional requested to explain the reasons behind the rating and to discuss what needed to be done to improve—but to no avail. Performance continued at the same low level and, eventually, the six were let go.

When word of the dismissal spread through the company, people responded with confusion and anxiety. After about a dozen consultants angrily complained to management, the CEO held two lengthy meetings where employees could air their concerns.

At the meetings, the professionals made a variety of claims. Some said the performance-evaluation process was unfair because judgments were subjective and biased and the criteria for minimum performance unclear. Others suspected that the real cause for the dismissals was economic and that the performance-evaluation procedure was just a fig leaf to hide the fact that the company was in trouble. Still others argued that the evaluation process was antilearning. If the company were truly a learning organization, as it claimed, then people performing below the minimum standard should be taught how to reach it. As one professional put it: "We were told that the company did not have an up-or-out policy. Up-or-out is inconsistent with learning. You misled us."

The CEO tried to explain the logic behind management's decision by grounding it in the facts of the case and by asking the professionals for any evidence that might contradict these facts.

Is there subjectivity and bias in the evaluation process? Yes, responded the CEO, but "we strive hard to reduce them. We are constantly trying to improve the process. If you have any ideas, please tell us. If you know of someone treated unfairly, please bring it up. If any of you feel that you have been treated unfairly, let's discuss it now or, if you wish, privately."

Is the level of minimum competence too vague? "We are working to define minimum competence more clearly," he answered. "In the case of the six, however, their performance was so poor that it wasn't difficult to reach a decision." Most of the six had received timely feedback about their problems. And in the two cases where people had not, the reason was that they had never taken the responsibility to seek out evaluations—and, indeed, had actively avoided them. "If you have any data to the contrary," the CEO added, "let's talk about it."

Were the six asked to leave for economic reasons? No, said the CEO. "We have more work than we can do, and letting professionals go is extremely costly for us. Do any of you have any information to the contrary?"

As to the company being antilearning, in fact, the entire evaluation process was designed to encourage learning. When a professional is performing below the minimum level, the CEO explained, "we jointly design remedial experiences with the individual. Then we look for signs of improvement. In these cases, either the professionals were reluctant to take on such assignments or they repeatedly failed when they did. Again, if you have information or evidence to the contrary, I'd like to hear about it."

The CEO concluded: "It's regrettable, but sometimes we make mistakes and hire the wrong people. If individuals don't produce and repeatedly prove themselves unable to improve, we don't know what else to do except dismiss them. It's just not fair to keep poorly performing individuals in the company. They earn an unfair share of the financial rewards."

Instead of responding with data of their own, the professionals simply repeated their accusations but in ways that consistently contradicted their claims. They said that a genuinely fair evaluation process would contain clear and documentable data about performance—but they were unable to provide firsthand examples of the unfairness that they implied colored the evaluation of the six dismissed employees. They argued that people shouldn't be judged by inferences unconnected to their actual performance—but they judged management in precisely this way. They insisted that management define clear, objective, and unambiguous performance standards—but they argued that any humane system would take into account that the performance of a professional cannot be precisely measured. Finally, they presented themselves as champions of learning—but they never proposed any criteria for assessing whether an individual might be unable to learn.

In short, the professionals seemed to hold management to a different level of performance than they held themselves. In their conversation at the meetings, they used many of the features of ineffective evaluation that they condemned—the absence of concrete data, for example, and the dependence on a circular logic of "heads we win, tails you lose." It is as if they were saying, "Here are the features of a fair performance-evaluation system. You should abide by them. But we don't have to when we are evaluating you."

Indeed, if we were to explain the professionals' behavior by articulating rules that would have to be in their heads in order for them to act the way they did, the rules would look something like this:

1. When criticizing the company, state your criticism in ways that you believe are valid—but also in ways that prevent

others from deciding for themselves whether your claim to validity is correct.

2. When asked to illustrate your criticisms, don't include any data that others could use to decide for themselves whether the illustrations are valid.

3. State your conclusions in ways that disguise their logical implications. If others point out those implications to you, deny them.

Of course, when such rules were described to the professionals, they found them abhorrent. It was inconceivable that these rules might explain their actions. And yet in defending themselves against this observation, they almost always inadvertently confirmed the rules.

LEARNING HOW TO REASON PRODUCTIVELY

If defensive reasoning is as widespread as I believe, then focusing on an individual's attitudes or commitment is never enough to produce real change. And as the previous example illustrates, neither is creating new organizational structures or systems. The problem is that even when people are genuinely committed to improving their performance and management has changed its structures in order to encourage the "right" kind of behavior, people still remain locked in defensive reasoning. Either they remain unaware of this fact, or if they do become aware of it, they blame others.

There is, however, reason to believe that organizations can break out of this vicious circle. Despite the strength of defensive reasoning, people genuinely strive to produce what they intend. They value acting competently. Their self-esteem is intimately tied up with behaving consistently and performing effectively. Companies can use these universal human tendencies to teach people how to reason in a new way—in effect, to change the master programs in their heads and thus reshape their behavior.

People can be taught how to recognize the reasoning they use when they design and implement their actions. They can begin to identify the inconsistencies between their espoused and actual theories of action. They can face up to the fact that they unconsciously design and implement actions that they do not intend. Finally, people can learn how to identify what individuals and groups do to create organizational defenses and how these defenses contribute to an organization's problems.

Once companies embark on this learning process, they will discover that the kind of reasoning necessary to reduce and overcome organizational defenses is the same kind of "tough reasoning" that underlies the effective use of ideas in strategy, finance, marketing, manufacturing, and other management disciplines. Any sophisticated strategic analysis, for example, depends on collecting valid data, analyzing it carefully, and constantly testing the inferences drawn from the data. The toughest tests are reserved for the conclusions. Good strategists make sure that their conclusions can withstand all kinds of critical questioning.

So too with productive reasoning about human behavior. The standard of analysis is just as high. Human resource programs no longer need to be based on "soft" reasoning but should be as analytical and as data-driven as any other management discipline.

Of course, that is not the kind of reasoning the consultants used when they encountered problems that were embarrassing or threatening. The data they collected was hardly objective. The inferences they made rarely became explicit. The conclusions they reached were largely self-serving, impossible for others to test, and as a result, "self-sealing," impervious to change.

How can an organization begin to turn this situation around, to teach its members how to reason productively? The first step is for managers at the top to examine critically and change their own theories-in-use. Until senior managers become aware of how they reason defensively and the counterproductive consequences that result, there will be little real progress. Any change activity is likely to be just a fad.

Change has to start at the top because otherwise defensive senior managers are likely to disown any transformation in reasoning patterns coming from below. If professionals or middle managers begin to change the way they reason and act, such changes are likely to appear strange—if not actually dangerous—to those at the top. The result is an unstable situation where senior managers still believe that it is a sign of caring and sensitivity to bypass and cover up difficult issues, while their subordinates see the very same actions as defensive.

The key to any educational experience designed to teach senior managers how to reason productively is to connect the program to real business problems. The best demonstration of the usefulness of productive reasoning is for busy managers to see how it can make a direct difference in their own performance and in that of the organization. This will not happen overnight. Managers need plenty of opportunity to practice the new skills. But once they grasp the powerful impact that productive reasoning can have on actual performance, they will have a strong incentive to reason productively not just in a training session but in all their work relationships.

One simple approach I have used to get this process started is to have participants produce a kind of rudimentary case study. The subject is a real business problem that the manager either wants to deal with or has tried unsuccessfully to address in the past. Writing the actual case usually takes less than an hour. But then the case becomes the focal point of an extended analysis.

For example, a CEO at a large organizational-development consulting company was pre-occupied with the problems caused by the intense competition among the various business functions represented by his four direct reports. Not only was he tired of having the problems dumped in his lap, but he was also worried about the impact the interfunctional conflicts were having on the organization's flexibility. He had even calculated that the money being spent to iron out disagreements amounted to hundreds of thousands of dollars every year. And the more fights there were, the more defensive people became, which only increased the costs to the organization.

In a paragraph or so, the CEO described a meeting he intended to have with his direct reports to address the problem. Next, he divided the paper in half, and on the right-hand side of the page, he wrote a scenario for the meeting—much like the script for a movie or play—describing what he would say and how his subordinates would likely respond. On the left-hand side of the page, he wrote down any thoughts and feelings that he would be likely to have during the meeting but that he wouldn't express for fear they would derail the discussion.

But instead of holding the meeting, the CEO analyzed this scenario *with* his direct reports. The case became the catalyst for a discussion in which the CEO learned several things about the way he acted with his management team.

He discovered that his four direct reports often perceived his conversations as counterproductive. In the guise of being "diplomatic," he would pretend that a consensus about the problem existed, when in fact none existed. The unintended result: instead of feeling reassured, his subordinates felt wary and tried to figure out "what is he *really* getting at."

The CEO also realized that the way he dealt with the competitiveness among department heads was completely contradictory. On the one hand, he kept urging them to "think of the organization as a whole." On the other, he kept calling for actions—department budget cuts, for example—that placed them directly in competition with each other.

Finally, the CEO discovered that many of the tacit evaluations and attributions he had listed turned out to be wrong. Since he had never expressed these assumptions, he had never found out just how wrong they were. What's more, he learned that much of what he thought he was hiding came through to his subordinates anyway—but with the added message that the boss was covering up.

The CEO's colleagues also learned about their own ineffective behavior. They learned by examining their own behavior as they tried to help the CEO analyze his case. They also learned by writing and analyzing cases of their own. They began to see that they too tended to bypass and cover up the real issues and that the CEO was often aware of it but did not say so. They too made inaccurate attributions and evaluations that they did not express. Moreover, the belief that they had to hide important ideas and feelings from the CEO and from each other in order not to upset anyone turned out to be mistaken. In the context of the case discussions, the entire senior management team was quite willing to discuss what had always been undiscussable.

In effect, the case study exercise legit-imizes talking about issues that people have never been able to address before. Such a discussion can be emotional—even painful. But for managers with the courage to persist, the payoff is great: management teams and entire organizations work more openly and more effectively and have greater options for behaving flexibly and adapting to particular situations.

When senior managers are trained in new reasoning skills, they can have a big impact

on the performance of the entire organization—even when other employees are still
reasoning defensively. The CEO who led the
meetings on the performance-evaluation
procedure was able to defuse dissatisfaction
because he didn't respond to professionals'
criticisms in kind but instead gave a clear
presentation of relevant data. Indeed, most
participants took the CEO's behavior to be a
sign that the company really acted on the values of participation and employee involvement that it espoused.

Of course, the ideal is for all the members
of an organization to learn how to reason
productively. This has happened at the company where the case team meeting took place.
Consultants and their managers are now
able to confront some of the most difficult

issues of the consultant-client relationship. To get a sense of the difference productive reasoning can make, imagine how the original conversation between the manager and case team might have gone had everyone engaged in effective reasoning. (The following dialogue is based on actual sessions I have attended with other case teams at the same company since the training has been completed.)

First, the consultants would have demonstrated their commitment to continuous improvement by being willing to examine their own role in the difficulties that arose during the consulting project. No doubt they would have identified their managers and the clients as part of the problem, but they would have gone on to admit that they had contributed to it as well. More important, they would have agreed with the manager that as they explored the various roles of clients, managers, and professionals, they would make sure to test any evaluations or attributions they might make against the data. Each individual would have encouraged the others to question his or her reasoning. Indeed, they would have insisted on it. And in turn, everyone would have understood that act of questioning not as a sign of mistrust or an invasion of privacy but as a valuable opportunity for learning.

The conversation about the manager's unwillingness to say no might look something like this:

Professional #1: "One of the biggest problems I had with the way you managed this case was that you seemed to be unable to say no when either the client or your superior made unfair demands." [Gives an example.]

Professional #2: "I have another example to add. [Describes a second example.] But I'd also like to say that we never really told you how we felt about this. Behind your back we were bad-mouthing you—you know, 'he's being such a wimp'—but we never came right out and said it."

Manager: "It certainly would have been helpful if you had said something. Was there anything I said or did that gave you the idea that you had better not raise this with me?"

Professional #3: "Not really. I think we didn't want to sound like we were whining."

Manager: "Well, I certainly don't think you sound like you're whining. But two thoughts come to mind. If I understand you correctly, you *were* complaining, but the complaining about me and my inability to say no was covered up. Second, if we had discussed this, I might have gotten the data I needed to be able to say no."

Notice that when the second professional describes how the consultants had covered up their complaints, the manager doesn't criticize her. Rather, he rewards her for being open by responding in kind. He focuses on the ways that he too may have contributed to the cover-up. Reflecting undefensively about his own role in the problem then makes it possible for the professionals to talk about their fears of appearing to be whining. The manager then agrees with the professionals that they shouldn't become complainers. At the same time, he points out the counterproductive consequences of covering up their complaints.

Another unresolved issue in the case team meeting concerned the supposed arrogance of the clients. A more productive conversation about that problem might go like this:

Manager: "You said that the clients were arrogant and uncooperative. What did they say and do?"

Professional #1: "One asked me if I had ever met a payroll. Another asked how long I've been out of school."

Professional #2: "One even asked me how old I was!"

Professional #3: "That's nothing. The worst is when they say that all we do is interview people, write a report based on what they tell us, and then collect our fees."

Manager: "The fact that we tend to be so young is a real problem for many of our clients. They get very defensive about it.

But I'd like to explore whether there is a way for them to freely express their views without our getting defensive . . ."

"What troubled me about your original responses was that you assumed you were right in calling the clients stupid. One thing I've noticed about consultants—in this company and others—is that we tend to defend ourselves by bad-mouthing the client."

Professional #1: "Right. After all, if they are genuinely stupid, then it's obviously not our fault that they aren't getting it!"

Professional #2: "Of course, that stance is antilearning and overprotective. By assuming that they can't learn, we absolve ourselves from having to."

{ 62 }

Professional #3: "And the more we all go along with the bad-mouthing, the more we reinforce each other's defensiveness."

Manager: "So what's the alternative? How can we encourage our clients to express their defensiveness and at the same time constructively build on it?"

Professional #1: "We all know that the real issue isn't our age; it's whether or not we are able to add value to the client's organization. They should judge us by what we produce. And if we aren't adding value, they should get rid of us—no matter how young or old we happen to be."

Manager: "Perhaps that is exactly what we should tell them."

In both these examples, the consultants and their manager are doing real work. They are learning about their own group dynamics and addressing some generic problems in client-consultant relationships. The insights they gain will allow them to act more effectively in the future—both as individuals and as a team. They are not just solving problems but developing a far deeper and more textured understanding of their role as members of the organization. They are laying the groundwork for continuous improvement that is truly continuous. They are learning how to learn.

ABOUT THE AUTHOR

Chris Argyris is the James Bryant Conant Professor Emeritus of Education and Organizational Behavior at Harvard University.

ALSO BY THIS AUTHOR

Harvard Business Review Articles

   "Double Loop Learning in Organizations"

   "Empowerment: The Emperor's New Clothes"

   "Good Communication that Blocks Learning"

   "Interpersonal Barriers to Decision Making"

   "Skilled Incompetence"

Article Summary

The Idea at Work

People often profess to be open to critique and new learning, but their actions suggest a very different set of governing values or theories-in-use:

- the desire to remain in unilateral control

- the goal of maximizing "winning" while minimizing "losing"

- the belief that negative feelings should be suppressed

- the desire to appear as rational as possible.

Taken together, these values betray a profoundly defensive posture: a need to avoid embarrassment, threat, or feelings of vulnerability and incompetence. This closed-loop reasoning explains why the mere encouragement of open inquiry can be intimidating to some. And it's especially relevant to the behavior of many of the most highly skilled and best-trained employees. Behind their high aspirations are an equally high fear of failure and a tendency to be ashamed when they don't live up to their high standards. Consequently, they become brittle and despondent in situations in which they don't excel immediately.

Fortunately, it *is* possible for individuals and organizations to develop more productive patterns of behavior. Two suggestions for how to make this happen:

1. *Apply the same kind of "tough reasoning" you use to conduct strategic analysis.* Collect the most objective data you can find.

Make your inferences explicit and test them constantly. Submit your conclusions to the toughest tests of all: make sure they aren't self-serving or impossible for others to verify.

2. *Senior managers must model the desired changes first.* When the leadership demonstrates its willingness to examine critically its own theories-in-use, changing them as indicated, everyone will find it easier to do the same.

Example: The CEO of an organizational-development firm created a case study to address real problems caused by the intense competition among his direct reports. In a paragraph, he described a meeting he intended to have with his subordinates. Then he wrote down what he planned to say, how he thought his subordinates would respond, as well as any thoughts or feelings he thought he might have but not express for fear of derailing the conversation. Instead of actually holding the meeting, he analyzed the scenario he had developed *with* his direct reports. The result was an illuminating conversation in which the CEO and his subordinates were able to circumvent the closed-loop reasoning that had characterized so many prior discussions.

WHAT MAKES
A LEADER?

HARVARD BUSINESS REVIEW
CLASSICS

WHAT MAKES A LEADER?

Daniel Goleman

Harvard Business Review Press
Boston, Massachusetts

Copyright 2017 Harvard Business School Publishing Corporation
Originally published in *Harvard Business Review* in January 2004
Reprint #R0401H
All rights reserved

Printed in the United States of America

10 9 8 7 6 5 4 3 2 1

The web addresses referenced in this book were live and correct at the time of the book's publication but may be subject to change.

Cataloging-in-Publication data is forthcoming.

ISBN: 978-1-63369-260-2
eISBN: 978-1-63369-261-9

The paper used in this publication meets the requirements of the American National Standard for Permanence of Paper for Publications and Documents in Libraries and Archives Z39.48-1992.

THE HARVARD BUSINESS REVIEW CLASSICS SERIES

Since 1922, *Harvard Business Review* has been a leading source of breakthrough ideas in management practice—many of which still speak to and influence us today. The HBR Classics series now offers you the opportunity to make these seminal pieces a part of your permanent management library. Each volume contains a groundbreaking idea that has shaped best practices and inspired countless managers around the world—and will change how you think about the business world today.

WHAT MAKES
A LEADER?

Every businessperson knows a story about a highly intelligent, highly skilled executive who was promoted into a leadership position only to fail at the job. And they also know a story about someone with solid—but not extraordinary—intellectual abilities and technical skills who was promoted into a similar position and then soared.

Such anecdotes support the widespread belief that identifying individuals with the "right stuff" to be leaders is more art than science. After all, the personal styles of superb leaders vary: Some leaders are subdued and analytical; others shout their manifestos from the mountaintops. And just as important, different situations call for different types of leadership. Most mergers need a sensitive negotiator at the helm, whereas many turnarounds require a more forceful authority.

I have found, however, that the most effective leaders are alike in one crucial way: They all have a high degree of what has come to be known as *emotional intelligence*. It's not that IQ and technical skills are irrelevant. They do matter, but mainly as "threshold capabilities"; that is, they are the entry-level requirements for executive positions. But my research, along with other recent studies, clearly shows that emotional intelligence is the sine qua non of leadership. Without it, a person can have the best training in the world, an incisive, analytical mind, and an endless supply of smart ideas, but he still won't make a great leader.

In the course of the past year, my colleagues and I have focused on how emotional intelligence operates at work. We have examined the relationship between emotional intelligence and effective performance, especially in leaders. And we have observed how emotional intelligence shows itself on the job. How can you tell if someone has high emotional intelligence, for example, and how can you recognize it in yourself? In the following pages, we'll explore these questions, taking each of the components of emotional intelligence—self-awareness, self-regulation, motivation, empathy, and social skill—in turn.

EVALUATING EMOTIONAL INTELLIGENCE

Most large companies today have employed trained psychologists to develop what are known as "competency models" to aid them in identifying, training, and promoting likely stars in the leadership firmament. The psychologists have also developed such models for lower-level positions. And in recent years, I have analyzed competency models from 188 companies, most of which were large and global and included the likes of Lucent Technologies, British Airways, and Credit Suisse.

In carrying out this work, my objective was to determine which personal capabilities drove outstanding performance within these organizations, and to what degree they did so. I grouped capabilities into three categories: purely technical skills like accounting and business planning; cognitive abilities like analytical reasoning; and competencies demonstrating emotional intelligence, such as the ability to work with others and effectiveness in leading change.

To create some of the competency models, psychologists asked senior managers at the companies to identify the capabilities that typified the organization's most outstanding leaders. To create other models, the psychologists used objective criteria, such as a division's profitability, to differentiate the star performers at senior levels within their organizations from the average ones. Those individuals were then extensively interviewed and tested, and their capabilities were compared. This process resulted in the creation of lists of ingredients for highly effective leaders. The lists ranged in length from seven to 15 items and included such ingredients as initiative and strategic vision.

When I analyzed all this data, I found dramatic results. To be sure, intellect was a driver of outstanding performance. Cognitive skills such as big-picture thinking and long-term vision were particularly important. But when I calculated the ratio of technical skills, IQ, and emotional intelligence as ingredients of excellent performance, emotional intelligence proved to be twice as important as the others for jobs at all levels.

Moreover, my analysis showed that emotional intelligence played an increasingly important role at the highest levels of the company, where differences in technical skills are of negligible importance. In other words, the higher the rank of a person considered to be a star performer, the more emotional intelligence capabilities showed up as the reason for his or her effectiveness. When I compared star performers with average ones in senior leadership positions, nearly 90% of the difference in their profiles was attributable to emotional intelligence factors rather than cognitive abilities.

Other researchers have confirmed that emotional intelligence not only distinguishes outstanding leaders but can also be linked to strong performance. The findings of the late David McClelland, the renowned researcher in human and organizational behavior, are a good example. In a 1996 study of a global food and beverage company, McClelland found that when senior managers had a critical mass of emotional intelligence capabilities, their divisions outperformed yearly earnings goals by 20%. Meanwhile, division leaders without that critical mass underperformed by almost the same amount. McClelland's findings, interestingly, held as true in the company's U.S. divisions as in its divisions in Asia and Europe.

In short, the numbers are beginning to tell us a persuasive story about the link between a company's success and the emotional intelligence of its leaders. And just as important, research is also demonstrating that people can, if they take the right approach, develop their emotional intelligence. (See the sidebar "Can Emotional Intelligence Be Learned?")

Can Emotional Intelligence Be Learned?

For ages, people have debated if leaders are born or made. So too goes the debate about emotional intelligence. Are people born with certain levels of empathy, for example, or do they acquire empathy as a result of life's experiences? The answer is both. Scientific inquiry strongly suggests that there is a genetic component to emotional intelligence. Psychological and developmental research indicates that nurture plays a role as well. How much of each perhaps will never be known, but research and practice clearly demonstrate that emotional intelligence can be learned.

One thing is certain: Emotional intelligence increases with age. There is an old-fashioned word for the phenomenon: maturity. Yet even with maturity, some people still need training to enhance their emotional intelligence. Unfortunately, far too many training programs that intend to build leadership skills—including emotional intelligence—are a waste of time and money. The problem is simple: They focus on the wrong part of the brain.

Emotional intelligence is born largely in the neurotransmitters of the brain's limbic system, which governs feelings, impulses, and drives. Research indicates that the limbic system learns best through motivation, extended practice, and feedback. Compare this with the kind of learning that goes on in the neocortex, which governs analytical and technical ability. The neocortex grasps concepts and logic. It is the part of the brain that figures out how to use a computer or make a sales call by reading a book. Not surprisingly—but mistakenly—it is also the part of the brain targeted by most training programs aimed at enhancing emotional intelligence. When such programs take, in effect, a neocortical approach, my research with the Consortium for Research on Emotional Intelligence in Organizations has shown they can even have a *negative* impact on people's job performance.

To enhance emotional intelligence, organizations must refocus their training to include the limbic system. They must help people break old behavioral habits and establish new ones. That not only takes much more time than conventional training programs, it also requires an individualized approach.

Imagine an executive who is thought to be low on empathy by her colleagues. Part of that deficit shows itself as an inability to listen; she interrupts people and doesn't pay close attention to what they're saying. To fix the problem, the executive needs to be motivated to change, and then she needs practice and feedback from others in the company. A colleague or coach could be tapped to let the executive know when she has been observed failing to listen. She would then have to replay the incident and give a better response; that is, demonstrate her ability to absorb what others are saying. And the executive could be directed to observe certain executives who listen well and to mimic their behavior.

With persistence and practice, such a process can lead to lasting results. I know one Wall Street executive who sought to improve his empathy—specifically his ability to read people's reactions and see their perspectives. Before beginning his quest, the executive's subordinates were terrified of working with him. People even went so far as to hide bad news from him. Naturally, he was shocked when finally confronted with these facts. He went home and told his family—but they only confirmed what he had heard at work. When their opinions on any given subject did not mesh with his, they, too, were frightened of him.

Enlisting the help of a coach, the executive went to work to heighten his empathy through practice and feedback. His first step was to take a vacation to a foreign country where he did not speak the language. While there, he monitored his reactions to the unfamiliar and his openness to people who were different from him. When he returned home, humbled by his week abroad, the executive asked his coach to shadow him for parts of the day, several times a week, to critique how he treated people with new or different perspectives. At the same time, he consciously used on-the-job interactions as opportunities to practice "hearing" ideas that differed from his. Finally, the executive had himself videotaped in meetings and asked those who worked for and with him to critique his ability to acknowledge and understand the feelings of others. It took several months, but the executive's emotional intelligence did ultimately rise, and the improvement was reflected in his overall performance on the job.

It's important to emphasize that building one's emotional intelligence cannot—will not—happen without sincere desire and concerted effort. A brief seminar won't help; nor can one buy a how-to manual. It is much harder to learn to empathize—to internalize empathy as a natural response to people—than it is to become adept at regression analysis. But it can be done. "Nothing great was ever achieved without enthusiasm," wrote Ralph Waldo Emerson. If your goal is to become a real leader, these words can serve as a guidepost in your efforts to develop high emotional intelligence.

SELF-AWARENESS

Self-awareness is the first component of emotional intelligence—which makes sense when one considers that the Delphic oracle gave the advice to "know thyself" thousands of years ago. Self-awareness means having a deep understanding of one's emotions, strengths, weaknesses, needs, and drives. People with strong self-awareness are neither overly critical nor unrealistically hopeful. Rather, they are honest—with themselves and with others.

People who have a high degree of self-awareness recognize how their feelings affect them, other people, and their job performance. Thus, a self-aware person who knows that tight deadlines bring out the worst in him plans his time carefully and gets his work done well in advance. Another person with high self-awareness will be able to work with a demanding client. She will understand the client's impact on her moods and the deeper reasons for her frustration. "Their trivial demands take us away from the real work that needs to be done," she might explain. And she will go one step further and turn her anger into something constructive.

Self-awareness extends to a person's understanding of his or her values and goals. Someone who is highly self-aware knows where he is headed and why; so, for example, he will be able to be firm in turning down a job offer that is tempting financially but does not fit with his principles or long-term goals. A person who lacks self-awareness is apt to make decisions that bring on inner turmoil by treading on buried values. "The money looked good so I signed on," someone might say two years into a job, "but the work means so little to me that I'm constantly bored." The decisions of self-aware people mesh with their values; consequently, they often find work to be energizing.

How can one recognize self-awareness? First and foremost, it shows itself as candor and an ability to assess oneself realistically. People with high self-awareness are able to speak accurately and openly—although not necessarily effusively or confessionally— about their emotions and the impact they have on their work. For instance, one manager I know of was skeptical about a new personal-shopper service that her company, a major department-store chain, was about to introduce. Without prompting from her team or her boss, she offered them an explanation: "It's hard for me to get behind the rollout of this service," she admitted, "because I really wanted to run the project, but I wasn't selected. Bear with me while I deal with that." The manager did indeed examine her feelings; a week later, she was supporting the project fully.

Such self-knowledge often shows itself in the hiring process. Ask a candidate to describe a time he got carried away by his feelings and did something he later regretted. Self-aware candidates will be frank in admitting to failure—and will often tell their tales with a smile. One of the hallmarks of self-awareness is a self-deprecating sense of humor.

Self-awareness can also be identified during performance reviews. Self-aware people know—and are comfortable talking about—their limitations and strengths, and they often demonstrate a thirst for constructive criticism. By contrast, people with low self-awareness interpret the message that they need to improve as a threat or a sign of failure.

Self-aware people can also be recognized by their self-confidence. They have a firm grasp of their capabilities and are less likely to set themselves up to fail by, for example, overstretching on assignments. They know, too, when to ask for help. And the risks they take on the job are calculated. They won't ask for a challenge that they know they can't handle alone. They'll play to their strengths.

Consider the actions of a midlevel employee who was invited to sit in on a strategy meeting with her company's top executives. Although she was the most junior person in the room, she did not sit there quietly, listening in awestruck or fearful silence. She knew she had a head for clear logic and the skill to present ideas persuasively, and she offered cogent suggestions about the company's strategy. At the same time, her self-awareness stopped her from wandering into territory where she knew she was weak.

Despite the value of having self-aware people in the workplace, my research indicates that senior executives don't often give self-awareness the credit it deserves when they look for potential leaders. Many executives mistake candor about feelings for "wimpiness" and fail to give due respect to employees who openly acknowledge their shortcomings. Such people are too readily dismissed as "not tough enough" to lead others.

In fact, the opposite is true. In the first place, people generally admire and respect candor. Furthermore, leaders are constantly required to make judgment calls that require a candid assessment of capabilities—their own and those of others. Do we have the management expertise to acquire a competitor? Can we launch a new product within six months? People who assess themselves honestly—that is, self-aware people—are well suited to do the same for the organizations they run.

SELF-REGULATION

Biological impulses drive our emotions. We cannot do away with them—but we can do much to manage them. Self-regulation, which is like an ongoing inner conversation, is the component of emotional intelligence that frees us from being prisoners of our feelings. People engaged in such a conversation feel bad moods and emotional impulses just as everyone else does, but they find ways to control them and even to channel them in useful ways.

Imagine an executive who has just watched a team of his employees present a botched analysis to the company's board of directors. In the gloom that follows, the executive might find himself tempted to pound on the table in anger or kick over a chair. He could leap up and scream at the group. Or he might maintain a grim silence, glaring at everyone before stalking off.

But if he had a gift for self-regulation, he would choose a different approach. He would pick his words carefully, acknowledging the team's poor performance without rushing to any hasty judgment. He would then step back to consider the reasons for the failure. Are they personal—a lack of effort? Are there any mitigating factors? What was his role in the debacle? After considering these questions, he would call the team together, lay out the incident's consequences, and offer his feelings about it. He would then present his analysis of the problem and a well-considered solution.

Why does self-regulation matter so much for leaders? First of all, people who are in control of their feelings and impulses—that is, people who are reasonable—are able to create an environment of trust and fairness. In such an environment, politics and infighting are sharply reduced and productivity is high. Talented people flock to the organization and aren't tempted to leave. And self-regulation has a trickle-down effect. No one wants to be known as a hot-head when the boss is known for her calm approach. Fewer bad moods at the top mean fewer throughout the organization.

Second, self-regulation is important for competitive reasons. Everyone knows that business today is rife with ambiguity and change. Companies merge and break apart regularly. Technology transforms work at a dizzying pace. People who have mastered their emotions are able to roll with the changes. When a new program is announced, they don't panic; instead, they are able to suspend judgment, seek out information, and listen to the executives as they explain the new program. As the initiative moves forward, these people are able to move with it.

Sometimes they even lead the way. Consider the case of a manager at a large manufacturing company. Like her colleagues, she had used a certain software program for five years. The program drove how she collected and reported data and how she thought about the company's strategy. One day, senior executives announced that a new program was to be installed that would radically change how information was gathered and assessed within the organization. While many people in the company complained bitterly about how disruptive the change would be, the manager mulled over the reasons for the new program and was convinced of its potential to improve performance. She eagerly attended training sessions—some of her colleagues refused to do so—and was eventually promoted to run several divisions, in part because she used the new technology so effectively.

I want to push the importance of self-regulation to leadership even further and make the case that it enhances integrity, which is not only a personal virtue but also an organizational strength. Many of the bad things that happen in companies are a function of impulsive behavior. People rarely plan to exaggerate profits, pad expense accounts, dip into the till, or abuse power for selfish ends. Instead, an opportunity presents itself, and people with low impulse control just say yes.

By contrast, consider the behavior of the senior executive at a large food company. The executive was scrupulously honest in his negotiations with local distributors. He would routinely lay out his cost structure in detail, thereby giving the distributors a realistic understanding of the company's pricing. This approach meant the executive couldn't always drive a hard bargain. Now, on occasion, he felt the urge to increase profits by withholding information about the company's costs. But he challenged that impulse—he saw that it made more sense in the long run to counteract it. His emotional self-regulation paid off in strong, lasting relationships with distributors that benefited the company more than any short-term financial gains would have.

The signs of emotional self-regulation, therefore, are easy to see: a propensity for reflection and thoughtfulness; comfort with ambiguity and change; and integrity—an ability to say no to impulsive urges.

Like self-awareness, self-regulation often does not get its due. People who can master their emotions are sometimes seen as cold fish—their considered responses are taken as a lack of passion. People with fiery temperaments are frequently thought of as "classic" leaders—their outbursts are considered hallmarks of charisma and power. But when such people make it to the top, their impulsiveness often works against them. In my research, extreme displays of negative emotion have never emerged as a driver of good leadership.

MOTIVATION

If there is one trait that virtually all effective leaders have, it is motivation. They are driven to achieve beyond expectations—their own and everyone else's. The key word here is *achieve*. Plenty of people are motivated by external factors, such as a big salary or the status that comes from having an impressive title or being part of a prestigious company.

By contrast, those with leadership potential are motivated by a deeply embedded desire to achieve for the sake of achievement.

If you are looking for leaders, how can you identify people who are motivated by the drive to achieve rather than by external rewards? The first sign is a passion for the work itself—such people seek out creative challenges, love to learn, and take great pride in a job well done. They also display an unflagging energy to do things better. People with such energy often seem restless with the status quo. They are persistent with their questions about why things are done one way rather than another; they are eager to explore new approaches to their work.

A cosmetics company manager, for example, was frustrated that he had to wait two weeks to get sales results from people in the field. He finally tracked down an automated phone system that would beep each of his salespeople at 5 p.m. every day. An automated message then prompted them to punch in their numbers—how many calls and sales they had made that day. The system shortened the feedback time on sales results from weeks to hours.

That story illustrates two other common traits of people who are driven to achieve. They are forever raising the performance bar, and they like to keep score. Take the performance bar first. During performance reviews, people with high levels of motivation might ask to be "stretched" by their superiors.

Of course, an employee who combines self-awareness with internal motivation will recognize her limits—but she won't settle for objectives that seem too easy to fulfill.

And it follows naturally that people who are driven to do better also want a way of tracking progress—their own, their team's, and their company's. Whereas people with low achievement motivation are often fuzzy about results, those with high achievement motivation often keep score by tracking such hard measures as profitability or market share. I know of a money manager who starts and ends his day on the Internet, gauging the performance of his stock fund against four industry-set benchmarks.

Interestingly, people with high motivation remain optimistic even when the score is against them. In such cases, self-regulation combines with achievement motivation to overcome the frustration and depression that come after a setback or failure. Take the case of an another portfolio manager at a large investment company. After several successful years, her fund tumbled for three consecutive quarters, leading three large institutional clients to shift their business elsewhere.

Some executives would have blamed the nosedive on circumstances outside their control; others might have seen the setback as evidence of personal failure. This portfolio manager, however, saw an opportunity to prove she could lead a turnaround. Two years later, when she was promoted to a very senior level in the company, she described the experience as "the best thing that ever happened to me; I learned so much from it."

Executives trying to recognize high levels of achievement motivation in their people can look for one last piece of evidence: commitment to the organization. When people love their jobs for the work itself, they often feel committed to the organizations that make that work possible. Committed employees are likely to stay with an organization even when they are pursued by headhunters waving money.

It's not difficult to understand how and why a motivation to achieve translates into strong leadership. If you set the performance bar high for yourself, you will do the same for the organization when you are in a position to do so. Likewise, a drive to surpass goals and an interest in keeping score can be contagious. Leaders with these traits can often build a team of managers around them with the same traits. And of course, optimism and organizational commitment are fundamental to leadership—just try to imagine running a company without them.

EMPATHY

Of all the dimensions of emotional intelligence, empathy is the most easily recognized. We have all felt the empathy of a sensitive teacher or friend; we have all been struck by its absence in an unfeeling coach or boss. But when it comes to business, we rarely hear people praised, let alone rewarded, for their empathy. The very word seems unbusinesslike, out of place amid the tough realities of the marketplace.

But empathy doesn't mean a kind of "I'm OK, you're OK" mushiness. For a leader, that is, it doesn't mean adopting other people's emotions as one's own and trying to please everybody. That would be a nightmare—it would make action impossible. Rather, empathy means thoughtfully considering employees' feelings—along with other factors—in the process of making intelligent decisions.

For an example of empathy in action, consider what happened when two giant brokerage companies merged, creating redundant jobs in all their divisions. One division manager called his people together and gave a gloomy speech that emphasized the number of people who would soon be fired. The manager of another division gave his people a different kind of speech. He was up-front about his own worry and confusion, and he promised to keep people informed and to treat everyone fairly.

The difference between these two managers was empathy. The first manager was too worried about his own fate to consider the feelings of his anxiety-stricken colleagues. The second knew intuitively what his people were feeling, and he acknowledged their fears with his words. Is it any surprise that the first manager saw his division sink as many demoralized people, especially the most talented, departed? By contrast, the second manager continued to be a strong leader, his best people stayed, and his division remained as productive as ever.

Empathy is particularly important today as a component of leadership for at least three reasons: the increasing use of teams; the rapid pace of globalization; and the growing need to retain talent.

Consider the challenge of leading a team. As anyone who has ever been a part of one can attest, teams are cauldrons of bubbling emotions. They are often charged with reaching a consensus—which is hard enough with two people and much more difficult as the numbers increase. Even in groups with as few as four or five members, alliances form and clashing agendas get set. A team's leader must be able to sense and understand the viewpoints of everyone around the table.

That's exactly what a marketing manager at a large information technology company was able to do when she was appointed to lead a troubled team. The group was in turmoil, overloaded by work and missing deadlines. Tensions were high among the members. Tinkering with procedures was not enough to bring the group together and make it an effective part of the company.

So the manager took several steps. In a series of one-on-one sessions, she took the time to listen to everyone in the group—what was frustrating them, how they rated their colleagues, whether they felt they had been ignored. And then she directed the team in a way that brought it together: She encouraged people to speak more openly about their frustrations, and she helped people raise constructive complaints during meetings. In short, her empathy allowed her to understand her team's emotional makeup. The result was not just heightened collaboration among members but also added business, as the team was called on for help by a wider range of internal clients.

Globalization is another reason for the rising importance of empathy for business leaders. Cross-cultural dialogue can easily lead to miscues and misunderstandings.

Empathy is an antidote. People who have it are attuned to subtleties in body language; they can hear the message beneath the words being spoken. Beyond that, they have a deep understanding of both the existence and the importance of cultural and ethnic differences.

Consider the case of an American consultant whose team had just pitched a project to a potential Japanese client. In its dealings with Americans, the team was accustomed to being bombarded with questions after such a proposal, but this time it was greeted with a long silence. Other members of the team, taking the silence as disapproval, were ready to pack and leave. The lead consultant gestured them to stop.

Although he was not particularly familiar with Japanese culture, he read the client's face and posture and sensed not rejection but interest—even deep consideration. He was right: When the client finally spoke, it was to give the consulting firm the job.

Finally, empathy plays a key role in the retention of talent, particularly in today's information economy. Leaders have always needed empathy to develop and keep good people, but today the stakes are higher. When good people leave, they take the company's knowledge with them.

That's where coaching and mentoring come in. It has repeatedly been shown that coaching and mentoring pay off not just in better performance but also in increased job satisfaction and decreased turnover. But what makes coaching and mentoring work best is the nature of the relationship. Outstanding coaches and mentors get inside the heads of the people they are helping. They sense how to give effective feedback. They know when to push for better performance and when to hold back. In the way they motivate their protégés, they demonstrate empathy in action.

In what is probably sounding like a refrain, let me repeat that empathy doesn't get much respect in business. People wonder how leaders can make hard decisions if they are "feeling" for all the people who will be affected. But leaders with empathy do more than sympathize with people around them: They use their knowledge to improve their companies in subtle but important ways.

SOCIAL SKILL

The first three components of emotional intelligence are self-management skills. The last two, empathy and social skill, concern a person's ability to manage relationships with others. As a component of emotional intelligence, social skill is not as simple as it sounds. It's not just a matter of friendliness, although people with high levels of social skill are rarely mean-spirited. Social skill, rather, is friendliness with a purpose: moving people in the direction you desire, whether that's agreement on a new marketing strategy or enthusiasm about a new product.

Socially skilled people tend to have a wide circle of acquaintances, and they have a knack for finding common ground with people of all kinds—a knack for building rapport. That doesn't mean they socialize continually; it means they work according to the assumption that nothing important gets done alone. Such people have a network in place when the time for action comes.

Social skill is the culmination of the other dimensions of emotional intelligence. People tend to be very effective at managing relationships when they can understand and control their own emotions and can

empathize with the feelings of others.
Even motivation contributes to social skill.
Remember that people who are driven to
achieve tend to be optimistic, even in the
face of setbacks or failure. When people
are upbeat, their "glow" is cast upon
conversations and other social encounters.
They are popular, and for good reason.

Because it is the outcome of the other
dimensions of emotional intelligence,
social skill is recognizable on the job in
many ways that will by now sound familiar.
Socially skilled people, for instance,
are adept at managing teams—that's
their empathy at work. Likewise, they
are expert persuaders—a manifestation
of self-awareness, self-regulation, and

empathy combined. Given those skills, good persuaders know when to make an emotional plea, for instance, and when an appeal to reason will work better. And motivation, when publicly visible, makes such people excellent collaborators; their passion for the work spreads to others, and they are driven to find solutions.

But sometimes social skill shows itself in ways the other emotional intelligence components do not. For instance, socially skilled people may at times appear not to be working while at work. They seem to be idly schmoozing—chatting in the hallways with colleagues or joking around with people who are not even connected to their "real" jobs. Socially skilled people, however, don't think it makes sense to arbitrarily limit the scope of their relationships. They build bonds widely because they know that in these fluid times, they may need help someday from people they are just getting to know today.

For example, consider the case of an executive in the strategy department of a global computer manufacturer. By 1993, he was convinced that the company's future lay with the Internet. Over the course of the next year, he found kindred spirits and used his social skill to stitch together a virtual community that cut across levels, divisions, and nations. He then used this de facto team to put up a corporate Web site, among the first by a major company. And, on his own initiative, with no budget or formal status, he

signed up the company to participate in an
annual Internet industry convention. Calling
on his allies and persuading various divisions
to donate funds, he recruited more than
50 people from a dozen different units to
represent the company at the convention.

Management took notice: Within a year
of the conference, the executive's team
formed the basis for the company's first
Internet division, and he was formally put in
charge of it. To get there, the executive had
ignored conventional boundaries, forging
and maintaining connections with people in
every corner of the organization.

Is social skill considered a key leadership
capability in most companies? The answer
is yes, especially when compared with the

other components of emotional intelligence. People seem to know intuitively that leaders need to manage relationships effectively; no leader is an island. After all, the leader's task is to get work done through other people, and social skill makes that possible. A leader who cannot express her empathy may as well not have it at all. And a leader's motivation will be useless if he cannot communicate his passion to the organization. Social skill allows leaders to put their emotional intelligence to work.

It would be foolish to assert that good old-fashioned IQ and technical ability are not important ingredients in strong leadership. But the recipe would not be complete without emotional intelligence. It was once thought that the components of emotional intelligence were "nice to have" in business leaders. But now we know that, for the sake of performance, these are ingredients that leaders "need to have."

It is fortunate, then, that emotional intelligence can be learned. The process is not easy. It takes time and, most of all, commitment. But the benefits that come from having a well-developed emotional intelligence, both for the individual and for the organization, make it worth the effort.

The five components of emotional intelligence at work

	Definition	Hallmarks
Self-awareness	The ability to recognize and understand your moods, emotions, and drives, as well as their effect on others	Self-confidence Realistic self-assessment Self-deprecating sense of humor
Self-regulation	The ability to control or redirect disruptive impulses and moods The propensity to suspend judgment—to think before acting	Trustworthiness and integrity Comfort with ambiguity Openness to change
Motivation	A passion to work for reasons that go beyond money or status A propensity to pursue goals with energy and persistence	Strong drive to achieve optimism, even in the face of failure organizational commitment

(Continued)

	Definition	**Hallmarks**
Empathy	The ability to understand the emotional makeup of other people Skill in treating people according to their emotional reactions	Expertise in building and retaining talent Cross-cultural sensitivity Service to clients and customers
Social skill	Proficiency in managing relationships and building networks An ability to find common ground and build rapport	Effectiveness in leading change Persuasiveness Expertise in building and leading teams

ABOUT THE AUTHOR

Daniel Goleman is a codirector of the Consortium for Research on Emotional Intelligence in Organizations at Rutgers University, coauthor of *Primal Leadership: Leading with Emotional Intelligence* (Harvard Business Review Press, 2013), and author of *The Brain and Emotional Intelligence: New Insights and Leadership: Selected Writings* (More Than Sound, 2011). His latest book is *A Force for Good: The Dalai Lama's Vision for Our World* (Bantam, 2015).

Article Summary

Idea in Brief

What distinguishes great leaders from merely good ones? It isn't IQ or technical skills, says Daniel Goleman. It's **emotional intelligence**: a group of five skills that enable the best leaders to maximize their own *and* their followers' performance. When senior managers at one company had a critical mass of EI capabilities, their divisions outperformed yearly earnings goals by 20%.

The EI skills are:

- *Self-awareness*—knowing one's strengths, weaknesses, drives, values, and impact on others

- *Self-regulation*—controlling or redirecting disruptive impulses and moods

- *Motivation*—relishing achievement for its own sake

- *Empathy*—understanding other people's emotional makeup

- *Social skill*—building rapport with others to move them in desired directions

We're each born with certain levels of EI skills. But we can strengthen these abilities through persistence, practice, and feedback from colleagues or coaches.

The most important management ideas all in one place.

STRATEGIC
INTENT

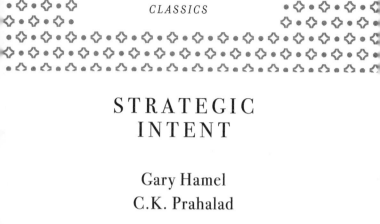

STRATEGIC
INTENT

Gary Hamel
C.K. Prahalad

Harvard Business Review Press
Boston, Massachusetts

Library of Congress Cataloging-in-Publication Data

Hamel, Gary.
  Strategic intent / Gary Hamel, C.K. Prahalad.
    p. cm. — (Harvard business review classics)
  ISBN 978-1-4221-3654-6 (paperback : perm. paper)
  1. Strategic planning.   I. Prahalad, C. K.   II. Title.
  HD30.28.H344 2010
  658.4′012—dc22

                   2010002892

THE HARVARD BUSINESS REVIEW CLASSICS SERIES

Since 1922, *Harvard Business Review* has been a leading source of breakthrough ideas in management practice—many of which still speak to and influence us today. The HBR Classics series now offers you the opportunity to make these seminal pieces a part of your permanent management library. Each volume contains a groundbreaking idea that has shaped best practices and inspired countless managers around the world—and will change how you think about the business world today.

STRATEGIC
INTENT

Today managers in many industries are working hard to match the competitive advantages of their new global rivals. They are moving manufacturing offshore in search of lower labor costs, rationalizing product lines to capture global scale economies, instituting quality circles and just-in-time production, and adopting Japanese human resource practices. When competitiveness still seems out of reach, they form strategic alliances—often with the very companies that upset the competitive balance in the first place.

Important as these initiatives are, few of them go beyond mere imitation. Too many companies are expending enormous energy simply to reproduce the cost and quality advantages their global competitors already enjoy. Imitation may be the sincerest form of flattery, but it will not lead to competitive revitalization. Strategies based on imitation are transparent to competitors who have already mastered them. Moreover, successful competitors rarely stand still. So it is not surprising that many executives feel trapped in a seemingly endless game of catch-up— regularly surprised by the new accomplishments of their rivals.

For these executives and their companies, regaining competitiveness will mean rethinking many of the basic concepts of strategy.[1] As "strategy" has blossomed, the competitiveness of Western companies has withered. This may be coincidence, but we think not. We believe that the application of concepts such as "strategic fit" (between resources and opportunities), "generic strategies" (low cost vs. differentiation vs. focus), and the "strategy hierarchy" (goals, strategies, and tactics) have often abetted the process of competitive decline. The new global competitors approach strategy from a perspective that is fundamentally different from that which underpins Western management thought. Against such competitors, marginal adjustments to current orthodoxies are no more likely to produce competitive revital-ization than are marginal improvements in operating efficiency. (The sidebar at the end of this article, "Remaking Strategy," describes our research and summarizes the two contrasting approaches to strategy we see in large, multinational companies.)

Few Western companies have an enviable track record anticipating the moves of new global competitors. Why? The explanation begins with the way most companies have approached competitor analysis. Typically, competitor analysis focuses on the existing resources (human, technical, and financial) of present competitors. The only companies seen as a threat are those with the resources to erode margins and market share in the next planning period. Resourcefulness, the pace at which new competitive advantages are being built, rarely enters in.

In this respect, traditional competitor analysis is like a snapshot of a moving car. By itself, the photograph yields little information about the car's speed or direction— whether the driver is out for a quiet Sunday drive or warming up for the Grand Prix. Yet many managers have learned through painful experience that a business's initial resource endowment (whether bountiful or meager) is an unreliable predictor of future global success.

Think back. In 1970, few Japanese companies possessed the resource base, manufacturing volume, or technical prowess of U.S. and European industry leaders. Komatsu was less than 35% as large as Caterpillar (measured by sales), was scarcely represented outside Japan, and relied on just one product line—small bulldozers—for most of its revenue. Honda was smaller than American Motors and had not yet begun to export cars to the United States. Canon's first halting steps in the reprographics business looked pitifully small compared with the $4 billion Xerox powerhouse.

If Western managers had extended their competitor analysis to include these companies, it would merely have underlined how dramatic the resource discrepancies between them were. Yet by 1985, Komatsu was a $2.8 billion company with a product scope encompassing a broad range of earth-moving equipment, industrial robots, and semi-conductors. Honda manufactured almost as many cars worldwide in 1987 as Chrysler. Canon had matched Xerox's global unit market share.

The lesson is clear: assessing the current tactical advantages of known competitors will not help you understand the resolution, stamina, and inventiveness of potential competitors. Sun-tzu, a Chinese military strategist, made the point 3,000 years ago: "All men can see the tactics whereby I conquer," he wrote, "but what none can see is the strategy out of which great victory is evolved."

Companies that have risen to global leadership over the past 20 years invariably began with ambitions that were out of all proportion to their resources and capabilities. But they created an obsession with winning at all levels of the organization and then sustained that obsession over the 10- to 20-year quest for global leadership. We term this obsession "strategic intent."

On the one hand, strategic intent envisions a desired leadership position and establishes the criterion the organization will use to chart its progress. Komatsu set out to "Encircle Caterpillar." Canon sought to "Beat Xerox." Honda strove to become a second Ford—an automotive pioneer. All are expressions of strategic intent.

At the same time, strategic intent is more than simply unfettered ambition. (Many companies possess an ambitious strategic intent yet fall short of their goals.) The concept also encompasses an active management process that includes: focusing the organization's attention on the essence of winning; motivating people by communicating the value of the target; leaving room for individual and team contributions; sustaining enthusiasm by providing new operational definitions as circumstances change; and using intent consistently to guide resource allocations.

STRATEGIC INTENT CAPTURES THE ESSENCE OF WINNING

The Apollo program—landing a man on the moon ahead of the Soviets—was as competitively focused as Komatsu's drive against Caterpillar. The space program became the scorecard for America's technology race with the USSR. In the turbulent information technology industry, it was hard to pick a single competitor as a target, so NEC's strategic intent, set in the early 1970s, was to acquire the technologies that would put it in the best position to exploit the convergence of computing and telecommunications. Other industry observers foresaw their convergence, but only NEC made convergence the guiding theme for subsequent strategic decisions by adopting "computing and communications" as its intent. For Coca-Cola, strategic intent has been to put a Coke within "arm's reach" of every consumer in the world.

STRATEGIC INTENT IS STABLE OVER TIME

In battles for global leadership, one of the most critical tasks is to lengthen the organization's attention span. Strategic intent provides consistency to short-term action, while leaving room for reinterpretation as new opportunities emerge. At Komatsu, encircling Caterpillar encompassed a succession of medium-term programs aimed at exploiting specific weaknesses in Caterpillar or building particular competitive advantages. When Caterpillar threatened Komatsu in Japan, for example, Komatsu responded by first improving quality, then driving down costs, then cultivating export markets, and then underwriting new product development.

STRATEGIC INTENT SETS A TARGET THAT DESERVES PERSONAL EFFORT AND COMMITMENT

Ask the CEOs of many American corporations how they measure their contributions to their companies' success and you're likely to get an answer expressed in terms of shareholder wealth. In a company that possesses a strategic intent, top management is more likely to talk in terms of global market leadership. Market share leadership typically yields shareholder wealth, to be sure. But the two goals do not have the same motivational impact. It is hard to imagine middle managers, let alone blue-collar employees, waking up each day with the sole thought of creating more shareholder wealth. But mightn't they feel different given the challenge to "Beat Benz"—the rallying cry at one Japanese auto producer? Strategic intent gives employees the only goal that is worthy of commitment: to unseat the best or remain the best, worldwide.

Many companies are more familiar with strategic planning than they are with strategic intent. The planning process typically acts as a "feasibility sieve." Strategies are accepted or rejected on the basis of whether managers can be precise about the "how" as well as the "what" of their plans. Are the milestones clear? Do we have the necessary skills and resources? How will competitors react? Has the market been thoroughly researched? In one form or another, the admonition "Be realistic!" is given to line managers at almost every turn.

But can you *plan* for global leadership? Did Komatsu, Canon, and Honda have detailed, 20-year "strategies" for attacking Western markets? Are Japanese and Korean managers better planners than their Western counterparts? No. As valuable as strategic planning is, global leadership is an objective that lies outside the range of planning. We know of few companies with highly developed planning systems that have managed to set a strategic intent. As tests of strategic fit become more stringent, goals that cannot be planned for fall by the wayside. Yet companies that are afraid to commit to goals that lie outside the range of planning are unlikely to become global leaders.

Although strategic planning is billed as a way of becoming more future oriented, most managers, when pressed, will admit that their strategic plans reveal more about today's problems than tomorrow's opportunities. With a fresh set of problems confronting managers at the beginning of every planning cycle, focus often shifts dramatically from year to year. And with the pace of change accelerating in most industries, the predictive horizon is becoming shorter and shorter. So plans do little more than project the present forward incrementally. The goal of strategic intent is to fold the future back into the present. The important question is not "How will next year be different from this year?" but "What must we do differently next year to get closer to our strategic intent?" Only with a carefully articulated and adhered to strategic intent will a succession of year-on-year plans sum up to global leadership.

Just as you cannot plan a 10- to 20-year quest for global leadership, the chance of falling into a leadership position by accident is also remote. We don't believe that global leadership comes from an undirected process of intrapreneurship. Nor is it the product of a skunkworks or other techniques for internal venturing. Behind such programs lies a nihilistic assumption: the organization is so hidebound, so orthodox ridden that the only way to innovate is to put a few bright people in a dark room, pour in some money, and hope that something wonderful will happen. In this "Silicon Valley" approach to innovation, the only role for top managers is to retrofit their corporate strategy to the entrepreneurial successes that emerge from below. Here the value added of top management is low indeed.

Sadly, this view of innovation may be consistent with reality in many large companies.[2] On the one hand, top management lacks any particular point of view about desirable ends beyond satisfying shareholders and keeping raiders at bay. On the other, the planning format, reward criteria, definition of served market, and belief in accepted industry practice all work together to tightly constrain the range of available means. As a result, innovation is necessarily an isolated activity. Growth depends more on the inventive capacity of individuals and small teams than on the ability of top management to aggregate the efforts of multiple teams towards an ambitious strategic intent.

In companies that overcame resource constraints to build leadership positions, we see a different relationship between means and ends. While strategic intent is clear about ends, it is flexible as to means—it leaves room for improvisation. Achieving strategic intent requires enormous creativity with respect to means: witness Fujitsu's use of strategic alliances in Europe to attack IBM. But this creativity comes in the service of a clearly prescribed end. Creativity is unbridled, but not uncorralled, because top management establishes the criterion against which employees can pre-test the logic of their initiatives. Middle managers must do more than deliver on promised financial targets; they must also deliver on the broad direction implicit in their organization's strategic intent.

Strategic intent implies a sizable stretch for an organization. Current capabilities and resources will not suffice. This forces the organization to be more inventive, to make the most of limited resources. Whereas the traditional view of strategy focuses on the degree of fit between existing resources and current opportunities, strategic intent creates an extreme misfit between resources and ambitions. Top management then challenges the organization to close the gap by systematically building new advantages. For Canon this meant first understanding Xerox's patents, then licensing technology to create a product that would yield early market experience, then gearing up internal R&D efforts, then licensing its own technology to other manufacturers to fund further R&D, then entering market segments in Japan and Europe where Xerox was weak, and so on.

In this respect, strategic intent is like a marathon run in 400-meter sprints. No one knows what the terrain will look like at mile 26, so the role of top management is to focus the organization's attention on the ground to be covered in the next 400 meters. In several companies, management did this by presenting the organization with a series of corporate challenges, each specifying the next hill in the race to achieve strategic intent. One year the challenge might be quality, the next total customer care, the next entry into new markets, the next a rejuvenated product line. As this example indicates, corporate challenges are a way to stage the acquisition of new competitive advantages, a way to identify the focal point for employees' efforts in the near to medium term. As with strategic intent, top management is specific about the ends (reducing product development times by 75%, for example) but less prescriptive about the means.

Like strategic intent, challenges stretch the organization. To preempt Xerox in the personal copier business, Canon set its engineers a target price of $1,000 for a home copier. At the time, Canon's least expensive copier sold for several thousand dollars. Trying to reduce the cost of existing models would not have given Canon the radical price-performance improvement it needed to delay or deter Xerox's entry into personal copiers. Instead, Canon engineers were challenged to reinvent the copier—a challenge they met by substituting a disposable cartridge for the complex image-transfer mechanism used in other copiers.

Corporate challenges come from analyzing competitors as well as from the foreseeable pattern of industry evolution. Together these reveal potential competitive openings and identify the new skills the organization will need to take the initiative away from better positioned players. The exhibit, "Building Competitive Advantage at Komatsu," illustrates the way challenges helped that company achieve its intent.

For a challenge to be effective, individuals and teams throughout the organization must understand it and see its implications for

Building Competitive Advantage at Komatsu

Corporate Challenge	Protect Komatsu's Home Market Against Caterpillar	Reduce Costs While Maintaining Quality
Programs	**early 1960s** Licensing deals with Cummins Engine, International Harvester, and Bucyrus-Erie to acquire technology and establish benchmarks **1961** Project A (For Ace) to advance the product quality of Komatsu's small and midsize bull-dozers above Caterpillar's **1962** Quality circles companywide to provide training for all employees	**1965** Cost Down (CD) Program **1966** Total CD program

Make Komatsu an International Enterprise and Build Export Markets	Respond to External Shocks That Threaten Markets	Create New Products and Markets
early 1960s Develop Eastern bloc countries	1975 V-10 program to reduce costs by 10% while maintaining quality; reduce parts by 20%; rationalize manufacturing system	late 1970s Accelerate product development to expand line
1967 Komatsu Europe marketing subsidiary established	1977 ¥180 program to budget companywide for 180 yen to the dollar when exchange rate was 240	1979 Future and Frontiers program to identify new businesses based on society needs and company's know-how
1970 Komatsu America established	1979 Project E to establish teams to redouble cost and quality efforts in response to oil crisis	1981 EPOCHS program to reconcile greater product variety with improved production efficiencies
1972 Project B to improve the durability and reliability and to reduce costs of large bulldozers		
1972 Project C to improve pay loaders		
1972 Project D to improve hydraulic excavators		
1974 Establish presales and service departments to assist newly industrializing countries in construction projects		

their own jobs. Companies that set corporate challenges to create new competitive advantages (as Ford and IBM did with quality improvement) quickly discover that engaging the entire organization requires top management to do the following:

- *Create a sense of urgency*, or quasi crisis, by amplifying weak signals in the environment that point up the need to improve, instead of allowing inaction to precipitate a real crisis. (Komatsu, for example, budgeted on the basis of worst-case exchange rates that overvalued the yen.)

- *Develop a competitor focus at every level through widespread use of competitive intelligence.* Every employee should be able to benchmark his or her efforts against best-in-class competitors so that the challenge becomes personal. (For example, Ford showed production-line workers videotapes of operations at Mazda's most efficient plant.)

- *Provide employees with the skills they need to work effectively*—training in statistical tools, problem solving, value engineering, and team building, for example.

- *Give the organization time to digest one challenge before launching another.* When competing initiatives overload the organization, middle managers often try to protect their people from the whipsaw of shifting priorities. But this "wait and see if they're serious this time" attitude ultimately destroys the credibility of corporate challenges.

- *Establish clear milestones and review mechanisms* to track progress and ensure that internal recognition and rewards reinforce desired behavior. The goal is to make the challenge inescapable for everyone in the company.

It is important to distinguish between the process of managing corporate challenges and the advantages that the process creates. Whatever the actual challenge may be—quality, cost, value engineering, or something else—there is the same need to engage employees intellectually and emotionally in the development of new skills. In each case, the challenge will take root only if senior executives and lower-level employees feel a reciprocal responsibility for competitiveness.

We believe workers in many companies have been asked to take a disproportionate share of the blame for competitive failure. In one U.S. company, for example, management had sought a 40% wage-package concession from hourly employees to bring labor costs into line with Far Eastern competitors. The result was a long strike and, ultimately, a 10% wage concession from employees on the line. However, direct labor costs in manufacturing accounted for less than 15% of total value added. The company thus succeeded in demoralizing its entire blue-collar workforce for the sake of a 1.5% reduction in total costs. Ironically, further analysis showed that their competitors' most significant costs savings came not from lower hourly wages but from better work methods invented by employees. You can imagine how eager the U.S. workers were to make similar contributions after the strike and concessions. Contrast this situation with what happened at Nissan when the yen strengthened: Top management took a big pay cut and then asked middle managers and line employees to sacrifice relatively less.

Reciprocal responsibility means shared gain and shared pain. In too many companies, the pain of revitalization falls almost exclusively on the employees least responsible for the enterprise's decline. Too often, workers are asked to commit to corporate goals without any matching commitment from top management—be it employment security, gain sharing, or an ability to influence the direction of the business. This one-sided approach to regaining competitiveness keeps many companies from harnessing the intellectual horsepower of their employees.

Creating a sense of reciprocal responsibility is crucial because competitiveness ultimately depends on the pace at which a company embeds new advantages deep within its organization, not on its stock of advantages at any given time. Thus we need to expand the concept of competitive advantage beyond the scorecard many managers now use: Are my costs lower? Will my product command a price premium?

Few competitive advantages are long lasting. Uncovering a new competitive advantage is a bit like getting a hot tip on a stock: the first person to act on the insight makes more money than the last. When the experience curve was young, a company that built capacity ahead of competitors, dropped prices to fill plants, and reduced costs as volume rose went to the bank. The first mover traded on the fact that competitors undervalued market share—they didn't price to capture additional share because they didn't understand how market share leadership could be translated into lower costs and better margins. But there is no more undervalued market share when each of 20 semiconductor companies builds enough capacity to serve 10% of the world market.

Keeping score of existing advantages is not the same as building new advantages. The essence of strategy lies in creating tomorrow's competitive advantages faster than competitors mimic the ones you possess today. In the 1960s, Japanese producers relied on labor and capital cost advantages. As Western manufacturers began to move production offshore, Japanese companies accelerated their investment in process technology and created scale and quality advantages. Then as their U.S. and European competitors rationalized manufacturing, they added another string to their bow by accelerating the rate of product development. Then they built global brands. Then they deskilled competitors through alliances and outsourcing deals. The moral? An organization's capacity to improve existing skills and learn new ones is the most defensible competitive advantage of all.

To achieve a strategic intent, a company must usually take on larger, better-financed competitors. That means carefully managing competitive engagements so that scarce resources are conserved. Managers cannot do that simply by playing the same game better—making marginal improvements to competitors' technology and business practices. Instead, they must fundamentally change the game in ways that disadvantage incumbents—devising novel approaches to market entry, advantage building, and competitive warfare. For smart competitors, the goal is not competitive imitation but competitive innovation, the art of containing competitive risks within manageable proportions.

Four approaches to competitive innovation are evident in the global expansion of Japanese companies. These are: building layers of advantage, searching for loose bricks, changing the terms of engagement, and competing through collaboration.

The wider a company's portfolio of advantages, the less risk it faces in competitive battles. New global competitors have built such portfolios by steadily expanding their arsenals of competitive weapons. They have moved inexorably from less defensible advantages such as low wage costs to more defensible advantages like global brands. The Japanese color television industry illustrates this layering process.

By 1967, Japan had become the largest producer of black-and-white television sets. By 1970, it was closing the gap in color televisions. Japanese manufacturers used their competitive advantage—at that time, primarily, low labor costs—to build a base in the private-label business, then moved quickly to establish world-scale plants. This investment gave them additional layers of advantage—quality and reliability—as well as further cost reductions from process improvements. At the same time, they recognized that these cost-based advantages were vulnerable to changes in labor costs, process and product technology, exchange rates, and trade policy. So throughout the 1970s, they also invested heavily in building channels and brands, thus creating another layer of advantage, a global franchise. In the late 1970s, they enlarged the scope of their products and businesses to amortize these grand investments, and by 1980 all the major players—Matsushita, Sharp, Toshiba, Hitachi, Sanyo—had established related sets of businesses that could support global marketing investments. More recently, they have been investing in regional manufacturing and design centers to tailor their products more closely to national markets.

These manufacturers thought of the various sources of competitive advantage as mutually desirable layers, not mutually exclusive choices. What some call competitive suicide–pursuing both cost and differentiation–is exactly what many competitors strive for.[3] Using flexible manufacturing technologies and better marketing intelligence, they are moving away from standardized "world products" to products like Mazda's minivan, developed in California expressly for the U.S. market.

Another approach to competitive innovation—searching for loose bricks— exploits the benefits of surprise, which is just as useful in business battles as it is in war. Particularly in the early stages of a war for global markets, successful new competitors work to stay below the response threshold of their larger, more powerful rivals. Staking out underdefended territory is one way to do this.

To find loose bricks, managers must have few orthodoxies about how to break into a market or challenge a competitor. For example, in one large U.S. multinational, we asked several country managers to describe what a Japanese competitor was doing in the local market. The first executive said, "They're coming at us in the low end.

Japanese companies always come in at the bottom." The second speaker found the comment interesting but disagreed: "They don't offer any low-end products in my market, but they have some exciting stuff at the top end. We really should reverse engineer that thing." Another colleague told still another story. "They haven't taken any business away from me," he said, "but they've just made me a great offer to supply components." In each country, their Japanese competitor had found a different loose brick.

The search for loose bricks begins with a careful analysis of the competitor's conventional wisdom: How does the company define its "served market"? What activities are most profitable? Which geographic markets are too troublesome to enter? The objective is not to find a corner of the industry (or niche) where larger competitors seldom tread but to build a base of attack just outside the market territory that industry leaders currently occupy. The goal is an uncontested profit sanctuary, which could be a particular product segment (the "low end" in motorcycles), a slice of the value chain (components in the computer industry), or a particular geographic market (Eastern Europe).

When Honda took on leaders in the motorcycle industry, for example, it began with products that were just outside the conventional definition of the leaders' product-market domains. As a result, it could build a base of operations in underdefended territory and then use that base to launch an expanded attack. What many competitors failed to see was Honda's strategic intent and its growing competence in engines and power trains. Yet even as Honda was selling 50cc motorcycles in the United States, it was already racing larger bikes in Europe—assembling the design skills and technology it would need for a systematic expansion across the entire spectrum of motor-related businesses.

Honda's progress in creating a core competence in engines should have warned competitors that it might enter a series of seemingly unrelated industries—automobiles, lawn mowers, marine engines, generators. But with each company fixated on its own market, the threat of Honda's horizontal diversification went unnoticed. Today companies like Matsushita and Toshiba are similarly poised to move in unexpected ways across industry boundaries. In protecting loose bricks, companies must extend their peripheral vision by tracking and anticipating the migration of global competitors across product segments, businesses, national markets, value-added stages, and distribution channels.

Changing the terms of engagement—refusing to accept the front runner's definition of industry and segment boundaries—represents still another form of competitive innovation. Canon's entry into the copier business illustrates this approach.

During the 1970s, both Kodak and IBM tried to match Xerox's business system in terms of segmentation, products, distribution, service, and pricing. As a result, Xerox had no trouble decoding the new entrants' intentions and developing countermoves. IBM eventually withdrew from the copier business, while Kodak remains a distant second in the large copier market that Xerox still dominates.

Canon, on the other hand, changed the terms of competitive engagement. While Xerox built a wide range of copiers, Canon standardized machines and components to reduce costs. Canon chose to distribute through office-product dealers rather than try to match Xerox's huge direct sales force.

It also avoided the need to create a national service network by designing reliability and serviceability into its product and then delegating service responsibility to the dealers. Canon copiers were sold rather than leased, freeing Canon from the burden of financing the lease base. Finally, instead of selling to the heads of corporate duplicating departments, Canon appealed to secretaries and department managers who wanted distributed copying. At each stage, Canon neatly sidestepped a potential barrier to entry.

Canon's experience suggests that there is an important distinction between barriers to entry and barriers to imitation. Competitors that tried to match Xerox's business system had to pay the same entry costs—the barriers to imitation were high. But Canon dramatically reduced the barriers to entry by changing the rules of the game.

Changing the rules also short-circuited Xerox's ability to retaliate quickly against its new rival. Confronted with the need to rethink its business strategy and organization, Xerox was paralyzed for a time. Xerox managers realized that the faster they downsized the product line, developed new channels, and improved reliability, the faster they would erode the company's traditional profit base. What might have been seen as critical success factors—Xerox's national sales force and service network, its large installed base of leased machines, and its reliance on service revenues—instead became barriers to retaliation. In this sense, competitive innovation is like judo: the goal is to use a larger competitor's weight against it. And that happens not by matching the leader's capabilities but by developing contrasting capabilities of one's own.

Competitive innovation works on the premise that a successful competitor is likely to be wedded to a "recipe" for success. That's why the most effective weapon new competitors possess is probably a clean sheet of paper. And why an incumbent's greatest vulnerability is its belief in accepted practice.

Through licensing, outsourcing agreements, and joint ventures, it is sometimes possible to win without fighting. For example, Fujitsu's alliances in Europe with Siemens and STC (Britain's largest computer maker) and in the United States with Amdahl yield manufacturing volume and access to Western markets. In the early 1980s, Matsushita established a joint venture with Thorn (in the United Kingdom), Telefunken (in Germany), and Thomson (in France), which allowed it to quickly multiply the forces arrayed against Philips in the battle for leadership in the European VCR business. In fighting larger global rivals by proxy, Japanese companies have adopted a maxim as old as human conflict itself: my enemy's enemy is my friend.

Hijacking the development efforts of potential rivals is another goal of competitive collaboration. In the consumer electronics war, Japanese competitors attacked traditional businesses like TVs and hi-fis while volunteering to manufacture "next generation" products like VCRs, camcorders, and compact disc players for Western rivals. They hoped their rivals would ratchet down development spending, and in most cases that is precisely what happened. But companies that abandoned their own development efforts seldom reemerged as serious competitors in subsequent new product battles.

Collaboration can also be used to calibrate competitors' strengths and weaknesses. Toyota's joint venture with GM, and Mazda's with Ford, give these automakers an invaluable vantage point for assessing the progress their U.S. rivals have made in cost reduction, quality, and technology. They can also learn how GM and Ford compete—when they will fight and when they won't. Of course, the reverse is also true: Ford and GM have an equal opportunity to learn from their partner-competitors.

The route to competitive revitalization we have been mapping implies a new view of strategy. Strategic intent assures consistency in resource allocation over the long term. Clearly articulated corporate challenges focus the efforts of individuals in the medium term. Finally, competitive innovation helps reduce competitive risk in the short term. This consistency in the long term, focus in the medium term, and inventiveness and involvement in the short term provide the key to leveraging limited resources in pursuit of ambitious goals. But just as there is a process of winning, so there is a process of surrender. Revitalization requires understanding that process too.

Given their technological leadership and access to large regional markets, how did U.S. and European countries lose their apparent birthright to dominate global industries? There is no simple answer. Few companies recognize the value of documenting failure. Fewer still search their own managerial orthodoxies for the seeds for competitive surrender. But we believe there is a pathology of surrender (summarized in "The Process of Surrender") that gives some important clues.

It is not very comforting to think that the essence of Western strategic thought can be reduced to eight rules for excellence, seven S's, five competitive forces, four product life-cycle stages, three generic strategies, and innumerable two-by-two matrices.[4] Yet for the past 20 years, "advances" in strategy have taken the form of ever more typologies, heuristics, and laundry lists, often with dubious empirical bases. Moreover, even reasonable concepts like the product life cycle, experience curve, product portfolios, and generic strategies often have toxic side effects: They reduce the number of strategic options management is willing to consider. They create a preference for selling businesses rather than defending them. They yield predictable strategies that rivals easily decode.

Strategy "recipes" limit opportunities for competitive innovation. A company may have 40 businesses and only four strategies— invest, hold, harvest, or divest. Too often strategy is seen as a positioning exercise in which options are tested by how they fit the existing industry structure. But current industry structure reflects the strengths of the industry leader; and playing by the leader's rules is usually competitive suicide.

Armed with concepts like segmentation, the value chain, competitor benchmarking, strategic groups, and mobility barriers, many managers have become better and better at drawing industry maps. But while they have been busy mapmaking, their competitors have been moving entire continents. The strategist's goal is not to find a niche within the existing industry space but to create new space that is uniquely suited to the company's own strengths, space that is off the map.

This is particularly true now that industry boundaries are becoming more and more unstable. In industries such as financial services and communications, rapidly changing technology, deregulation, and globalization have undermined the value of traditional industry analysis. Mapmaking skills are worth little in the epicenter of an earthquake. But an industry in upheaval presents opportunities for ambitious companies to redraw the map in their favor, so long as they can think outside traditional industry boundaries.

Concepts like "mature" and "declining" are largely definitional. What most executives mean when they label a business mature is that sales growth has stagnated in their current geographic markets for existing products sold through existing channels. In such cases, it's not the industry that is mature, but the executives' conception of the industry. Asked if the piano business was mature, a senior executive in Yamaha replied, "Only if we can't take any market share from anybody anywhere in the world and still make money. And anyway, we're not in the 'piano' business, we're in the 'keyboard' business." Year after year, Sony has revitalized its radio and tape recorder businesses, despite the fact that other manufacturers long ago abandoned these businesses as mature.

A narrow concept of maturity can foreclose a company from a broad stream of future opportunities. In the 1970s, several U.S. companies thought that consumer electronics had become a mature industry. What could possibly top the color TV? they asked themselves. RCA and GE, distracted by opportunities in more "attractive" industries like mainframe computers, left Japanese producers with a virtual monopoly in VCRs, camcorders, and compact disc players. Ironically, the TV business, once thought mature, is on the verge of a dramatic renaissance. A $20 billion-a-year business will be created when high-definition television is launched in the United States. But the pioneers of television may capture only a small part of this bonanza.

Most of the tools of strategic analysis are focused domestically. Few force managers to consider global opportunities and threats. For example, portfolio planning portrays top management's investment options as an array of businesses rather than as an array of geographic markets. The result is predictable: As businesses come under attack from foreign competitors, the company attempts to abandon them and enter others in which the forces of global competition are not yet so strong. In the short term, this may be an appropriate response to waning competitiveness, but there are fewer and fewer businesses in which a domestic-oriented company can find refuge. We seldom hear such companies asking: Can we move into emerging markets overseas ahead of our global rivals and prolong the profitability of this business? Can we counterattack in our global competitors' home market and slow the pace of their expansion? A senior executive in one successful global company made a telling comment: "We're glad to find a competitor managing by the portfolio concept—we can almost predict how much share we'll have to take away to put the business on the CEO's 'sell list.'"

Companies can also be overcommitted to organizational recipes, such as strategic business units and the decentralization an SBU structure implies. Decentralization is seductive because it places the responsibility for success or failure squarely on the shoulders of line managers. Each business is assumed to have all the resources it needs to execute its strategies successfully, and in this no-excuses environment, it is hard for top management to fail. But desirable as clear lines of responsibility and accountability are, competitive revitalization requires positive value added from top management.

Few companies with a strong SBU orientation have built successful global distribution and brand positions. Investments in a global brand franchise typically transcend the resources and risk propensity of a single business. While some Western companies have had global brand positions for 30 or 40 years or more (Heinz, Siemens, IBM, Ford, and Kodak, for example), it is hard to identify any American or European company that has created a new global brand franchise in the last 10 to 15 years. Yet, Japanese companies have created a score or more—NEC, Fujitsu, Panasonic (Matsushita), Toshiba, Sony, Seiko, Epson, Canon, Minolta, and Honda, among them.

General Electric's situation is typical. In many of its businesses, this American giant has been almost unknown in Europe and Asia. GE made no coordinated effort to build a global corporate franchise. Any GE business with international ambitions had to bear

the burden of establishing its credibility
and credentials in the new market alone.
Not surprisingly, some once-strong GE
businesses opted out of the difficult task of
building a global brand position. In contrast,
smaller Korean companies like Samsung,
Daewoo, and Lucky Gold Star are busy
building global-brand umbrellas that will
ease market entry for a whole range of businesses. The underlying principle is simple:
economies of scope may be as important as
economies of scale in entering global markets. But capturing economies of scope
demands interbusiness coordination that
only top management can provide.

We believe that inflexible SBU-type
organizations have also contributed to the

deskilling of some companies. For a single SBU, incapable of sustaining investment in a core competence such as semiconductors, optical media, or combustion engines, the only way to remain competitive is to purchase key components from potential (often Japanese or Korean) competitors. For an SBU defined in product market terms, competitiveness means offering an end product that is competitive in price and performance. But that gives an SBU manager little incentive to distinguish between external sourcing that achieves "product embodied" competitiveness and internal development that yields deeply embedded organizational competences that can be exploited across multiple businesses. Where upstream component manufacturing activities are seen as cost centers with cost-plus transfer pricing, additional investment in the core activity may seem a less profitable use of capital than investment in downstream activities. To make matters worse, internal accounting data may not reflect the competitive value of retaining control over core competence.

Together a shared global corporate brand franchise and shared core competence act as mortar in many Japanese companies. Lacking this mortar, a company's businesses are truly loose bricks—easily knocked out by global competitors that steadily invest in core competences. Such competitors can co-opt domestically oriented companies into long-term sourcing dependence and capture the economies of scope of global brand investment through interbusiness coordination.

Last in decentralization's list of dangers is the standard of managerial performance typically used in SBU organizations. In many companies, business unit managers are rewarded solely on the basis of their performance against return on investment targets. Unfortunately, that often leads to denominator management because executives soon discover that reductions in investment and head count—the denominator—"improve" the financial ratios by which they are measured more easily than growth in the numerator—revenues. It also fosters a hair-trigger sensitivity to industry downturns that can be very costly. Managers who are quick to reduce investment and dismiss workers find it takes much longer to regain lost skills and catch up on investment when the industry turns upward again. As a result, they lose market share in every business cycle. Particularly in industries where there is fierce competition for the best people and where competitors invest relentlessly, denominator management creates a retrenchment ratchet.

The concept of the general manager as a movable peg reinforces the problem of denominator management. Business schools are guilty here because they have perpetuated the notion that a manager with net present value calculations in one hand and portfolio planning in the other can manage any business anywhere.

In many diversified companies, top management evaluates line managers on numbers alone because no other basis for dialogue exists. Managers move so many times as part of their "career development" that they often do not understand the nuances of the businesses they are managing. At GE, for example, one fast-track manager heading an important new venture had moved across five businesses in five years. His series of quick successes finally came to an end when he confronted a Japanese competitor whose managers had been plodding along in the same business for more than a decade.

Regardless of ability and effort, fast-track managers are unlikely to develop the deep business knowledge they need to discuss technology options, competitors' strategies, and global opportunities substantively. Invariably, therefore, discussions gravitate to "the numbers," while the value added of managers is limited to the financial and planning savvy they carry from job to job. Knowledge of the company's internal planning and accounting systems substitutes for substantive knowledge of the business, making competitive innovation unlikely.

When managers know that their assignments have a two- to three-year time frame, they feel great pressure to create a good track record fast. This pressure often takes one of two forms. Either the manager does not commit to goals whose time line extends beyond his or her expected tenure. Or ambitious goals are adopted and squeezed into an unrealistically short time frame. Aiming to be number one in a business is the essence of strategic intent; but imposing a three- to four-year horizon on the effort simply invites disaster. Acquisitions are made with little attention to the problems of integration. The organization becomes overloaded with initiatives. Collaborative ventures are formed without adequate attention to competitive consequences.

Almost every strategic management theory and nearly every corporate planning system is premised on a strategy hierarchy in which corporate goals guide business unit strategies and business unit strategies guide functional tactics.[5] In this hierarchy, senior management makes strategy and lower levels execute it. The dichotomy between formulation and implementation is familiar and widely accepted. But the strategy hierarchy undermines competitiveness by fostering an elitist view of management that tends to disenfranchise most of the organization. Employees fail to identify with corporate goals or involve themselves deeply in the work of becoming more competitive.

The strategy hierarchy isn't the only explanation for an elitist view of management, of course. The myths that grow up around successful top managers—"Lee Iacocca saved Chrysler," "De Benedetti rescued Olivetti," "John Sculley turned Apple around"—perpetuate it. So does the turbulent business environment. Middle managers buffeted by circumstances that seem to be beyond their control desperately want to believe that top management has all the answers. And top management, in turn, hesitates to admit it does not for fear of demoralizing lower-level employees.

The result of all this is often a code of silence in which the full extent of a company's competitiveness problem is not widely shared. We interviewed business unit managers in one company, for example, who were extremely anxious because top management wasn't talking openly about the competitive challenges the company faced. They assumed the lack of communication indicated a lack of awareness on their senior managers' part. But when asked whether they were open with their own employees, these same managers replied that while they could face up to the problems, the people below them could not. Indeed, the only time the workforce heard about the company's competitiveness problems was during wage negotiations when problems were used to extract concessions.

Unfortunately, a threat that everyone perceives but no one talks about creates more anxiety than a threat that has been clearly identified and made the focal point for the problem-solving efforts of the entire company. That is one reason honesty and humility on the part of top management may be the first prerequisite of revitalization. Another reason is the need to make participation more than a buzzword.

Programs such as quality circles and total customer service often fall short of expectations because management does not recognize that successful implementation requires more than administrative structures. Difficulties in embedding new capabilities are typically put down to "communication" problems, with the unstated assumption that if only downward communication were more effective—"if only middle management would get the message straight"—the new program would quickly take root. The need for upward communication is often ignored, or assumed to mean nothing more than feedback. In contrast, Japanese companies win, not because they have smarter managers, but because they have developed ways to harness the "wisdom of the anthill." They realize that top managers are a bit like the astronauts who circle the earth in the space shuttle. It may be the astronauts who get all the glory, but everyone knows that the real intelligence behind the mission is located firmly on the ground.

Where strategy formulation is an elitist activity it is also difficult to produce truly creative strategies. For one thing, there are not enough heads and points of view in divisional or corporate planning departments to challenge conventional wisdom. For another, creative strategies seldom emerge from the annual planning ritual. The starting point for next year's strategy is almost always this year's strategy. Improvements are incremental. The company sticks to the segments and territories it knows, even though the real opportunities may be elsewhere. The impetus for Canon's pioneering entry into the personal copier business came from an overseas sales subsidiary—not from planners in Japan.

The goal of the strategy hierarchy remains valid—to ensure consistency up and down the organization. But this consistency is better derived from a clearly articulated strategic intent than from inflexibly applied top-down plans. In the 1990s, the challenge will be to enfranchise employees to invent the means to accomplish ambitious ends.

We seldom found cautious administrators among the top managements of companies that came from behind to challenge incumbents for global leadership. But in studying organizations that had surrendered, we invariably found senior managers who, for whatever reason, lacked the courage to commit their companies to heroic goals—goals that lay beyond the reach of planning and existing resources. The conservative goals they set failed to generate pressure and enthusiasm for competitive innovation or give the organization much useful guidance. Financial targets and vague mission statements just cannot provide the consistent direction that is a prerequisite for winning a global competitive war.

This kind of conservatism is usually blamed on the financial markets. But we believe that in most cases investors' so-called short-term orientation simply reflects their lack of confidence in the ability of senior managers to conceive and deliver stretch goals. The chairman of one company complained bitterly that even after improving return on capital employed to over 40% (by ruthlessly divesting lackluster businesses and downsizing others), the stock market held the company to an 8:1 price/earnings ratio. Of course the market's message was clear: "We don't trust you. You've shown no ability to achieve profitable growth. Just cut out the slack, manage the denominators, and perhaps you'll be taken over by a company that can use your resources more creatively." Very little in the track record of most large Western companies warrants the confidence of the stock market. Investors aren't hopelessly short-term, they're justifiably skeptical.

We believe that top management's caution reflects a lack of confidence in its own ability to involve the entire organization in revitalization—as opposed to simply raising financial targets. Developing faith in the organization's ability to deliver on tough goals, motivating it to do so, focusing its attention long enough to internalize new capabilities—this is the real challenge for top management. Only by rising to this challenge will senior managers gain the courage they need to commit themselves and their companies to global leadership.

Remaking Strategy

Over the last ten years, our research on global competition, international alliances, and multinational management has brought us into close contact with senior managers in America, Europe, and Japan. As we tried to unravel the reasons for success and surrender in global markets, we became more and more suspicious that executives in Western and Far Eastern companies often operated with very different conceptions of competitive strategy. Understanding these differences, we thought, might help explain the conduct and outcome of competitive battles as well as supplement traditional explanations for Japan's ascendance and the West's decline.

We began by mapping the implicit strategy models of managers who had participated in our research. Then we built detailed histories of selected competitive battles. We searched for evidence of divergent views of strategy, competitive advantage, and the role of top management.

Two contrasting models of strategy emerged. One, which most Western managers will recognize, centers on the problem of maintaining strategic fit. The other centers on the problem of leveraging resources. The two are not mutually exclusive, but they represent a significant difference in emphasis—an emphasis that deeply affects how competitive battles get played out over time.

Both models recognize the problem of competing in a hostile environment with limited resources. But while the emphasis in the first is on trimming ambitions to match available resources, the emphasis in the second is on leveraging resources to reach seemingly unattainable goals.

Both models recognize that relative competitive advantage determines relative profitability. The first emphasizes the search for advantages that are inherently sustainable, the second emphasizes the need to accelerate organizational learning to outpace competitors in building new advantages.

Both models recognize the difficulty of competing against larger competitors. But while the first leads to a search for niches (or simply dissuades the company from challenging an entrenched competitor), the second produces a quest for new rules that can devalue the incumbent's advantages.

Both models recognize that balance in the scope of an organization's activities reduces risk. The first seeks to reduce financial risk by building a balanced portfolio of cash-generating and cash-consuming businesses. The second seeks to reduce competitive risk by ensuring a well-balanced and sufficiently broad portfolio of advantages.

Both models recognize the need to disaggregate the organization in a way that allows top management to differentiate among the investment needs of various planning units. In the first model, resources are allocated to product-market units in which relatedness is defined by common products, channels, and customers. Each business is assumed to own all the critical skills it needs to execute its strategy successfully. In the second, investments are made in core competences (microprocessor controls or electronic imaging, for example) as well as in product-market units. By tracking these investments across businesses, top management works to assure that the plans of individual strategic units don't undermine future developments by default.

Both models recognize the need for consistency in action across organizational levels.

In the first, consistency between corporate and business levels is largely a matter of conforming to financial objectives. Consistency between business and functional levels comes by tightly restricting the means the business uses to achieve its strategy—establishing standard operating procedures, defining the served market, adhering to accepted industry practices. In the second model, business-corporate consistency comes from allegiance to a particular strategic intent. Business-functional consistency comes from allegiance to intermediate-term goals or challenges with lower level employees encouraged to invent how those goals will be achieved.

The Process of Surrender

In the battles for global leadership that have taken place during the last two decades, we have seen a pattern of competitive attack and retrenchment that was remarkably similar across industries. We call this the process of surrender.

The process started with unseen intent. Not possessing long-term, competitor-focused goals themselves, Western companies did not ascribe such intentions to their rivals. They also calculated the threat posed by potential competitors in terms of their existing resources rather than their resourcefulness. This led to systematic underestimation of smaller rivals who were fast gaining technology through licensing arrangements, acquiring market understanding from downstream OEM partners, and improving product quality and manufacturing productivity through company-wide employee involvement programs. Oblivious of the strategic intent and intangible advantages of their rivals, American and European businesses were caught off guard.

Adding to the competitive surprise was the fact that the new entrants typically attacked the periphery of a market (Honda in small motorcycles, Yamaha in grand pianos, Toshiba in small black-and-white televisions) before going head-to-head with incumbents. Incumbents often misread these attacks, seeing them as

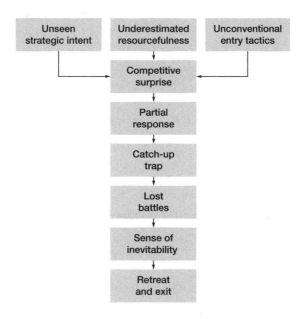

part of a niche strategy and not as a search for
"loose bricks." Unconventional market entry
strategies (minority holdings in less developed

countries, use of nontraditional channels, extensive corporate advertising) were ignored or dismissed as quirky. For example, managers we spoke with said Japanese companies' position in the European computer industry was nonexistent. In terms of brand share that's nearly true, but the Japanese control as much as one-third of the manufacturing value added in the hardware sales of European-based computer businesses. Similarly, German auto producers claimed to feel unconcerned over the proclivity of Japanese producers to move upmarket. But with its low-end models under tremendous pressure from Japanese producers, Porsche has now announced that it will no longer make "entry level" cars.

Western managers often misinterpreted their rivals' tactics. They believed that Japanese and Korean companies were competing solely on the basis of cost and quality. This typically produced a partial response to those competitors' initiatives: moving manufacturing offshore, outsourcing, or instituting a quality program. Seldom was the full extent of the competitive threat appreciated—the multiple layers of advantage, the expansion across related product segments, the development of global brand positions. Imitating the currently visible tactics of rivals put Western businesses into a perpetual catch-up trap. One by one, companies lost battles and came to see surrender as inevitable. Surrender was not inevitable, of course, but the attack was staged in a way that disguised ultimate intentions and sidestepped direct confrontation.

NOTES

1. Among the first to apply the concept of strategy to management were H. Igor Ansoff in *Corporate Strategy: An Analytic Approach to Business Policy for Growth and Expansion* (New York: McGraw-Hill, 1965) and Kenneth R. Andrews in *The Concept of Corporate Strategy* (Homewood, Ill.: Dow Jones-Irwin, 1971).

2. Robert A. Burgelman, "A Process Model of Internal Corporate Venturing in the Diversified Major Firm," *Administrative Science Quarterly*, June 1983.

3. For example, see Michael E. Porter, *Competitive Strategy* (New York: Free Press, 1980).

4. Strategic frameworks for resource allocation in diversified companies are summarized in Charles W. Hofer and Dan E. Schendel, *Strategy Formulation: Analytical Concepts* (St. Paul, Minn.: West Publishing, 1978).

5. For example, see Peter Lorange and Richard F. Vancil, *Strategic Planning Systems* (Englewood Cliffs, N.J.: Prentice-Hall, 1977).

ABOUT THESE AUTHORS

Gary Hamel is Visiting Professor of Strategic and International Management at the London Business School; cofounder of Strategos, an international consulting company; and director of the Management Innovation Lab.

C.K. Prahalad is the Paul and Ruth McCracken Distinguished University Professor of Strategy at the University of Michigan's Ross School of Business.

ALSO BY THESE AUTHORS

Gary Hamel
***Harvard Business Review* Articles**
"Core Competence of the Corporation"
with C.K. Prahalad

"Moon Shots for Management"

"Quest for Resilience"
with Liisa Valikangas

"Why, What, and How of Management
Innovation"

Harvard Business Press Books

Alliance Advantage: The Act of Creating Value Through Partnering
with Yves L. Doz

Competing for the Future
with C.K. Prahalad

The Future of Management

Leading the Revolution

C.K. Prahalad
Harvard Business Review **Articles**
"Core Competence of the Corporation"
with Gary Hamel

"Serving the World's Poor, Profitably"
with Allen Hammond

"Why Sustainability Is Now the Key Driver of Innovation"
with Ram Nidumolu and M.R. Rangaswami

Harvard Business Press Books
Competing for the Future
with Gary Hamel

The End of Corporate Imperialism
with Kenneth Lieberthal

Future of Competition: Co-Creating Unique Value with Customers
with Venkatram Ramaswamy

Article Summary

The Idea in Brief

If your company is struggling to outsmart formidable rivals, beware the flaws of traditional strategic planning approaches. They cause managers to misjudge the threat posed by more inventive and determined players, and prompt them to scale down their competitive aspirations to match current resources.

Managers who secure a leadership position for their company approach strategy from a very different angle. They nurture ambitions out of all proportion to their firm's current resources and capabilities. They fuel an obsessive will to win at every level of the organization—and sustain it over decades. And they define a long-term *strategic intent* that captures employees' imaginations and clarifies criteria for success—for example, Canon set out to "Beat Xerox." The payoff? Their companies take the lead and *keep* it—trapping also-rans in an endless game of catch-up.

The Idea in Practice

Turn Strategic Intent into Reality

Picture strategic intent as a marathon run in 400-meter sprints. You can't know what the terrain at mile 26 looks like, so you have to focus your company's attention on the next 400 meters. How? Present corporate challenges—each specifying the next hill in the race:

- **Create a sense of urgency.** Avoid future crises by exaggerating current indicators of potential threats. Heavy equipment manufacturer Komatsu budgeted based on worst-case exchange rates with an overvalued yen.

- **Personalize challenges.** When employees see exactly what best-in-class competitors are doing, they become personally focused on winning. Ford fired up workers with videos of Mazda's most efficient plant.

- **Give employees needed skills.** Provide training in statistical tools, problem solving, and team building.

- **Tackle one challenge at a time.** You'll avoid organizational overload and conflicting priorities.

Stay Ahead of Your Competition

With scarcer resources than your rivals', you need to continually outsmart your better-financed competition. Competitive innovation can help. Consider these approaches:

- **Build layers of advantages**. Don't rely on just one source of advantage, such as cheap labor. Also build your brand, increase your distribution channels, and tailor your products to unique markets.

- **Stake out undefended territory.** Honda identified "low end" motorcycles as an un-contested market. While selling 50cc bikes in the United States, it raced bigger ones in Europe—assembling the design skills and technology it needed to dominate the entire business. Rivals never saw Honda's strategic intent and growing competence in engines and power trains.

- **Change the terms of engagement.** While Xerox built a wide range of copiers it leased to corporate copy centers through a huge sales force, Canon standardized copy machines and components to reduce costs, sold its offerings outright through office-product dealers, and appealed to people who wanted their own machines. By developing capabilities that contrasted with Xerox's, Canon created a new "recipe" for success, short-circuiting Xerox's ability to retaliate quickly.

- **Compete through collaboration.** Electronics manufacturer Fujitsu's alliances with Siemens and British computer maker STC and with Amdahl in the United States boosted their manufacturing capacity and opened doors to Western markets.

BLUE OCEAN
LEADERSHIP

HARVARD BUSINESS REVIEW

CLASSICS

BLUE OCEAN LEADERSHIP

W. Chan Kim and
Renée Mauborgne

Harvard Business Review Press
Boston, Massachusetts

Copyright 2017 Harvard Business School Publishing Corporation
Originally published in *Harvard Business Review* in May 2014
Reprint #R1405C
All rights reserved

Printed in the United States of America

10 9 8 7 6 5 4 3

The web addresses referenced in this book were live and correct at the time of the book's publication but may be subject to change.

Cataloging-in-Publication data is forthcoming.

ISBN: 978-1-63369-264-0
eISBN: 978-1-63369-265-7

The paper used in this publication meets the requirements of the American National Standard for Permanence of Paper for Publications and Documents in Libraries and Archives Z39.48-1992.

THE HARVARD BUSINESS REVIEW CLASSICS SERIES

Since 1922, *Harvard Business Review* has been a leading source of breakthrough ideas in management practice—many of which still speak to and influence us today. The HBR Classics series now offers you the opportunity to make these seminal pieces a part of your permanent management library. Each volume contains a groundbreaking idea that has shaped best practices and inspired countless managers around the world—and will change how you think about the business world today.

BLUE OCEAN
LEADERSHIP

It's a sad truth about the workplace: just 30% of employees are actively committed to doing a good job. According to Gallup's 2013 *State of the American Workplace* report, 50% of employees merely put their time in, while the remaining 20% act out their discontent in counterproductive ways, negatively influencing their coworkers, missing days on the job, and driving customers away through poor service. Gallup estimates that the 20% group alone costs the

US economy around half a trillion dollars each year.

What's the reason for the widespread employee disengagement? According to Gallup, poor leadership is a key cause.

Most executives—not just those in America—recognize that one of their biggest challenges is closing the vast gulf between the potential and the realized talent and energy of the people they lead. As one CEO put it, "We have a large workforce that has an appetite to do a good job up and down the ranks. If we can transform them—tap into them through effective leadership—there will be an awful lot of people out there doing an awful lot of good."

Of course, managers don't intend to be poor leaders. The problem is that they lack a clear understanding of just what changes it would take to bring out the best in everyone and achieve high impact. We believe that leaders can obtain this understanding through an approach we call "blue ocean leadership." It draws on our research on blue ocean strategy, our model for creating new market space by converting noncustomers into customers, and applies its concepts and analytic frameworks to help leaders release the blue ocean of unexploited talent and energy in their organizations—rapidly and at low cost.

The underlying insight is that leadership, in essence, can be thought of as a service that people in an organization "buy" or "don't buy." Every leader in that sense has customers: the bosses to whom the leader must deliver performance, and the followers who need the leader's guidance and support to achieve. When people value your leadership practices, they in effect buy your leadership. They're inspired to excel and act with commitment. But when employees don't buy your leadership, they disengage, becoming noncustomers of your leadership. Once we started thinking about leadership in this way, we began to see that the concepts and frameworks we were developing to create new demand by converting noncustomers into customers could be adapted to help leaders convert disengaged employees into engaged ones.

Over the past 10 years we and Gavin Fraser, a Blue Ocean Strategy Network expert, have interviewed hundreds of people in organizations to understand where leadership was falling short and how it could be transformed while conserving leaders' most precious resource: time. In this article we present the results of our research.

KEY DIFFERENCES FROM CONVENTIONAL LEADERSHIP APPROACHES

Blue ocean leadership rapidly brings about a step change in leadership strength. It's distinct from traditional leadership development approaches in several overarching ways. Here are the three most salient:

Focus on acts and activities

Over many years a great deal of research has generated insights into the values, qualities, and behavioral styles that make for good leadership, and these have formed the basis of development programs and executive coaching. The implicit assumption is that changes in values, qualities, and behavioral styles ultimately translate into high performance.

But when people look back on these programs, many struggle to find evidence of notable change. As one executive put it, "Without years of dedicated efforts, how can you transform a person's character or behavioral traits? And can you really measure and assess whether leaders are embracing and internalizing these personal traits and styles? In theory, yes, but in reality it's hard at best."

Blue ocean leadership, by contrast, focuses on *what acts and activities leaders need to undertake* to boost their teams' motivation and business results, not on *who leaders need to be*. This difference in emphasis is important.

{ 6 }

It is markedly easier to change people's acts and activities than their values, qualities, and behavioral traits. Of course, altering a leader's activities is not a complete solution, and having the right values, qualities, and behavioral traits matters. But activities are something that any individual can change, given the right feedback and guidance.

Connect closely to market realities

Traditional leadership development programs tend to be quite generic and are often detached from what firms stand for in the eyes of customers and from the market results people are expected to achieve. In contrast, under blue ocean leadership, the people who face market realities are asked for their direct input on how their leaders hold them back and what those leaders could do to help them best serve customers and other key stakeholders. And when people are engaged in defining the leadership practices that will enable them to thrive, and *those practices are connected to the market realities* against which they need to perform, they're highly motivated to create the best possible profile for leaders and to make the new solutions work. Their willing cooperation maximizes the acceptance of new profiles for leadership while minimizing implementation costs.

Distribute leadership across all management levels

Most leadership programs focus on executives and their potential for impact now and in the future. But the key to a successful organization is having empowered leaders at every level, because outstanding organizational performance often comes down to the motivation and actions of middle and frontline leaders, who are in closer contact with the market. As one senior executive put it, "The truth is that we, the top management, are not in the field to fully appreciate the middle and frontline actions. We need effective leaders at every level to maximize corporate performance."

Blue ocean leadership is designed to be applied across the three distinct management levels: *top, middle*, and *frontline*. It calls for profiles for leaders that are tailored to the very different tasks, degrees of power, and environments you find at each level. Extending leadership capabilities deep into the front line unleashes the latent talent and drive of a critical mass of employees, and creating strong distributed leadership significantly enhances performance across the organization.

THE FOUR STEPS OF BLUE OCEAN LEADERSHIP

Now let's walk through how to put blue ocean leadership into practice. It involves four steps.

1. See your leadership reality

A common mistake organizations make is to discuss changes in leadership before resolving differences of opinion over what leaders are actually doing. Without a common understanding of where leadership stands and is falling short, a forceful case for change cannot be made.

Achieving this understanding is the objective of the first step. It takes the form of what we call as-is Leadership Canvases, analytic visuals that show just how managers at each level invest their time and effort, as perceived by the customers of their leadership. An organization begins the process by creating a canvas for each of its three management levels.

A team of 12 to 15 senior managers is typically selected to carry out this project. The people chosen should cut across functions and be recognized as good leaders in the company so that the team has immediate credibility. The team is then broken into three smaller subteams, each focused on one level and charged with interviewing its relevant leadership customers—both bosses and subordinates—and ensuring that a representative number of each are included.

The aim is to uncover how people experience current leadership and to start a companywide conversation about what leaders do and should do at each level. The customers of leaders are asked which acts and activities—good and bad—their leaders spend most of their time on, and which are key to motivation and performance but are neglected by their leaders. Getting at the specifics is important; the as-is canvases must be grounded in acts and activities that reflect each level's specific market reality and performance goals. This involves a certain amount of probing.

At a company we'll call British Retail Group (BRG), many interviewees commented that middle managers spent much of their time playing politics. The subteam focused on that level pushed for clarification and discovered that two acts principally accounted for this judgment. One was that the leaders tended to divide responsibility among people, which created uncertainty about accountability—and some internal competitiveness. The result was a lot of finger-pointing and the perception that the leaders were playing people against one another. The subteam also found that the leaders spent much of their time in meetings with senior management. This led subordinates to conclude that their leaders were more interested in maximizing political "face time" and spinning news than in being present to support them.

After four to six weeks of interviews, subteam members come together to create as-is Leadership Profiles by pooling their findings and determining, based on frequency of citation, the dominant leadership acts and activities at each level. To help the subteams focus on what really matters, we typically ask for no more than 10 to 15 leadership acts and activities per level. These get registered on the horizontal axis of the as-is canvas, and the extent to which leaders do them is registered on the vertical axis. The cap of 10 to 15 prevents the canvas from becoming a statement of everything and nothing.

The result is almost always eye-opening. It's not uncommon to find that 20% to 40% of the acts and activities of leaders at all three levels provide only questionable value to those above and below them. It's also not uncommon to find that leaders are underinvesting in 20% to 40% of the acts and activities that interviewees at their level cite as important.

At BRG, the canvas for senior managers revealed that their customers thought they spent most of their time on essentially middle-management acts and activities, while the canvas of middle managers indicated that they seemed to be absorbed in protecting bureaucratic procedures. Frontline leaders were seen to be focused on trying to keep their bosses happy by doing things like deferring customer queries to them, which satisfied their desire to be in control. When we asked team members to describe each canvas in a tagline, an exercise that's part of the process, they labeled the frontline Leadership Profile "Please the Boss," the middle-manager profile "Control and Play Safe," and the senior manager profile "Focus on the Day-to-Day." (For an example, see the exhibit "What middle managers actually do.")

The implications were depressing. The biggest "aha" for the subteams was that senior managers appeared to have scarcely any time to do the real job of top management—thinking, probing, identifying opportunities on the horizon, and gearing up the organization to capitalize on them. Faced with firsthand, repeated evidence of the shortcomings of leadership practices, the subteams could not defend the current Leadership Profiles. The canvases made a strong case for change at all three levels; it was clear that people throughout the organization wished for it.

2. Develop alternative Leadership Profiles

At this point the subteams are usually eager to explore what effective Leadership Profiles would look like at each level. To achieve this, they go back to their interviewees with two sets of questions.

The first set is aimed at pinpointing the extent to which each act and activity on the canvas is either a cold spot (absorbing leaders' time but adding little or no value) or a hot spot (energizing employees and inspiring them to apply their talents, but currently underinvested in by leaders or not addressed at all).

The second set prompts interviewees to think beyond the bounds of the company and focus on effective leadership acts they've observed outside the organization, in particular those that could have a strong impact if adopted by internal leaders at their level. Here fresh ideas emerge about what

leaders could be doing but aren't. This is
not, however, about benchmarking against
corporate icons; employees' personal experiences are more likely to produce insights.
Most of us have come across people in our
lives who have had a disproportionately
positive influence on us. It might be a sports
coach, a schoolteacher, a scoutmaster, a
grandparent, or a former boss. Whoever
those role models are, it's important to get
interviewees to detail which acts and activities they believe would add real value for
them if undertaken by their current leaders.

To process the findings from the second round of interviews, the subteams
apply an analytic tool we call the Blue
Ocean Leadership Grid (see the table by

the same name). For each leadership level the interview results get incorporated into this grid. Typically, we start with the cold-spot acts and activities, which go into the Eliminate or Reduce quadrants depending on how negatively interviewees judge them. This energizes the subteams right away, because people immediately perceive the benefits of stopping leaders from doing things that add little or no value. Cutting back on those activities also gives leaders the time and space they need to raise their game. Without that breathing room, a step change in leadership strength would remain largely wishful thinking, given leaders' already full plates. From the cold spots we move to the hot spots, which go into the Raise quadrant if they involve current acts and activities or Create for those not currently performed at all by leaders. With this input, the subteams draft two to four "to-be" canvases for each leadership level. These analytic visuals illustrate Leadership Profiles that can lift individual and organizational performance, and juxtapose them against the as-is Leadership Profiles. The subteams produce a range of leadership models, rather than stop at one set of possibilities, to thoroughly explore new leadership space.

3. Select to-be Leadership Profiles

After two to three weeks of drawing and redrawing their Leadership Canvases, the subteams present them at what we call a "leadership fair." Fair attendees include board members and top, middle, and front-line managers.

The event starts with members of the original senior team behind the effort describing the process and presenting the three as-is canvases. With those three visuals, the team establishes why change is necessary, confirms that comments from interviewees at all levels were taken into account, and sets the context against which the to-be Leadership Profiles can be understood and appreciated. Although the as-is canvases often present a sobering reality, as they did at BRG, the Leadership Profiles are shown and discussed only at the aggregate level. That makes individual leaders more open to change, because they feel that everyone is in the same boat.

With the stage set, the subteams present the to-be profiles, hanging their canvases on the walls so that the audience can easily see them. Typically, the subteam that focused on frontline leaders will go first. After the presentation, the attendees are each given three Post-it notes and told to put one next to their favorite Leadership Profile. And if they find that canvas especially compelling, they can put up to three Post-its on it.

After all the votes are in, the company's senior executives probe the attendees about why they voted as they did. The same process is then repeated for the two other leadership levels. (We find it easier to deal with each level separately and sequentially, and that doing so increases voters' recall of the discussion.)

After about four hours everyone in attendance has a clear picture of the current Leadership Profile of each level, the completed Blue Ocean Leadership Grids, and a selection of to-be Leadership Profiles that could create a significant change in leadership performance. Armed with this information and the votes and comments of attendees, the top managers convene outside the fair room and decide which to-be Leadership Profile to move forward on at each level. Then they return and explain their decisions to the fair's participants.

At BRG, more than 125 people voted on the profiles, and fair attendees greeted the three that were selected with enthusiasm. The tagline for frontline leaders' to-be profile was "Cut Through the Crap." (Sadly, this was later refined to "Cut Through to Serve Customers.") In this profile, frontline leaders did not defer the vast majority of customer queries to middle management and spent less time jumping through procedural hoops. Their time was directed to training frontline personnel to deliver on company promises on the spot, resolve customer problems, quickly help customers in distress, and make meaningful cross-sales— leadership acts and activities that fired up the frontline workers, were sure to excite customers, and would have a direct impact on the company's bottom line.

"Liberate, Coach, and Empower" was the tagline for middle management's to-be profile. Here leaders' time and attention shifted from controlling to supporting employees.

This involved eliminating and reducing a range of oversight activities—such as requiring weekly reports on customer calls received and funds spent on office supplies—that sapped people's energy and kept frontline leaders at their desks. The profile also included new actions aimed at managing, disseminating, and integrating the knowledge of frontline leaders and their staff. In practical terms, this meant spending much more time providing face-to-face coaching and feedback.

The tagline for the to-be profile of senior management was "Delegate and Chart the Company's Future." With the acts and activities of frontline and middle managers reset, senior managers would be freed up to devote a significant portion of their time to thinking about the big picture—the changes in the industry and their implications for strategy and the organization. They would spend less time putting out fires.

The board members who attended the leadership fair felt strongly that the to-be Leadership Profiles supported the interests of customers as well as shareholders' profit and growth objectives. The frontline leaders were energized and ready to charge ahead. Senior managers went from feeling towed under the waves by all the middle-management duties they had to coordinate and attend to, to feeling as if they could finally get their heads above water and see the beauty of the ocean they had to chart.

The trickiest to-be Leadership Profile was middle management's. Letting go of control and empowering the people below them can be tough for folks in this organizational tier. But the to-be Leadership Profiles of both frontline and senior management helped clear the path to change at this level.

4. Institutionalize new leadership practices

After the fair is over, the original subteam members communicate the results to the people they interviewed who were not at the fair.

Organizations then distribute the agreed-on to-be profiles to the leaders at each level. The subteam members hold meetings with leaders to walk them through their canvases, explaining what should be eliminated, reduced, raised, and created. This step reinforces the buy-in that the initiative has been building by briefing leaders throughout the organization on key findings at each step of the process and tapping many of them for input. And because every leader is in effect the buyer of another level of leadership, all managers will be working to change, knowing that their bosses will be doing the same thing on the basis of input they directly provided.

The leaders are then charged with passing the message along to their direct reports and explaining to them how the new Leadership Profiles will allow them to be more effective. To keep the new profiles top of mind, the to-be canvases are pinned up prominently in the offices of both the leaders and their reports. Leaders are tasked with holding regular monthly meetings at which they gather their direct reports' feedback on how well they're making the transition to the new profiles. All comments must be illustrated with specific examples. Has the leader cut back on the acts and activities that were to be eliminated and reduced in the new Leadership Profile? If yes, how? If not, in what instances was she still engaging in them? Likewise, is she focusing more on what does add value and doing the new activities in her profile? Though the meetings can be unnerving at first—both for employees who have to critique the boss and for the bosses whose actions are being exposed to scrutiny—it doesn't take long before a team spirit and mutual respect take hold, as all people see how the changes in leadership are positively influencing their performance.

Through the changes highlighted by the to-be profiles, BRG was able to deepen its leadership strength and achieve high impact at lower cost. Consider the results produced just at the frontline level: Turnover of BRG's 10,000-plus frontline employees dropped from about 40% to 11% in the first year, reducing both recruitment and training costs by some 50%. The total savings, including those from decreased absenteeism, amounted to more than $50 million that year. On top of that, BRG's customer satisfaction scores climbed by over 30%, and leaders at all levels reported feeling less stressed, more energized by their ability to act, and more confident that they were making a greater contribution to the company, customers, and their own personal development.

EXECUTION IS BUILT INTO THE FOUR STEPS

Any change initiative faces skepticism. Think of it as the "bend over—here it comes again" syndrome. While blue ocean leadership also meets such a reaction initially, it counters it by building good execution into the process. The four steps are founded on the principles of fair process: engagement, explanation, and expectation clarity. The power of these principles cannot be overstated, and we have written extensively about their impact on the quality of execution for over 20 years. (See, for example, our article "Fair Process: Managing in the Knowledge Economy," HBR, July–August 1997.)

In the leadership development context, the application of fair process achieves buy-in and ownership of the to-be Leadership Profiles and builds trust, preparing the ground for implementation. The principles are applied in a number of ways, with the most important practices being:

- *Respected senior managers spearhead the process.* Their engagement is not ceremonial; they conduct interviews and draw the canvases. This strongly signals the importance of the initiative, which makes people at all levels feel respected and gives senior managers a visceral sense of what actions are needed to create a step change in leadership performance. Here's a typical employee reaction: "At first, I thought this was just one of those initiatives where management loves to talk about the need for change but then essentially goes back to doing what they've always done. But when I saw that leading senior managers were driving the process and rolling up their sleeves to push the change, I thought to myself, 'Hmm . . . they may just finally mean it.'"

- *People are engaged in defining what leaders should do.* Since the to-be profiles are generated with the employees' own input, people have confidence in the changes made. The process also makes them feel more deeply engaged with their leaders, because they have greater ownership of what their leaders are doing. Here's what people told us: "Senior management said they were going to come and talk to people at all levels to understand what we need our leaders to do and not do, so we could thrive. And I thought, 'I'll believe it when someone comes knocking on my door.' And then they knocked."

- *People at all levels have a say in the final decision.* A slice of the organization across the three management levels gets to vote in selecting the new Leadership Profiles. Though the top managers have the final say on the to-be profiles and may not choose those with the most votes, they are required to provide a clear, sound explanation for their decisions in front of all attendees. Here's some typical feedback: "The doubts we had that our comments were just paid lip service to were dispelled when we saw how our inputs were figured into the to-be profiles. We realized then that our voices were heard."

- *It's easy to assess whether expectations are being met.* Clarity about what needs to change to move from the as-is to the to-be Leadership Profiles makes it simple to monitor progress. The monthly review meetings between leaders and their direct reports help the organization check whether it's making headway. We've found that those meetings keep leaders honest, motivate them to continue with change, and build confidence in both the process and the sincerity of the leaders. By collecting feedback from those meetings, top management can assess how rapidly leaders are making the shift from their as-is to their to-be Leadership Profiles, which becomes a key input in annual performance evaluations. This is what people say: "With the one-page visual of our old and new Leadership Profiles, we can easily track the progress in moving from the old to the new. In it, everyone can see with clarity precisely where we are in closing the gap."

Essentially, the gift that fair process confers is trust and, hence, voluntary cooperation, a quality vital to the leader-follower relationship. Anyone who has ever worked in an organization understands how important trust is. If you trust the process and the people you work for, you're willing to go the extra mile and give your best. If you don't trust them, you'll stick to the letter of the law that binds your contract with the organization and devote your energy to protecting your position and fighting over turf rather than to winning customers and creating value. Not only will your abilities be wasted, but they will often work against your organization's performance.

BECOMING A BLUE OCEAN LEADER

We never cease to be amazed by the talent and energy we see in the organizations we study. Sadly, we are equally amazed by how much of it is squandered by poor leadership. Blue ocean leadership can help put an end to that.

The Leadership Canvases give people a concrete, visual framework in which they can surface and discuss the improvements leaders need to make. The fairness of the process makes the implementation and monitoring of those changes far easier than in traditional top-down approaches. Moreover, blue ocean leadership achieves a transformation with less time and effort, because leaders are not trying to alter who they are and break the habits of a lifetime. They are simply changing the tasks they carry out. Better yet, one of the strengths of blue ocean leadership is its scalability. You don't have to wait for your company's top leadership to launch this process. Whatever management level you belong to, you can awaken the sleeping potential of your people by taking them through the four steps.

Are you ready to be a blue ocean leader?

TABLE 1

The Blue Ocean Leadership Grid

The Blue Ocean Leadership Grid is an analytic tool that challenges people to think about which acts and activities leaders should do less of because they hold people back, and which leaders should do more of because they inspire people to give their all. Current activities from the leaders' "as-is" profiles (which may add value or not), along with new activities that employees believe would add a lot of value if leaders started doing them, are assigned to the four categories in the grid. Organizations then use the grids to develop new profiles of effective leadership.

Eliminate	Reduce	Raise	Create
What acts and activities do leaders invest their time and intelligence in that should be eliminated?	What acts and activities do leaders invest their time and intelligence in that should be reduced well below their current level?	What acts and activities do leaders invest their time and intelligence in that should be raised well above their current level?	What acts and activities should leaders invest their time and intelligence in that they currently don't undertake?

What middle managers actually do

As-is Leadership Canvases show the activities that employees see leaders engaging in, and the amount of time and energy they think leaders spend on each. The canvas below, for middle managers at the retail company BRG, reveals that people viewed them as rule enforcers who played it safe.

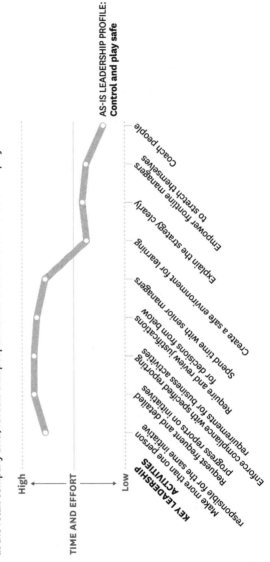

TIME AND EFFORT

High

Low

AS-IS LEADERSHIP PROFILE: Control and play safe

KEY LEADERSHIP ACTIVITIES

- Make more than one person responsible for the same initiative
- Request frequent and detailed progress reports on initiatives
- Enforce compliance with specified requirements for business activities
- Require and review justifications for decisions from below
- Spend time with senior managers
- Create a safe environment for learning
- Explain the strategy clearly
- Empower frontline managers to stretch themselves
- Coach people

To-be Leadership Canvas

Frontline managers: Serve customers, not the boss

Current activities of BRG's frontline leaders vs. the activities employees think they should be doing:

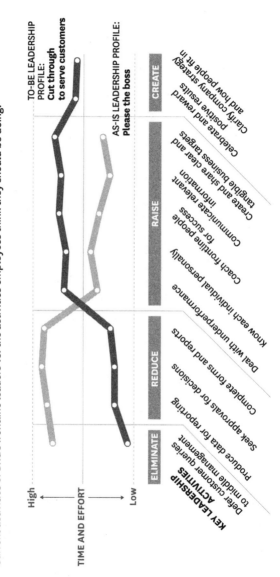

To-be Leadership Canvas

Middle managers: More coaching, less control

Current activities of BRG's midlevel leaders vs. the activities employees think they should be doing:

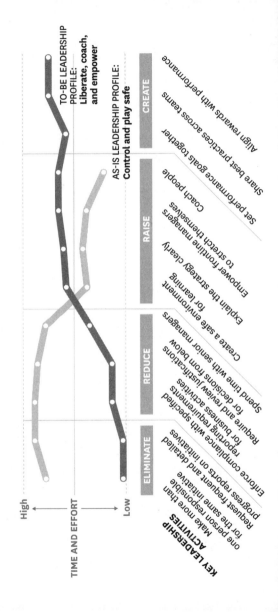

TIME AND EFFORT — High / Low

TO-BE LEADERSHIP PROFILE: **Liberate, coach, and empower**

AS-IS LEADERSHIP PROFILE: **Control and play safe**

KEY LEADERSHIP ACTIVITIES

ELIMINATE
- Request more than one person responsible for the same initiative
- Request frequent and detailed progress reports on initiatives

REDUCE
- Enforce compliance with specified reporting requirements for business activities
- Require justifications for decisions from below
- Spend time with senior managers

RAISE
- Create a safe environment for learning
- Explain the strategy clearly
- Empower frontline managers to stretch themselves
- Coach people

CREATE
- Set performance goals together
- Share best practices across teams
- Align rewards with performance

To-be Leadership Canvas

Senior managers: From the day-to-day to the big picture

Current activities of BRG's senior managers vs. the activities employees think they should be doing:

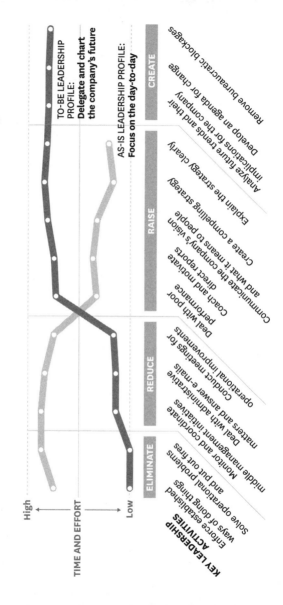

TIME AND EFFORT — High ← → Low

ELIMINATE
- Enforce established ways of doing things
- Solve operational problems and put out fires
- Monitor and coordinate middle management initiatives
- Deal with administrative matters and answer e-mails

REDUCE
- Conduct meetings for operational improvements
- Deal with poor performance

RAISE
- Coach and motivate direct reports
- Communicate the company's vision and what it means to people
- Create a compelling strategy
- Explain the strategy clearly
- Analyze future trends and their implications for the company

CREATE
- Develop an agenda for change
- Remove bureaucratic blockages

KEY LEADERSHIP ACTIVITIES

TO-BE LEADERSHIP PROFILE:
Delegate and chart the company's future

AS-IS LEADERSHIP PROFILE:
Focus on the day-to-day

ABOUT THE AUTHORS

W. Chan Kim and *Renée Mauborgne* are professors at INSEAD, the world's second-largest business school, and codirectors of the INSEAD Blue Ocean Strategy Institute. They are the authors of *Blue Ocean Strategy*, which is recognized as one of the most iconic and impactful strategy books ever written. The theory of blue ocean strategy has been actively embraced by companies, governments, and nonprofits across the globe and is currently being taught in more than eighteen hundred universities around the world. *Blue Ocean Strategy* is a best-seller across five continents. It has sold over 3.6 million copies and has been published in a record-breaking 44 languages. Kim and Mauborgne are ranked in the top three of the Thinkers50 global list of top management thinkers and were named among the world's top five best business school professors by MBA Rankings. They have received numerous academic and management awards around the globe, including the Nobels Colloquia Prize for Leadership on Business and Economic Thinking, the Carl S. Sloane Award by the Association of Management Consulting Firms, the Leadership Hall of Fame by *Fast Company* magazine, and the

Eldridge Haynes Prize by the Academy of International Business, among others. Kim and Mauborgne are Fellows of the World Economic Forum in Davos. Mauborgne is a member of President Barack Obama's Board of Advisors on Historically Black Colleges and Universities (HBCUs). Kim is an advisory member for the European Union and is an advisor for several countries.

ALSO BY THESE AUTHORS

Harvard Business Review Press Books

*Blue Ocean Strategy, Expanded Edition:
How to Create Uncontested Market Space
and Make the Competition Irrelevant*

*The W. Chan Kim and Renée Mauborgne
Blue Ocean Strategy Reader*

Harvard Business Review Articles

"Blue Ocean Strategy"

"Charting Your Company's Future"

"Creating New Market Space"

"Fair Process: Managing in the Knowledge Economy"

"How Strategy Shapes Structure"

"Knowing a Winning Business Idea When You See One"

"Red Ocean Traps"

"Tipping Point Leadership"

"Value Innovation: The Strategic Logic of High Growth"

Article Summary

Idea in Brief

The Problem

According to Gallup, only 30% of employees actively apply their talent and energy to move their organizations forward. Fifty percent are just putting their time in, while the remaining 20% act out their discontent in counterproductive ways. Gallup estimates that the 20% group alone costs the US economy around half a trillion dollars each year. A main cause of employee disengagement is poor leadership, Gallup says.

The Solution

A new approach called blue ocean leadership can release the sea of unexploited talent and energy in organizations. It involves a four-step process that allows leaders to gain a clear understanding of just what changes it would take to bring out the best in their people, while conserving their most precious resource: time. An analytic tool, the Leadership Canvas, shows leaders what activities they need to eliminate, reduce, raise, and create to convert disengaged employees into engaged ones.

Case in Point

A British retail group applied blue ocean leadership to redefine what effectiveness meant for frontline, midlevel, and senior leaders. The impact was significant. On the front line, for example, employee turnover dropped from about 40% to 11% in the first year, reducing recruitment and training costs by 50%. Factoring in reduced absenteeism, the group saved more than $50 million in the first year, while customer satisfaction scores climbed by over 30%.

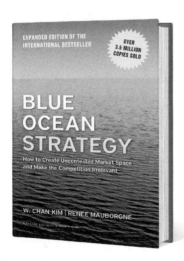

The most important management ideas all in one place.

We hope you enjoyed this book from *Harvard Business Review*. For the best ideas HBR has to offer turn to HBR's 10 Must Reads Boxed Set. From books on leadership and strategy to managing yourself and others, this 6-book collection delivers articles on the most essential business topics to help you succeed.

HBR's 10 Must Reads Series

The definitive collection of ideas and best practices on our most sought-after topics from the best minds in business.

- Change Management
- Collaboration
- Communication
- Emotional Intelligence
- Innovation
- Leadership
- Making Smart Decisions

- Managing Across Cultures
- Managing People
- Managing Yourself
- Strategic Marketing
- Strategy
- Teams
- The Essentials

hbr.org/mustreads

Buy for your team, clients, or event.
Visit hbr.org/bulksales for quantity discount rates.

HARVARD BUSINESS REVIEW
CLASSICS

LEADERSHIP THAT GETS RESULTS

Daniel Goleman

Harvard Business Review Press
Boston, Massachusetts

Copyright 2017 Harvard Business School Publishing Corporation
Originally published in *Harvard Business Review* in March 2000
Reprint #R00204
All rights reserved

Printed in the United States of America

10 9 8 7 6 5 4 3 2 1

The web addresses referenced in this book were live and correct at the time of the book's publication but may be subject to change.

Cataloging-in-Publication data is forthcoming.

ISBN: 978-1-63369-262-6
eISBN: 978-1-63369-263-3

The paper used in this publication meets the requirements of the American National Standard for Permanence of Paper for Publications and Documents in Libraries and Archives Z39.48-1992.

LEADERSHIP THAT GETS RESULTS

Ask any group of businesspeople the question "What do effective leaders do?" and you'll hear a sweep of answers. Leaders set strategy; they motivate; they create a mission; they build a culture. Then ask "What should leaders do?" If the group is seasoned, you'll likely hear one response: the leader's singular job is to get results.

But how? The mystery of what leaders can and ought to do in order to spark the best performance from their people is age-old. In recent years, that mystery has spawned an entire cottage industry: literally thousands of "leadership experts" have made careers of testing and coaching executives, all in pursuit of creating businesspeople who can turn bold objectives—be they strategic, financial, organizational, or all three—into reality.

Still, effective leadership eludes many people and organizations. One reason is that until recently, virtually no quantitative research has demonstrated which precise leadership behaviors yield positive results. Leadership experts proffer advice based on inference, experience, and instinct. Sometimes that advice is which precise leadership behaviors yield positive results.

Leadership experts proffer advice based on inference, experience, and instinct. Sometimes that advice is right on target; sometimes it's not.

But new research by the consulting firm Hay/McBer, which draws on a random sample of 3,871 executives selected from a database of more than 20,000 executives worldwide, takes much of the mystery out of effective leadership. The research found six distinct leadership styles, each springing from different components of emotional intelligence. The styles, taken individually, appear to have a direct and unique impact on the working atmosphere of a company, division, or team, and in turn, on its financial performance. And perhaps most important, the research indicates that leaders with the best results do not rely on only one leadership style; they use most of them in a given week—seamlessly and in different measure—depending on the business situation. Imagine the styles, then, as the array of clubs in a golf pro's bag. Over the course of a game, the pro picks and chooses clubs based on the demands of the shot. Sometimes he has to ponder his selection, but usually it is automatic. The pro senses the challenge ahead, swiftly pulls out the right tool, and elegantly puts it to work. That's how high-impact leaders operate, too.

What are the six styles of leadership? None will shock workplace veterans. Indeed, each style, by name and brief description alone, will likely resonate with anyone who leads, is led, or as is the case with most of us, does both. *Coercive leaders* demand immediate compliance. *Authoritative leaders* mobilize people toward a vision. *Affiliative leaders* create emotional bonds and harmony. *Democratic leaders* build consensus through participation. *Pacesetting leaders* expect excellence and self-direction. And *coaching leaders* develop people for the future.

Close your eyes and you can surely imagine a colleague who uses any one of these styles. You most likely use at least one yourself. What is new in this research, then, is its implications for action. First, it offers a fine-grained understanding of how different leadership styles affect performance and results. Second, it offers clear guidance on when a manager should switch between them. It also strongly suggests that switching flexibly is well advised. New, too, is the research's finding that each leadership style springs from different components of emotional intelligence.

MEASURING LEADERSHIP'S IMPACT

It has been more than a decade since research first linked aspects of emotional intelligence to business results. The late David McClelland, a noted Harvard University psychologist, found that leaders with strengths in a critical mass of six or more emotional intelligence competencies were far more effective than peers who lacked such strengths. For instance, when he analyzed the performance of division heads at a global food and beverage company, he found that among leaders with this critical mass of competence, 87% placed in the top third for annual salary bonuses based on their business performance. More telling, their divisions on average outperformed yearly revenue targets by 15% to 20%. Those executives who lacked emotional intelligence were rarely rated as outstanding in their annual performance reviews, and their divisions underperformed by an average of almost 20%.

Our research set out to gain a more molecular view of the links among leadership and emotional intelligence, and climate and performance. A team of McClelland's colleagues headed by Mary Fontaine and Ruth Jacobs from Hay/McBer studied data about or observed thousands of executives, noting specific behaviors and their impact on climate. How did each individual motivate direct reports? Manage change initiatives? Handle crises? It was in a later phase of the research that we identified which emotional intelligence capabilities drive the six leadership styles. How does he rate in terms of self-control and social skill? Does a leader show high or low levels of empathy?

The team tested each executive's immediate sphere of influence for its climate. "Climate" is not an amorphous term. First defined by psychologists George Litwin and Richard Stringer and later refined by McClelland and his colleagues, it refers to six key factors that influence an organization's working environment: its flexibility—that is, how free employees feel to innovate unencumbered by red tape; their sense of responsibility to the organization; the level of standards that people set; the sense of accuracy about performance feedback and aptness of rewards; the clarity people have about mission and values; and finally, the level of commitment to a common purpose.

We found that all six leadership styles have a measurable effect on each aspect of climate. (For details, see the sidebar "Getting Molecular: The Impact of Leadership Styles on Drivers of Climate" on page 62.) Further, when we looked at the impact of climate on financial results—such as return on sales, revenue growth, efficiency, and profitability—we found a direct correlation between the two. Leaders who used styles that positively affected the climate had decidedly better financial results than those who did not. That is not to say that organizational climate is the only driver of performance. Economic conditions and competitive dynamics matter enormously. But our analysis strongly suggests that climate accounts for nearly a third of results. And that's simply too much of an impact to ignore.

THE STYLES IN DETAIL

Executives use six leadership styles, but only four of the six consistently have a positive effect on climate and results. Let's look then at each style of leadership in detail. (For a summary of the material that follows, see the chart "The Six Leadership Styles at a Glance" on page 64.)

The coercive style

The computer company was in crisis mode—its sales and profits were falling, its stock was losing value precipitously, and its shareholders were in an uproar. The board brought in a new CEO with a reputation as a turnaround artist. He set to work chopping jobs, selling off divisions, and making the tough decisions that should have been executed years before. The company was saved, at least in the short-term.

From the start, though, the CEO created a reign of terror, bullying and demeaning his executives, roaring his displeasure at the slightest misstep. The company's top echelons were decimated not just by his erratic firings but also by defections. The CEO's direct reports, frightened by his tendency to blame the bearer of bad news, stopped bringing him any news at all. Morale was at an all-time low—a fact reflected in another downturn in the business after the short-term recovery. The CEO was eventually fired by the board of directors.

It's easy to understand why of all the leadership styles, the coercive one is the least effective in most situations. Consider what the style does to an organization's climate. Flexibility is the hardest hit. The leader's extreme top-down decision making kills new ideas on the vine. People feel so disrespected that they think, "I won't even bring my ideas up—they'll only be shot down." Likewise, people's sense of responsibility evaporates: unable to act on their own initiative, they lose their sense of ownership and feel little accountability for their performance. Some become so resentful they adopt the attitude, "I'm not going to help this bastard."

Coercive leadership also has a damaging effect on the rewards system. Most high-performing workers are motivated by more than money—they seek the satisfaction of work well done. The coercive style erodes such pride. And finally, the style undermines one of the leader's prime tools—motivating people by showing them how their job fits into a grand, shared mission. Such a loss, measured in terms of diminished clarity and commitment, leaves people alienated from their own jobs, wondering, "How does any of this matter?"

Given the impact of the coercive style, you might assume it should never be applied. Our research, however, uncovered a few occasions when it worked masterfully. Take the case of a division president who was brought in to change the direction of a food company that was losing money. His first act was to have the executive conference room demolished. To him, the room—with its long marble table that looked like "the deck of the Starship Enterprise"—symbolized the tradition-bound formality that was paralyzing the company. The destruction of the room, and the subsequent move to a smaller, more informal setting, sent a message no one could miss, and the division's culture changed quickly in its wake.

That said, the coercive style should be used only with extreme caution and in the few situations when it is absolutely imperative, such as during a turnaround or when a hostile takeover is looming. In those cases, the coercive style can break failed business habits and shock people into new ways of working. It is always appropriate during a genuine emergency, like in the aftermath of an earthquake or a fire. And it can work with problem employees with whom all else has failed. But if a leader relies solely on this style or continues to use it once the emergency passes, the long-term impact of his insensitivity to the morale and feelings of those he leads will be ruinous.

The authoritative style

Tom was the vice president of marketing at a floundering national restaurant chain that specialized in pizza. Needless to say, the company's poor performance troubled the senior managers, but they were at a loss for what to do. Every Monday, they met to review recent sales, struggling to come up with fixes. To Tom, the approach didn't make sense. "We were always trying to figure out why our sales were down last week. We had the whole company looking backward instead of figuring out what we had to do tomorrow."

Tom saw an opportunity to change people's way of thinking at an off-site strategy meeting. There, the conversation began with stale truisms: the company had to drive up shareholder wealth and increase return on assets. Tom believed those concepts didn't have the power to inspire a restaurant manager to be innovative or to do better than a good-enough job.

So Tom made a bold move. In the middle of a meeting, he made an impassioned plea for his colleagues to think from the customer's perspective. Customers want convenience, he said. The company was not in the restaurant business, it was in the business of distributing high-quality, convenient-to-get pizza. That notion—and nothing else—should drive everything the company did.

With his vibrant enthusiasm and clear vision—the hallmarks of the authoritative style—Tom filled a leadership vacuum at the company. Indeed, his concept became the core of the new mission statement. But this conceptual breakthrough was just the beginning. Tom made sure that the mission statement was built into the company's strategic planning process as the designated driver of growth. And he ensured that the vision was articulated so that local restaurant managers understood they were the key to the company's success and were free to find new ways to distribute pizza.

Changes came quickly. Within weeks, many local managers started guaranteeing fast, new delivery times. Even better, they started to act like entrepreneurs, finding ingenious locations to open new branches: kiosks on busy street corners and in bus and train stations, even from carts in airports and hotel lobbies.

Tom's success was no fluke. Our research indicates that of the six leadership styles, the authoritative one is most effective, driving up every aspect of climate. Take clarity. The authoritative leader is a visionary; he motivates people by making clear to them how their work fits into a larger vision for the organization. People who work for such leaders understand that what they do matters and why. Authoritative leadership also maximizes commitment to the organization's goals and strategy. By framing the individual tasks within a grand vision, the authoritative leader defines standards that revolve around that vision. When he gives performance feedback—whether positive or negative—the singular criterion is whether or not that performance furthers the vision. The standards for success are clear to all, as are the rewards. Finally, consider the style's impact on flexibility. An authoritative leader states the end but generally gives people plenty of leeway to devise their own means. Authoritative leaders give people the freedom to innovate, experiment, and take calculated risks.

Because of its positive impact, the authoritative style works well in almost any business situation. But it is particularly effective when a business is adrift. An authoritative leader charts a new course and sells his people on a fresh long-term vision.

The authoritative style, powerful though it may be, will not work in every situation.

The approach fails, for instance, when a leader is working with a team of experts or peers who are more experienced than he is; they may see the leader as pompous or out-of-touch. Another limitation: if a manager trying to be authoritative becomes overbearing, he can undermine the egalitarian spirit of an effective team. Yet even with such caveats, leaders would be wise to grab for the authoritative "club" more often than not. It may not guarantee a hole in one, but it certainly helps with the long drive.

The affiliative style

If the coercive leader demands, "Do what I say," and the authoritative urges, "Come with me," the affiliative leader says, "People come first." This leadership style revolves around people—its proponents value individuals and their emotions more than tasks and goals. The affiliative leader strives to keep employees happy and to create harmony among them. He manages by building strong emotional bonds and then reaping the benefits of such an approach, namely fierce loyalty. The style also has a markedly positive effect on communication. People who like one another a lot talk a lot. They share ideas; they share inspiration. And the style drives up flexibility; friends trust one another, allowing habitual innovation and risk taking. Flexibility also rises because the affiliative leader, like a parent who adjusts household rules for a maturing adolescent, doesn't impose unnecessary strictures on how employees get their work done. They give people the freedom to do their job in the way they think is most effective.

As for a sense of recognition and reward for work well done, the affiliative leader offers ample positive feedback. Such feedback has special potency in the workplace because it is all too rare: outside of an annual review, most people usually get no feedback on their day-to-day efforts—or only negative feedback. That makes the affiliative leader's positive words all the more motivating. Finally, affiliative leaders are masters at building a sense of belonging. They are, for instance, likely to take their direct reports out for a meal or a drink, one-on-one, to see

how they're doing. They will bring in a cake
to celebrate a group accomplishment. They
are natural relationship builders.

Joe Torre, the heart and soul of the New
York Yankees, is a classic affiliative leader.
During the 1999 World Series, Torre tended
ably to the psyches of his players as they
endured the emotional pressure cooker of
a pennant race. All season long, he made a
special point to praise Scott Brosius, whose
father had died during the season, for stay-
ing committed even as he mourned. At the
celebration party after the team's final game,
Torre specifically sought out right fielder
Paul O'Neill. Although he had received
the news of his father's death that morning, O'Neill chose to play in the decisive

game—and he burst into tears the moment it ended. Torre made a point of acknowledging O'Neill's personal struggle, calling him a "warrior." Torre also used the spotlight of the victory celebration to praise two players whose return the following year was threatened by contract disputes. In doing so, he sent a clear message to the team and to the club's owner that he valued the players immensely—too much to lose them.

Along with ministering to the emotions of his people, an affiliative leader may also tend to his own emotions openly. The year Torre's brother was near death awaiting a heart transplant, he shared his worries with his players. He also spoke candidly with the team about his treatment for prostate cancer.

The affiliative style's generally positive impact makes it a good all-weather approach, but leaders should employ it particularly when trying to build team harmony, increase morale, improve communication, or repair broken trust. For instance, one executive in our study was hired to replace a ruthless team leader. The former leader had taken credit for his employees' work and had attempted to pit them against one another. His efforts ultimately failed, but the team he left behind was suspicious and weary. The new executive managed to mend the situation by unstintingly showing emotional honesty and rebuilding ties. Several months in, her leadership had created a renewed sense of commitment and energy.

Despite its benefits, the affiliative style should not be used alone. Its exclusive focus on praise can allow poor performance to go uncorrected; employees may perceive that mediocrity is tolerated. And because affiliative leaders rarely offer constructive advice on how to improve, employees must figure out how to do so on their own. When people need clear directives to navigate through complex challenges, the affiliative style leaves them rudderless. Indeed, if overly relied on, this style can actually steer a group to failure. Perhaps that is why many affiliative leaders, including Torre, use this style in close conjunction with the authoritative style. Authoritative leaders state a vision, set standards, and let people know how their work is furthering the group's goals. Alternate that with the caring, nurturing approach of the affiliative leader, and you have a potent combination.

The democratic style

Sister Mary ran a Catholic school system in a large metropolitan area. One of the schools— the only private school in an impoverished neighborhood—had been losing money for years, and the archdiocese could no longer afford to keep it open. When Sister Mary eventually got the order to shut it down, she didn't just lock the doors. She called a meeting of all the teachers and staff at the school and explained to them the details of the financial crisis—the first time anyone working at the school had been included in the business side of the institution. She asked for their ideas on ways to keep the school open and on how to handle the closing, should it come to that. Sister Mary spent much of her time at the meeting just listening.

She did the same at later meetings for school parents and for the community and during a successive series of meetings for the school's teachers and staff. After two months of meetings, the consensus was clear: the school would have to close. A plan was made to transfer students to other schools in the Catholic system.

The final outcome was no different than if Sister Mary had gone ahead and closed the school the day she was told to. But by allowing the school's constituents to reach that decision collectively, Sister Mary received none of the backlash that would have accompanied such a move. People mourned the loss of the school, but they understood its inevitability. Virtually no one objected.

Compare that with the experiences of a priest in our research who headed another Catholic school. He, too, was told to shut it down. And he did—by fiat. The result was disastrous: parents filed lawsuits, teachers and parents picketed, and local newspapers ran editorials attacking his decision. It took a year to resolve the disputes before he could finally go ahead and close the school.

Sister Mary exemplifies the democratic style in action—and its benefits. By spending time getting people's ideas and buy-in, a leader builds trust, respect, and commitment. By letting workers themselves have a say in decisions that affect their goals and how they do their work, the democratic leader drives up flexibility and responsibility. And by listening to employees' concerns, the democratic leader learns what to do to keep morale high. Finally, because they have a say in setting their goals and the standards for evaluating success, people operating in a democratic system tend to be very realistic about what can and cannot be accomplished.

However, the democratic style has its drawbacks, which is why its impact on climate is not as high as some of the other styles. One of its more exasperating consequences can be endless meetings where ideas are mulled over, consensus remains elusive, and the only visible result is scheduling more meetings. Some democratic leaders use the style to put off making crucial decisions, hoping that enough thrashing things out will eventually yield a blinding insight. In reality, their people end up feeling confused and leaderless. Such an approach can even escalate conflicts.

When does the style work best? This approach is ideal when a leader is himself uncertain about the best direction to take and needs ideas and guidance from able employees. And even if a leader has a strong vision, the democratic style works well to generate fresh ideas for executing that vision.

The democratic style, of course, makes much less sense when employees are not competent or informed enough to offer sound advice. And it almost goes without saying that building consensus is wrong-headed in times of crisis. Take the case of a CEO whose computer company was severely threatened by changes in the market. He always sought consensus about what to do. As competitors stole customers and customers' needs changed, he kept appointing committees to consider the situation. When the market made a sudden shift because of a new technology, the CEO froze in his tracks.

The board replaced him before he could appoint yet another task force to consider the situation. The new CEO, while occasionally democratic and affiliative, relied heavily on the authoritative style, especially in his first months.

The pacesetting style

Like the coercive style, the pacesetting style has its place in the leader's repertory, but it should be used sparingly. That's not what we expected to find. After all, the hallmarks of the pacesetting style sound admirable. The leader sets extremely high performance standards and exemplifies them himself. He is obsessive about doing things better and faster, and he asks the same of everyone around him.

He quickly pinpoints poor performers and demands more from them. If they don't rise to the occasion, he replaces them with people who can. You would think such an approach would improve results, but it doesn't.

In fact, the pacesetting style destroys climate. Many employees feel overwhelmed by the pacesetter's demands for excellence, and their morale drops. Guidelines for working may be clear in the leader's head, but she does not state them clearly; she expects people to know what to do and even thinks, "If I have to tell you, you're the wrong person for the job." Work becomes not a matter of doing one's best along a clear course so much as second-guessing what the leader wants. At the same time, people often feel that the pacesetter doesn't trust them to work in their own way or to take initiative. Flexibility and responsibility evaporate; work becomes so task focused and routinized it's boring.

As for rewards, the pacesetter either gives no feedback on how people are doing or jumps in to take over when he thinks they're lagging. And if the leader should leave, people feel directionless—they're so used to "the expert" setting the rules. Finally, commitment dwindles under the regime of a pacesetting leader because people have no sense of how their personal efforts fit into the big picture.

For an example of the pacesetting style, take the case of Sam, a biochemist in R&D

at a large pharmaceutical company. Sam's superb technical expertise made him an early star: he was the one everyone turned to when they needed help. Soon he was promoted to head of a team developing a new product. The other scientists on the team were as competent and self-motivated as Sam; his métier as team leader became offering himself as a model of how to do first-class scientific work under tremendous deadline pressure, pitching in when needed. His team completed its task in record time.

But then came a new assignment: Sam was put in charge of R&D for his entire division. As his tasks expanded and he had to articulate a vision, coordinate projects, delegate responsibility, and help develop others, Sam began to slip. Not trusting that his subordinates were as capable as he was, he became a micromanager, obsessed with details and taking over for others when their performance slackened. Instead of trusting them to improve with guidance and development, Sam found himself working nights and weekends after stepping in to take over for the head of a floundering research team. Finally, his own boss suggested, to his relief, that he return to his old job as head of a product development team.

Although Sam faltered, the pacesetting style isn't always a disaster. The approach works well when all employees are self-motivated, highly competent, and need little direction or coordination—for example, it can work for leaders of highly skilled and self-motivated professionals, like R&D groups or legal teams. And, given a talented team to lead, pacesetting does exactly that: gets work done on time or even ahead of schedule. Yet like any leadership style, pace-setting should never be used by itself.

The coaching style

A product unit at a global computer company had seen sales plummet from twice as much as its competitors to only half as much. So Lawrence, the president of the manufacturing division, decided to close the unit and reassign its people and products. Upon hearing the news, James, the head of the doomed unit, decided to go over his boss's head and plead his case to the CEO.

What did Lawrence do? Instead of blowing up at James, he sat down with his rebellious direct report and talked over not just the decision to close the division but also James's future. He explained to James how moving to another division would help him develop new skills. It would make him a better leader and teach him more about the company's business.

Lawrence acted more like a counselor than a traditional boss. He listened to James's concerns and hopes, and he shared his own. He said he believed James had grown stale in his current job; it was, after all, the only place he'd worked in the company. He predicted that James would blossom in a new role.

The conversation then took a practical turn. James had not yet had his meeting with the CEO—the one he had impetuously demanded when he heard of his division's closing. Knowing this—and also knowing that the CEO unwaveringly supported the closing—Lawrence took the time to coach James on how to present his case in that meeting. "You don't get an audience with the CEO very often," he noted, "let's make sure you impress him with your thoughtfulness." He advised James not to plead his personal case but to focus on the business unit: "If he thinks you're in there for your own glory, he'll throw you out faster than you walked through the door." And he urged him to put his ideas in writing; the CEO always appreciated that.

Lawrence's reason for coaching instead of scolding? "James is a good guy, very talented and promising," the executive explained to us, "and I don't want this to derail his career. I want him to stay with the company, I want him to work out, I want him to learn, I want him to benefit and grow. Just because he screwed up doesn't mean he's terrible."

Lawrence's actions illustrate the coaching style par excellence. Coaching leaders help employees identify their unique strengths and weaknesses and tie them to their personal and career aspirations. They encourage employees to establish long-term

development goals and help them concep-
tualize a plan for attaining them. They make
agreements with their employees about
their role and responsibilities in enacting
development plans, and they give plentiful
instruction and feedback. Coaching leaders
excel at delegating; they give employees
challenging assignments, even if that means
the tasks won't be accomplished quickly. In
other words, these leaders are willing to put
up with short-term failure if it furthers long-
term learning.

Of the six styles, our research found that
the coaching style is used least often. Many
leaders told us they don't have the time in
this high-pressure economy for the slow and
tedious work of teaching people and helping

them grow. But after a first session, it takes little or no extra time. Leaders who ignore this style are passing up a powerful tool: its impact on climate and performance are markedly positive.

Admittedly, there is a paradox in coaching's positive effect on business performance because coaching focuses primarily on personal development, not on immediate work-related tasks. Even so, coaching improves results. The reason: it requires constant dialogue, and that dialogue has a way of pushing up every driver of climate. Take flexibility. When an employee knows his boss watches him and cares about what he does, he feels free to experiment. After all, he's sure to get quick and constructive feedback. Similarly, the ongoing dialogue of coaching guarantees that people know what is expected of them and how their work fits into a larger vision or strategy. That affects responsibility and clarity. As for commitment, coaching helps there, too, because the style's implicit message is, "I believe in you, I'm investing in you, and I expect your best efforts." Employees very often rise to that challenge with their heart, mind, and soul.

The coaching style works well in many business situations, but it is perhaps most effective when people on the receiving end are "up for it." For instance, the coaching style works particularly well when employees are already aware of their weaknesses and would like to improve their performance.

Similarly, the style works well when employees realize how cultivating new abilities can help them advance. In short, it works best with employees who want to be coached.

By contrast, the coaching style makes little sense when employees, for whatever reason, are resistant to learning or changing their ways. And it flops if the leader lacks the expertise to help the employee along. The fact is, many managers are unfamiliar with or simply inept at coaching, particularly when it comes to giving ongoing performance feedback that motivates rather than creates fear or apathy. Some companies have realized the positive impact of the style and are trying to make it a core competence. At some companies, a significant portion of annual bonuses are tied to an executive's development of his or her direct reports. But many organizations have yet to take full advantage of this leadership style. Although the coaching style may not scream "bottom-line results," it delivers them.

LEADERS NEED MANY STYLES

Many studies, including this one, have shown that the more styles a leader exhibits, the better. Leaders who have mastered four or more—especially the authoritative, democratic, affiliative, and coaching styles— have the very best climate and business performance. And the most effective leaders switch flexibly among the leadership styles as needed. Although that may sound daunting, we witnessed it more often than you might guess, at both large corporations and tiny start-ups, by seasoned veterans who could explain exactly how and why they lead and by entrepreneurs who claim to lead by gut alone.

Such leaders don't mechanically match their style to fit a checklist of situations—they are far more fluid. They are exquisitely sensitive to the impact they are having on others and seamlessly adjust their style to get the best results. These are leaders, for example, who can read in the first minutes of conversation that a talented but underperforming employee has been demoralized by an unsympathetic, do-it-the-way-I-tell-you manager and needs to be inspired through a reminder of why her work matters. Or that leader might choose to reenergize the employee by asking her about her dreams and aspirations and finding ways to make her job more challenging. Or that initial conversation might signal that the employee needs an ultimatum: improve or leave.

For an example of fluid leadership in action, consider Joan, the general manager of a major division at a global food and beverage company. Joan was appointed to her job while the division was in a deep crisis. It had not made its profit targets for six years; in the most recent year, it had missed by $50 million. Morale among the top management team was miserable;

mistrust and resentments were rampant. Joan's directive from above was clear: turn the division around.

Joan did so with a nimbleness in switching among leadership styles that is rare. From the start, she realized she had a short window to demonstrate effective leadership and to establish rapport and trust. She also knew that she urgently needed to be informed about what was not working, so her indent first task was to listen to key people.

Her first week on the job she had lunch and dinner meetings with each member of the management team. Joan sought to get each person's understanding of the current situation. But her focus was not so much on learning how each person diagnosed the problem as on getting to know each manager as a person. Here Joan employed the affiliative style: she explored their lives, dreams, and aspirations.

She also stepped into the coaching role, looking for ways she could help the team members achieve what they wanted in their careers. For instance, one manager who had been getting feedback that he was a poor team player confided his worries to her. He thought he was a good team member, but he was plagued by persistent complaints. Recognizing that he was a talented executive and a valuable asset to the company, Joan made an agreement with him to point out (in private) when his actions undermined his goal of being seen as a team player.

She followed the one-on-one conversations with a three-day offsite meeting. Her goal here was team building, so that everyone would own whatever solution for the business problems emerged. Her initial stance at the off-site meeting was that of a democratic leader. She encouraged everyone to express freely their frustrations and complaints.

The next day, Joan had the group focus on solutions: each person made three specific proposals about what needed to be done. As Joan clustered the suggestions, a natural consensus emerged about priorities for the business, such as cutting costs. As the group came up with specific action plans, Joan got the commitment and buy-in she sought.

With that vision in place, Joan shifted into the authoritative style, assigning accountability for each follow-up step to specific executives and holding them responsible for their accomplishment. For example, the division had been dropping prices on products without increasing its volume. One obvious solution was to raise prices, but the previous VP of sales had dithered and had let the problem fester. The new VP of sales now had responsibility to adjust the price points to fix the problem.

Over the following months, Joan's main stance was authoritative. She continually articulated the group's new vision in a way that reminded each member of how his or her role was crucial to achieving these goals. And, especially during the first few weeks of the plan's implementation, Joan felt that the urgency of the business crisis justified an occasional shift into the coercive style should someone fail to meet his or her responsibility. As she put it, "I had to be brutal about this follow-up and make sure this stuff happened. It was going to take discipline and focus."

The results? Every aspect of climate improved. People were innovating. They were talking about the division's vision and crowing about their commitment to new, clear goals. The ultimate proof of Joan's fluid leadership style is written in black ink: after only seven months, her division exceeded its yearly profit target by $5 million.

EXPANDING YOUR REPERTORY

Few leaders, of course, have all six styles in their repertory, and even fewer know when and how to use them. In fact, as we have brought the findings of our research into many organizations, the most common responses have been, "But I have only two of those!" and, "I can't use all those styles. It wouldn't be natural."

Such feelings are understandable, and in some cases, the antidote is relatively simple. The leader can build a team with members who employ styles she lacks. Take the case of a VP for manufacturing. She successfully ran a global factory system largely by using the affiliative style. She was on the road constantly, meeting with plant managers, attending to their pressing concerns, and letting them know how much she cared about them personally. She left the division's strategy—extreme efficiency—to a trusted lieutenant with a keen understanding of technology, and she delegated its performance standards to a colleague who was adept at the authoritative approach. She also had a pacesetter on her team who always visited the plants with her.

An alternative approach, and one I would recommend more, is for leaders to expand their own style repertories. To do so, leaders must first understand which emotional intelligence competencies underlie the leadership styles they are lacking. They can then work assiduously to increase their quotient of them.

For instance, an affiliative leader has strengths in three emotional intelligence competencies: in empathy, in building relationships, and in communication. Empathy—sensing how people are feeling in the moment—allows the affiliative leader to respond to employees in a way that is highly congruent with that person's emotions, thus building rapport. The affiliative leader also displays a natural ease in forming new relationships, getting to know someone as a person, and cultivating a bond. Finally, the outstanding affiliative leader has mastered the art of interpersonal communication, particularly in saying just the right thing or making the apt symbolic gesture at just the right moment.

So if you are primarily a pacesetting leader who wants to be able to use the affiliative style more often, you would need to improve your level of empathy and, perhaps, your skills at building relationships or communicating effectively. As another example, an authoritative leader who wants to add the democratic style to his repertory might need to work on the capabilities of collaboration and communication. Such advice about adding capabilities may seem simplistic—"Go change yourself"—but enhancing emotional intelligence is entirely possible with practice. (For more on how to improve emotional intelligence, see the sidebar "Growing Your Emotional Intelligence" on page 72.)

MORE SCIENCE, LESS ART

Like parenthood, leadership will never be an exact science. But neither should it be a complete mystery to those who practice it. In recent years, research has helped parents understand the genetic, psychological, and behavioral components that affect their "job performance." With our new research, leaders, too, can get a clearer picture of what it takes to lead effectively. And perhaps as important, they can see how they can make that happen.

The business environment is continually changing, and a leader must respond in kind. Hour to hour, day to day, week to week, executives must play their leadership styles like a pro—using the right one at just the right time and in the right measure. The pay-off is in the results.

NOTE

Daniel Goleman consults with Hay/McBer on leadership development.

Daniel Goleman

Getting Molecular: The Impact of Leadership Styles on Drivers of Climate

Our research investigated how each leadership style affected the six drivers of climate, or working atmosphere. The figures below show the correlation between each leadership style and each aspect of climate. So, for instance, if we look at the climate driver of flexibility, we see that the coercive style has a –.28 correlation while the democratic style has a .28 correlation, equally strong in the opposite direction. Focusing on the authoritative leadership style, we find that it has a .54 correlation with rewards—strongly positive—and a .21 correlation with responsibility—positive, but not as strong. In other words, the style's correlation with rewards was more than twice that with responsibility.

According to the data, the authoritative leadership style has the most positive effect on climate, but three others—affiliative, democratic, and coaching—follow close behind. That said, the research indicates that no style should be relied on exclusively, and all have at least short-term uses.

	Coercive	Authoritative	Affiliative	Democratic	Pacesetting	Coaching
Flexibility	−.28	.32	.27	.28	−.07	.17
Responsibility	−.37	.21	.16	.23	.04	.08
Standards	.02	.38	.31	.22	−.27	.39
Rewards	−.18	.54	.48	.42	−.29	.43
Clarity	−.11	.44	.37	.35	−.28	.38
Commitment	−.13	.35	.34	.26	−.20	.27
Overall impact on climate	−.26	.54	.46	.43	−.25	.42

The Six Leadership Styles at a Glance

Our research found that leaders use six styles, each springing from different components of emotional intelligence. Here is a summary of the styles, their origin, when they work best, and their impact on an organization's climate and thus its performance.

	Coercive	Authoritative
The leader's modus operandi	Demands immediate compliance	Mobilizes people toward a vision
The style in a phrase	"Do what I tell you."	"Come with me."
Underlying emotional intelligence competencies	Drive to achieve, initiative, self-control	Self-confidence, empathy, change catalyst
When the style works best	In a crisis, to kick start a turnaround, or with problem employees	When changes require a new vision, or when a clear direction is needed
Overall impact on climate	Negative	Most strongly positive

	Affiliative	**Democratic**
The leader's modus operandi	Creates harmony and builds emotional bonds	Forges consensus through participation
The style in a phrase	"People come first."	"What do you think?"
Underlying emotional intelligence competencies	Empathy, building relationships, communication	Collaboration, team leadership, communication
When the style works best	To heal rifts in a team or to motivate people during stressful circumstances	To build buy-in or consensus, or to get input from valuable employees
Overall impact on climate	Positive	Positive

	Pacesetting	Coaching
The leader's modus operandi	Sets high standards for performance	Develops people for the future
The style in a phrase	"Do as I do, now."	"Try this."
Underlying emotional intelligence competencies	Conscientiousness, drive to achieve, initiative	Developing others, empathy, self-awareness
When the style works best	To get quick results from a highly motivated and competent team	To help an employee improve performance or develop long-term strengths
Overall impact on climate	Negative	Positive

Emotional Intelligence: A Primer

Emotional intelligence—the ability to manage ourselves and our relationships effectively—consists of four fundamental capabilities: self-awareness, self-management, social awareness, and social skill. Each capability, in turn, is composed of specific sets of competencies. Below is a list of the capabilities and their corresponding traits.

Self-Awareness

- *Emotional self-awareness:* the ability to read and understand your emotions as well as recognize their impact on work performance, relationships, and the like.

- *Accurate self-assessment:* a realistic evaluation of your strengths and limitations.

- *Self-confidence:* a strong and positive sense of self-worth.

Self-Management

- *Self-control:* the ability to keep disruptive emotions and impulses under control.

- *Trustworthiness:* a consistent display of honesty and integrity.

- *Conscientiousness:* the ability to manage yourself and your responsibilities.

- *Adaptability:* skill at adjusting to changing situations and overcoming obstacles.

- *Achievement orientation:* the drive to meet an internal standard of excellence.

- *Initiative:* a readiness to seize opportunities.

Social Awareness

- *Empathy:* skill at sensing other people's emotions, understanding their perspective, and taking an active interest in their concerns.

- *Organizational awareness:* the ability to read the currents of organizational life, build decision networks, and navigate politics.

- *Service orientation:* the ability to recognize and meet customers' needs.

Social Skill

- *Visionary leadership:* the ability to take charge and inspire with a compelling vision.

- *Influence:* the ability to wield a range of persuasive tactics.

- *Developing others:* the propensity to bolster the abilities of others through feedback and guidance.

- *Communication:* skill at listening and at sending clear, convincing, and well-tuned messages.

- *Change catalyst:* proficiency in initiating new ideas and leading people in a new direction.

- *Conflict management:* the ability to de-escalate disagreements and orchestrate resolutions.

- *Building bonds:* proficiency at cultivating and maintaining a web of relationships.

- *Teamwork and collaboration:* competence at promoting cooperation and building teams.

Growing Your Emotional Intelligence

Unlike IQ, which is largely genetic—it changes little from childhood—the skills of emotional intelligence can be learned at any age. It's not easy, however. Growing your emotional intelligence takes practice and commitment. But the payoffs are well worth the investment.

Consider the case of a marketing director for a division of a global food company. Jack, as I'll call him, was a classic pacesetter: high-energy, always striving to find better ways to get things done, and too eager to step in and take over when, say, someone seemed about to miss a deadline. Worse, Jack was prone to pounce on anyone who didn't seem to meet his standards, flying off the handle if a person merely deviated from completing a job in the order Jack thought best.

Jack's leadership style had a predictably disastrous impact on climate and business results. After two years of stagnant performance, Jack's boss suggested he seek out a coach. Jack wasn't pleased but, realizing his own job was on the line, he complied.

The coach, an expert in teaching people how to increase their emotional intelligence, began with a 360-degree evaluation of Jack. A diagnosis from multiple viewpoints is essential in improving emotional intelligence because those who need the most help usually have blind spots. In fact, our research found that top-performing leaders overestimate their strengths on, at most, one emotional intelligence ability, whereas poor performers overrate themselves on four or more. Jack was not that far off, but he did rate himself more glowingly than his direct reports, who gave him especially low grades on emotional self-control and empathy.

Initially, Jack had some trouble accepting the feedback data. But when his coach showed him how those weaknesses were tied to his inability to display leadership styles dependent on those competencies—especially the authoritative, affiliative, and coaching styles—Jack realized he had to improve if he wanted to advance in the company. Making such a connection is essential. The reason: improving emotional intelligence isn't done in a weekend or during a seminar—it takes diligent practice on the job, over several months. If people do not see the value of the change, they will not make that effort.

Once Jack zeroed in on areas for improvement and committed himself to making the effort, he and his coach worked up a plan to turn his day-to-day job into a learning laboratory. For instance, Jack discovered he was empathetic when things were calm, but in a crisis, he tuned out others. This tendency hampered his ability to listen to what people were telling him in the very moments he most needed to do so. Jack's plan required him to focus on his behavior during tough situations. As soon as he felt himself tensing up, his job was to immediately step back, let the other person speak, and then ask clarifying questions. The point was to not act judgmental or hostile under pressure.

The change didn't come easily, but with practice Jack learned to defuse his flare-ups by entering into a dialogue instead of launching a harangue. Although he didn't always agree with them, at least he gave people a chance to make their case. At the same time, Jack also practiced giving his direct reports more positive feedback and reminding them of how their work contributed to the group's mission. And he restrained himself from micromanaging them.

Jack met with his coach every week or two to review his progress and get advice on specific problems. For instance, occasionally Jack would find himself falling back on his old pacesetting tactics—cutting people off, jumping in to take over, and blowing up in a rage. Almost immediately, he would regret it. So he and his coach dissected those relapses to figure out what triggered the old ways and what to do the next time a similar moment arose. Such "relapse prevention" measures inoculate people against future lapses or just giving up. Over a six-month period, Jack made real improvement. His own records showed he had reduced the number of flare-ups from one or more a day at the beginning to just one or two a month. The climate had improved sharply, and the division's numbers were starting to creep upward.

Why does improving an emotional intelligence competence take months rather than days? Because the emotional centers of the brain, not just the neocortex, are involved. The neocortex, the thinking brain that learns technical skills and purely cognitive abilities, gains knowledge very quickly, but the emotional brain does not. To master a new behavior, the emotional centers need repetition and practice. Improving your emotional intelligence, then, is akin to changing your habits. Brain circuits that carry leadership habits have to unlearn the old ones and replace them with the new. The more often a behavioral sequence is repeated, the stronger the underlying brain circuits become. At some point, the new neural pathways become the brain's default option. When that happened, Jack was able to go through the paces of leadership effortlessly, using styles that worked for him—and the whole company.

ABOUT THE AUTHOR

Daniel Goleman is a codirector of the
Consortium for Research on Emotional
Intelligence in Organizations at Rutgers
University, coauthor of *Primal Leadership:
Leading with Emotional Intelligence*
(Harvard Business Review Press, 2013),
and author of *The Brain and Emotional
Intelligence: New Insights and Leadership:
Selected Writings* (More Than Sound,
2011). His latest book is *A Force For Good:
The Dalai Lama's Vision for Our World*
(Bantam, 2015).

Article Summary

Idea in Brief

Many managers mistakenly assume that leadership style is a function of personality rather than strategic choice. Instead of choosing the one style that suits their temperament, they should ask which style best addresses the demands of a particular situation.

Research has shown that the most successful leaders have strengths in the following emotional intelligence competencies: **self-awareness, self-regulation, motivation, empathy**, and

social skill. There are six basic styles of leadership; each makes use of the key components of emotional intelligence in different combinations. The best leaders don't know just one style of leadership—they're skilled at several, and have the flexibility to switch between styles as the circumstances dictate.

Idea in Practice

Managers often fail to appreciate how profoundly the organizational climate can influence financial results. It can account for nearly a third of financial performance. Organizational climate, in turn, is influenced by leadership style—by the way that managers motivate direct reports, gather and use information, make decisions, manage change initiatives, and handle crises. There are six basic leadership styles. Each derives from different emotional intelligence competencies, works best in particular situations, and affects the organizational climate in different ways.

1. *The coercive style*. This "Do what I say" approach can be very effective in a turnaround situation, a natural disaster, or when working with problem employees. But in most situations, coercive leadership inhibits the organization's flexibility and dampens employees' motivation.

2. *The authoritative style*. An authoritative leader takes a "Come with me" approach: she states the overall goal but gives people the freedom to choose their own means of achieving it. This style works especially well when a business is adrift. It is less effective when the leader is working with a team of experts who are more experienced than he is.

3. *The affiliative style*. The hallmark of the affiliative leader is a "People come first" attitude. This style is particularly useful for building team harmony or increasing morale. But its exclusive focus on praise can allow poor performance to go uncorrected. Also, affiliative leaders rarely offer advice, which often leaves employees in a quandary.

4. *The democratic style*. This style's impact on organizational climate is not as high as you might imagine. By giving workers a voice in decisions, democratic leaders build organizational flexibility and responsibility and help generate fresh ideas. But sometimes the price is endless meetings and confused employees who feel leaderless.

5. *The pacesetting style*. A leader who sets high performance standards and exemplifies them himself has a very positive impact on

employees who are self-motivated and highly competent. But other employees tend to feel overwhelmed by such a leader's demands for excellence—and to resent his tendency to take over a situation.

6. *The coaching style.* This style focuses more on personal development than on immediate work-related tasks. It works well when employees are already aware of their weaknesses and want to improve, but not when they are resistant to changing their ways.

The more styles a leader has mastered, the better. In particular, being able to switch among the authoritative, affiliative, democratic, and coaching styles as conditions dictate creates the best organizational climate and optimizes business performance.

MANAGING
YOUR BOSS

HARVARD BUSINESS REVIEW
CLASSICS

MANAGING
YOUR BOSS

John J. Gabarro and
John P. Kotter

Harvard Business Review Press
Boston, Massachusetts

Library of Congress Cataloging-in-Publication Data
Gabarro, John J.
  Managing your boss / John J. Gabarro, John P. Kotter.
    p. cm. — (Harvard business review classics)
  ISBN 978-1-4221-2288-4
  1. Managing your boss. 2. Interpersonal relations. I. Kotter,
John P., 1947- II. Title.
  HF5548.83.G33 2008
  650.1′3–dc22
                                            2007037488

The paper used in this publication meets the requirements of the
American National Standard for Permanence of Paper for Publications and Documents in Libraries and Archives Z39.48-1992.

THE
HARVARD BUSINESS REVIEW
CLASSICS SERIES

Since 1922, *Harvard Business Review* has been a leading source of breakthrough ideas in management practice—many of which still speak to and influence us today. The HBR Classics series now offers you the opportunity to make these seminal pieces a part of your permanent management library. Each volume contains a groundbreaking idea that has shaped best practices and inspired countless managers around the world—and will change how you think about the business world today.

MANAGING
YOUR BOSS

To many people, the phrase "managing your boss" may sound unusual or suspicious. Because of the traditional top-down emphasis in most organizations, it is not obvious why you need to manage relationships upward—unless, of course, you would do so for personal or political reasons. But we are not referring to political maneuvering or to apple polishing. We are using the term to mean the process of consciously working with your superior to obtain the best possible results for you, your boss, and the company.

Recent studies suggest that effective managers take time and effort to manage not only relationships with their subordinates but also those with their bosses. These studies also show that this essential aspect of management is sometimes ignored by otherwise talented and aggressive managers. Indeed, some managers who actively and effectively supervise subordinates, products, markets, and technologies assume an almost passively reactive stance vis-à-vis their bosses. Such a stance almost always hurts them and their companies.

If you doubt the importance of managing your relationship with your boss or how difficult it is to do so effectively, consider for a moment the following sad but telling story.

Frank Gibbons was an acknowledged manufacturing genius in his industry and, by any profitability standard, a very effective executive. In 1973, his strengths propelled him into the position of vice president of manufacturing for the second largest and most profitable company in its industry. Gibbons was not, however, a good manager of people. He knew this, as did others in his company and his industry. Recognizing this weakness, the president made sure that those who reported to Gibbons were good at working with people and could compensate for his limitations. The arrangement worked well.

In 1975, Philip Bonnevie was promoted into a position reporting to Gibbons. In keeping with the previous pattern, the president selected Bonnevie because he had an excellent track record and a reputation for being good with people. In making that selection, however, the president neglected to notice that, in his rapid rise through the organization, Bonnevie had always had good-to-excellent bosses. He had never been forced to manage a relationship with a difficult boss. In retrospect, Bonnevie admits he had never thought that managing his boss was a part of his job.

Fourteen months after he started working for Gibbons, Bonnevie was fired. During that same quarter, the company reported a net loss for the first time in seven years. Many of those who were close to these events say that they don't really understand what happened. This much is known, however: While the company was bringing out a major new product—a process that required sales, engineering, and manufacturing groups to coordinate decisions very carefully—a whole series of misunderstandings and bad feelings developed between Gibbons and Bonnevie.

For example, Bonnevie claims Gibbons was aware of and had accepted Bonnevie's decision to use a new type of machinery to make the new product; Gibbons swears he did not. Furthermore, Gibbons claims he made it clear to Bonnevie that introduction of the product was too important to the company in the short run to take any major risks.

As a result of such misunderstandings, planning went awry: A new manufacturing plant was built that could not produce the new product designed by engineering, in the volume desired by sales, at a cost agreed on by the executive committee. Gibbons blamed Bonnevie for the mistake. Bonnevie blamed Gibbons.

Of course, one could argue that the problem here was caused by Gibbons's inability to manage his subordinates. But one can make just as strong a case that the problem was related to Bonnevie's inability to manage his boss. Remember, Gibbons was not having difficulty with any other subordinates. More-over, given the personal price paid by Bonnevie (being fired and having his reputation within the industry severely tarnished), there was little consolation in saying the problem was that Gibbons was poor at managing subordinates. Everyone already knew that.

We believe that the situation could have turned out differently had Bonnevie been more adept at understanding Gibbons and at managing his relationship with him. In this case, an inability to manage upward was unusually costly. The company lost $2 million to $5 million, and Bonnevie's career was, at least temporarily, disrupted. Many less costly cases similar to this probably occur regularly in all major corporations, and the cumulative effect can be very destructive.

MISREADING THE BOSS-SUBORDINATE RELATIONSHIP

People often dismiss stories like the one we just related as being merely cases of personality conflict. Because two people can on occasion be psychologically or temperamentally incapable of working together, this can be an apt description. But more often, we have found, a personality conflict is only a part of the problem—sometimes a very small part.

Bonnevie did not just have a different personality from Gibbons, he also made or had unrealistic assumptions and expectations about the very nature of boss-subordinate relationships. Specifically, he did not recognize that his relationship to Gibbons involved *mutual dependence* between two *fallible* human beings. Failing to recognize this, a manager typically either avoids trying to manage his or her relationship with a boss or manages it ineffectively.

Some people behave as if their bosses were not very dependent on them. They fail to see how much the boss needs their help and cooperation to do his or her job effectively. These people refuse to acknowledge that the boss can be severely hurt by their actions and needs cooperation, dependability, and honesty from them.

Some people see themselves as not very dependent on their bosses. They gloss over how much help and information they need from the boss in order to perform their own jobs well. This superficial view is particularly damaging when a manager's job and decisions affect other parts of the organization, as was the case in Bonnevie's situation. A manager's immediate boss can play a critical role in linking the manager to the rest of the organization, making sure the manager's priorities are consistent with organizational needs, and in securing the resources the manager needs to perform well. Yet some managers need to see themselves as practically self-sufficient, as not needing the critical information and resources a boss can supply.

Many managers, like Bonnevie, assume that the boss will magically know what information or help their subordinates need and provide it to them. Certainly, some bosses do an excellent job of caring for their subordinates in this way, but for a manager to expect that from all bosses is dangerously unrealistic. A more reasonable expectation for managers to have is that modest help will be forthcoming. After all, bosses are only human. Most really effective managers accept this fact and assume primary responsibility for their own careers and development. They make a point of seeking the information and help they need to do a job instead of waiting for their bosses to provide it.

In light of the foregoing, it seems to us that managing a situation of mutual dependence among fallible human beings requires the following:

1. That you have a good understanding of the other person and yourself, especially regarding strengths, weaknesses, work styles, and needs.

2. That you use this information to develop and manage a healthy working relationship—one that is compatible with both people's work styles and assets, is characterized by mutual expectations, and meets the most critical needs of the other person.

This combination is essentially what we have found highly effective managers doing.

UNDERSTANDING THE BOSS

Managing your boss requires that you gain an understanding of the boss and his or her context, as well as your own situation. All managers do this to some degree, but many are not thorough enough.

At a minimum, you need to appreciate your boss's goals and pressures, his or her strengths and weaknesses. What are your boss's organizational and personal objectives, and what are his or her pressures, especially those from his or her own and others at the same level? What are your boss's long suits and blind spots? What is the preferred style of working? Does your boss like to get information through memos, formal meetings, or phone calls? Does he or she thrive on conflict or try to minimize it? Without this information, a manager is flying blind when dealing with the boss, and unnecessary conflicts, misunderstandings, and problems are inevitable.

In one situation we studied, a top-notch marketing manager with a superior performance record was hired into a company as a vice president "to straighten out the marketing and sales problems." The company, which was having financial difficulties, had recently been acquired by a larger corporation. The president was eager to turn it around and gave the new marketing vice president free rein—at least initially. Based on his previous experience, the new vice president correctly diagnosed that greater market share was needed for the company and that strong product management was required to bring that about. Following that logic, he made a number of pricing decisions that were aimed at increasing high-volume business.

When margins declined and the financial situation did not improve, however, the president increased pressure on the new vice president. Believing that the situation would eventually correct itself as the company gained back market share, the vice president resisted the pressure.

When by the second quarter, margins and profits had still failed to improve, the president took direct control over all pricing decisions and put all items on a set level of margin, regardless of volume. The new vice president began to find himself shut out by the president, and their relationship deteriorated. In fact, the vice president found the president's behavior bizarre. Unfortunately, the president's new pricing scheme also failed to increase margins, and by the fourth quarter, both the president and the vice president were fired.

What the new vice president had not known until it was too late was that improving marketing and sales had been only *one* of the president's goals. His most immediate goal had been to make the company more profitable—quickly.

Nor had the new vice president known that his boss was invested in this short-term priority for personal as well as business reasons. The president had been a strong advocate of the acquisition within the parent company, and his personal credibility was at stake.

The vice president made three basic errors. He took information supplied to him at face value, he made assumptions in areas where he had no information, and—what was most damaging—he never actively tried to clarify what his boss's objectives were. As a result, he ended up taking actions that were actually at odds with the president's priorities and objectives.

Managers who work effectively with their bosses do not behave this way. They seek out information about the boss's goals and problems and pressures. They are alert for opportunities to question the boss and others around him or her to test their assumptions. They pay attention to clues in the boss's behavior. Although it is imperative that they do this especially when they begin working with a new boss, effective managers also do this on an ongoing basis because they recognize that priorities and concerns change.

Being sensitive to a boss's work style can be crucial, especially when the boss is new. For example, a new president who was organized and formal in his approach replaced a man who was informal and intuitive. The new president worked best when he had written reports. He also preferred formal meetings with set agendas.

One of his division managers realized this need and worked with the new president to identify the kinds and frequency of information and reports that the president wanted. This manager also made a point of sending background information and brief agendas ahead of time for their discussions. He found that with this type of preparation their meetings were very useful. Another interesting result was he found that with adequate preparation his new boss was even more effective at brainstorming problems than his more informal and intuitive predecessor had been.

In contrast, another division manager never fully understood how the new boss's work style differed from that of his predecessor. To the degree that he did sense it, he experienced it as too much control. As a result, he seldom sent the new president the background information he needed, and the president never felt fully prepared for meetings with the manager. In fact, the president spent much of this time when they met trying to get information that he felt he should have had earlier. The boss experienced these meetings as frustrating and inefficient, and the subordinate often found himself thrown off guard by the questions that the president asked. Ultimately, this division manager resigned.

The difference between the two division managers just described was not so much one of ability or even adaptability. Rather, one of the men was more sensitive to his boss's work style than the other and to the implications of his boss's needs.

UNDERSTANDING YOURSELF

The boss is only one-half of the relationship. You are the other half, as well as the part over which you have more direct control. Developing an effective working relationship requires, then, that you know your own needs, strengths and weaknesses, and personal style.

You are not going to change either your basic personality structure or that of your boss. But you can become aware of what it is about you that impedes or facilitates working with your boss and, with that awareness, take actions that make the relationship more effective.

For example, in one case we observed, a manager and his superior ran into problems whenever they disagreed. The boss's typical response was to harden his position and overstate it. The manager's reaction was then to raise the ante and intensify the forcefulness of his argument. In doing this, he channeled his anger into sharpening his attacks on the logical fallacies he saw in his boss's assumptions. His boss in turn would become even more adamant about holding his original position. Predictably, this escalating cycle resulted in the subordinate avoiding whenever possible any topic of potential conflict with his boss.

In discussing this problem with his peers, the manager discovered that his reaction to the boss was typical of how he generally reacted to counterarguments—but with a difference. His response would overwhelm his peers but not his boss. Because his attempts to discuss this problem with his boss were unsuccessful, he concluded that the only way to change the situation was to deal with his own instinctive reactions. Whenever the two reached an impasse, he would check his own impatience and suggest that they break up and think about it before getting together again. Usually when they renewed their discussion, they had digested their differences and were more able to work them through.

Gaining this level of self-awareness and acting on it are difficult but not impossible. For example, by reflecting over his past experiences, a young manager learned that he was not very good at dealing with difficult and emotional issues where people were involved. Because he disliked those issues and realized that his instinctive responses to them were seldom very good, he developed a habit of touching base with his boss whenever such a problem arose. Their discussions always surfaced ideas and approaches the manager had not considered. In many cases, they also identified specific actions the boss could take to help.

Although a superior-subordinate relationship is one of mutual dependence, it is also one in which the subordinate is typically more dependent on the boss than the other way around. This dependence inevitably results in the subordinate feeling a certain degree of frustration, sometimes anger, when his actions or options are constrained by his boss's decisions. This is a normal part of life and occurs in the best of relationships. The way in which a manager handles these frustrations largely depends on his or her predisposition toward dependence on authority figures.

Some people's instinctive reaction under these circumstances is to resent the boss's authority and to rebel against the boss's decisions. Sometimes a person will escalate a conflict beyond what is appropriate. Seeing the boss almost as an institutional enemy, this type of manager will often, without being conscious of it, fight with the boss just for the sake of fighting. The subordinate's reactions to being constrained are usually strong and sometimes impulsive. He or she sees the boss as someone who, by virtue of the role, is a hindrance to progress, an obstacle to be circumvented or at best tolerated.

Psychologists call this pattern of reactions counterdependent behavior. Although a counterdependent person is difficult for most superiors to manage and usually has a history of strained relationships with superiors, this sort of manager is apt to have even more trouble with a boss who tends to be directive or authoritarian. When the manager acts on his or her negative feelings, often in subtle and nonverbal ways, the boss sometimes does become the enemy. Sensing the subordinate's latent hostility, the boss will lose trust in the subordinate or his or her judgment and then behave even less openly.

Paradoxically, a manager with this type of predisposition is often a good manager of his or her own people. He or she will many times go out of the way to get support for them and will not hesitate to go to bat for them.

At the other extreme are managers who swallow their anger and behave in a very compliant fashion when the boss makes what they know to be a poor decision. These managers will agree with the boss even when a disagreement might be welcome or when the boss would easily alter a decision if given more information. Because they bear no relationship to the specific situation at hand, their responses are as much an overreaction as those of counterdependent managers. Instead of seeing the boss as an enemy, these people deny their anger—the other extreme—and tend to see the boss as if he or she were an all-wise parent who should know best, should take responsibility for their careers, train them in all they need to know, and protect them from overly ambitious peers.

Both counterdependence and overdependence lead managers to hold unrealistic views of what a boss is. Both views ignore that most bosses, like everyone else, are imperfect and fallible. They don't have unlimited time, encyclopedic knowledge, or extrasensory perception; nor are they evil enemies. They have their own pressures and concerns that are sometimes at odds with the wishes of the subordinate—and often for good reason.

Altering predispositions toward authority, especially at the extremes, is almost impossible without intensive psychotherapy (psychoanalytic theory and research suggest that such predispositions are deeply rooted in a person's personality and upbringing). However, an awareness of these extremes and the range between them can be very useful in understanding where your own predispositions fall and what the implications are for how you tend to behave in relation to your boss.

If you believe, on the one hand, that you have some tendencies toward counterdependence, you can understand and even predict what your reactions and overreactions are likely to be. If, on the other hand, you believe you have some tendencies toward overdependence, you might question the extent to which your overcompliance or inability to confront real differences may be making both you and your boss less effective.

DEVELOPING AND MANAGING THE RELATIONSHIP

With a clear understanding of both your boss and yourself, you can *usually* establish a way of working together that fits both of you, that is characterized by unambiguous mutual expectations, and that helps you both be more productive and effective. The "Checklist for Managing Your Boss" at the end of this article summarizes some things such a relationship consists of. Following are a few more.

Compatible Work Styles

Above all else, a good working relationship with a boss accommodates differences in work style. For example, in one situation we studied, a manager (who had a relatively good relationship with his superior) realized that during meetings his boss would often become inattentive and sometimes brusque. The subordinate's own style tended to be discursive and exploratory. He would often digress from the topic at hand to deal with background factors, alternative approaches, and so forth. His boss preferred to discuss problems with a minimum of background detail and became impatient and distracted whenever his subordinate digressed from the immediate issue.

Recognizing this difference in style, the manager became terser and more direct during meetings with his boss. To help himself do this, before meetings, he would develop brief agendas that he used as a guide. Whenever he felt that a digression was needed, he explained why. This small shift in his own style made these meetings more effective and far less frustrating for both of them.

Subordinates can adjust their styles in response to their bosses' preferred method for receiving information. Peter Drucker divides bosses into "listeners" and "readers." Some bosses like to get information in report form so they can read and study it. Others work better with information and reports presented in person so they can ask questions. As Drucker points out, the implications are obvious. If your boss is a listener, you brief him or her in person, *then* follow it up with a memo. If your boss is a reader, you cover important items or proposals in a memo or report, *then* discuss them.

Other adjustments can be made according to a boss's decision-making style. Some bosses prefer to be involved in decisions and problems as they arise. These are high-involvement managers who like to keep their hands on the pulse of the operation. Usually their needs (and your own) are best satisfied if you touch base with them on an ad hoc basis. A boss who has a need to be involved will become involved one way or another, so there are advantages to including him or her at your initiative. Other bosses prefer to delegate—they don't want to be involved. They expect you to come to them with major problems and inform them about any important changes.

Creating a compatible relationship also involved drawing on each other's strengths and making up for each other's weaknesses. Because he knew that the boss—the vice president of engineering—was not very good at monitoring his employees' problems, one manager we studied made a point of doing it himself. The stakes were high: the engineers and technicians were all union members, the company worked on a customer-contract basis, and the company had recently experienced a serious strike.

The manager worked closely with his boss, along with people in the scheduling department and the personnel office, to make sure that potential problems were avoided. He also developed an informal arrangement through which his boss would review with him any proposed changes in personnel or assignment policies before taking action. The boss valued his advice and credited his subordinate for improving both the performance of the division and the labor-management climate.

Mutual Expectations

The subordinate who passively assumes that he or she knows what the boss expects is in for trouble. Of course, some superiors will spell out their expectations very explicitly and in great detail. But most do not. And although many corporations have systems that provide a basis for communicating expectations (such as formal planning processes, career planning reviews, and performance appraisal reviews), these systems never work perfectly. Also, between these formal reviews, expectations invariably change.

Ultimately, the burden falls on the subordinate to find out what the boss's expectations are. They can be both broad (such as what kinds of problems the boss wishes to be

informed about and when) as well as very specific (such things as when a particular project
should be completed and what kinds of information the boss needs in the interim).

Getting a boss who tends to be vague or not
explicit to express expectations can be difficult. But effective managers find ways to get
that information. Some will draft a detailed
memo covering key aspects of their work and
then send it to their boss for approval. They
then follow this up with a face-to-face discussion in which they go over each item in the
memo. A discussion like this will often surface
virtually all of the boss's expectations.

Other effective managers will deal with an
inexplicit boss by initiating an ongoing series
of informal discussions about "good management" and "our objectives." Still others find

useful information more indirectly through those who used to work for the boss and through the formal planning systems in which the boss makes commitments to his or her own superior. Which approach you choose, of course, should depend on your understanding of your boss's style.

Developing a workable set of mutual expectations also requires that you communicate your own expectations to the boss, find out if they are realistic, and influence the boss to accept the ones that are important to you. Being able to influence the boss to value your expectations can be particularly important if the boss is an overachiever. Such a boss will often set unrealistically high standards that need to be brought into line with reality.

A Flow of Information

How much information a boss needs about what a subordinate is doing will vary significantly depending on the boss's style, the situation he or she is in, and the confidence the boss has in the subordinate. But it is not uncommon for a boss to need more information than the subordinate would naturally supply or for the subordinate to think the boss knows more than he or she really does. Effective managers recognize that they probably underestimate what their bosses need to know and make sure they find ways to keep them informed through processes that fit their styles.

Managing the flow of information upward is particularly difficult if the boss does not like to hear about problems. Although many people would deny it, bosses often give off signals they want to hear only good news. They show great displeasure—usually non-verbally—when someone tells them about a problem. Ignoring individual achievement, they may even evaluate more favorably subordinates who do not bring problems to them.

Nevertheless, for the good of the organization, the boss, and the subordinate, a superior needs to hear about failures as well as successes. Some subordinates deal with a good-news-only boss by finding indirect ways to get the necessary information to him or her, such as a management information system. Others see to it that potential problems, whether in the form of good surprises or bad news, are communicated immediately.

Dependability and Honesty

Few things are more disabling to a boss than a subordinate on whom he cannot depend, whose work he cannot trust. Almost no one is intentionally undependable, but many managers are inadvertently so because of oversight or uncertainty about the boss's priorities. A commitment to an optimistic delivery date may please a superior in the short term but become a source of displeasure if not honored. It's difficult for a boss to rely on a subordinate who repeatedly slips deadlines. As one president (describing a subordinate) put it: "I'd rather he be more consistent even if he delivered fewer peak successes—at least I could rely on him."

Nor are many managers intentionally dis-
honest with their bosses. But it is easy to
shade the truth and play down issues. Current
concerns often become future surprise problems. It's almost impossible for bosses to
work effectively if they cannot rely on a fairly
accurate reading from their subordinates. Because it undermines credibility, dishonesty is
perhaps the most troubling trait a subordinate
can have. Without a basic level of trust, a boss
feels compelled to check all of a subordinate's
decisions, which makes it difficult to delegate.

Good Use of Time and Resources

Your boss is probably as limited in his or
her store of time, energy, and influence as
you are. Every request you make of your boss
uses up some of these resources, so it's wise

to draw on these resources selectively. This may sound obvious, but many managers use up their boss's time (and some of their own credibility) over relatively trivial issues.

One vice president went to great lengths to get his boss to fire a meddlesome secretary in another department. His boss had to use considerable influence to do it. Understandably, the head of the other department was not pleased. Later, when the vice president wanted to tackle more important problems, he ran into trouble. By using up blue chips on a relatively trivial issue, he had made it difficult for him and his boss to meet more important goals.

No doubt, some subordinates will resent that on top of all their other duties, they also need to take time and energy to manage their relationships with their bosses. Such managers fail to realize the importance of this activity and how it can simplify their jobs by eliminating potentially severe problems. Effective managers recognize that this part of their work is legitimate. Seeing themselves as ultimately responsible for what they achieve in an organization, they know they need to establish and manage relationships with everyone on whom they depend—and that includes the boss.

Checklist for Managing Your Boss

Make sure you understand your boss and his or her context, including:

- ☐ Goals and objectives
- ☐ Pressures

- ☐ Strengths, weaknesses, blind spots
- ☐ Preferred work style

Assess yourself and your needs, including:

- ☐ Strengths and weaknesses
- ☐ Personal style
- ☐ Predisposition toward dependence on authority figures

Develop and maintain a relationship that:

- ☐ Fits both your needs and styles
- ☐ Is characterized by mutual expectations
- ☐ Keeps your boss informed
- ☐ Is based on dependability and honesty
- ☐ Selectively uses your boss's time and resources

ABOUT THE AUTHORS

John J. Gabarro is the UPS Foundation Professor of Human Resource Management, Emeritus at Harvard Business School.

John P. Kotter is the Konosuke Matsushita Professor of Leadership, Emeritus at Harvard Business School.

ALSO BY THESE AUTHORS

John J. Gabarro

Harvard Business Press Books

Breaking Through: The Making of Minority Executives in Corporate America
with David A. Thomas

The Dynamics of Taking Charge

Managing People and Organizations

When Professionals Have to Lead
with Thomas J. DeLong, John J. Gabarro,
Robert J. Lees, and Helen Rees

John J. Gabarro and John P. Kotter

***Harvard Business Review* Articles**

"When a New Manager Takes Charge"

John P. Kotter

Harvard Business Press Books

John P. Kotter on What Leaders Really Do

Leading Change

The Heart of Change: Real-Life Stories of How People Change Their Organizations
with Dan S. Cohen

Harvard Business Review Articles

"Choosing Strategies for Change"

"Leading Change: Why Transformation Efforts Fail"

"Power, Dependence, and Effective Management"

"What Leaders Really Do"

"What Effective General Managers Really Do"

Article Summary

The Idea in Brief

Managing our *bosses*? Isn't that merely manipulation? Corporate cozying up? Out-and-out apple polishing? In fact, we manage our bosses for very good reasons: to get resources to do the best job, not only for ourselves, but for our bosses and our companies as well. We actively pursue a healthy and productive working relationship based on mutual respect and understanding—understanding our own and our bosses' strengths, weaknesses, goals, work styles, and needs. Here's what can happen when we don't:

Example: A new president with a formal work style replaced someone who'd been looser, more intuitive. The new president preferred written reports and structured meetings. One of his managers found this too controlling. He seldom sent background information, and was often blindsided by unanticipated questions. His boss found their meetings inefficient and frustrating. The manager had to resign.

In contrast, here's how another manager's sensitivity to this same boss's style really paid off:

Example: This manager identified the kinds and frequency of information the president wanted. He sent ahead background reports and discussion agendas. The result? Highly productive meetings and even more innovative problem solving than with his previous boss.

Managers often don't realize how much their bosses depend on them. They need cooperation, reliability, and honesty from their direct reports. Many managers also don't realize how much *they* depend on their bosses—for links to the rest of the organization, for setting priorities, and for obtaining critical resources.

Recognizing this mutual dependence, effective managers seek out information about the boss's concerns and are sensitive to his work style. They also understand how their own attitudes toward authority can sabotage the relationship. Some see the boss as the enemy and fight him at every turn; others are overly compliant, viewing the boss as an all-wise parent.

The Idea in Practice

You can benefit from this mutual dependence and develop a very productive relationship with your boss by focusing on:

- *Compatible work styles.* Bosses process information differently. "Listeners" prefer to be briefed in person so they can ask questions. "Readers" want to process written information first, and then meet to discuss.

Decision-making styles also vary. Some bosses are highly involved. Touch base with them frequently. Others prefer to delegate. Inform them about important decisions you've already made.

- *Mutual expectations.* Don't passively assume you know what the boss expects. Find out. With some bosses, write detailed outlines of your work for their approval. With others, carefully planned discussions are key.

Also, communicate *your* expectations to find out if they are realistic. Persuade the boss to accept the most important ones.

- *Information flow.* Managers typically underestimate what their bosses need to know—

and what they *do* know. Keep the boss informed through processes that fit his style.
Be forthright about both good and bad news.

- *Dependability and honesty.* Trustworthy subordinates only make promises they can keep
  and don't shade the truth or play down difficult issues.

- *Good use of time and resources.* Don't
  waste your boss's time with trivial issues.
  Selectively draw on his time and resources
  to meet the most important goals—yours,
  his, and the company's.

HOW TO
WRITE A GREAT
BUSINESS PLAN

HARVARD BUSINESS REVIEW
CLASSICS

HOW TO WRITE A GREAT BUSINESS PLAN

William A. Sahlman

Harvard Business Review Press
Boston, Massachusetts

Library of Congress Cataloging-in-Publication Data
Sahlman, William Andrews.
  How to write a great business plan / William A. Sahlman.
    p. cm. — (Harvard business review classics)
  ISBN 978-1-4221-2142-9
  1. Business planning—Handbooks, manuals, etc. I. Title.
  HD30.28.S234 2008
  658.4′01—dc22

                                    2007041317

THE
HARVARD BUSINESS REVIEW
CLASSICS SERIES

Since 1922, *Harvard Business Review* has
been a leading source of breakthrough ideas
in management practice—many of which still
speak to and influence us today. The HBR
Classics series now offers you the opportunity
to make these seminal pieces a part of your
permanent management library. Each volume contains a groundbreaking idea that has
shaped best practices and inspired countless
managers around the world—and will change
how you think about the business world today.

HOW TO
WRITE A GREAT
BUSINESS PLAN

F ew areas of business attract as much attention as new ventures, and few aspects of new-venture creation attract as much attention as the business plan. Countless books and articles in the popular press dissect the topic. A growing number of annual business-plan contests are springing up across the United States and, increasingly, in other countries. Both graduate and undergraduate schools devote entire courses to the subject. Indeed, judging by all the hoopla surrounding business plans, you would think that the only things standing between a would-be entrepreneur and spectacular success are glossy five-color charts, a bundle of meticulous-looking spreadsheets, and a decade of month-by-month financial projections.

Nothing could be further from the truth. In my experience with hundreds of entrepreneurial start-ups, business plans rank no higher than 2—on a scale from 1 to 10—as a predictor of a new venture's success. (For intrapreneurial start-ups, see "Business Plans: For Entrepreneurs Only?" at the end of this article.) And sometimes, in fact, the more elaborately crafted the document, the more likely the venture is to, well, flop, for lack of a more euphemistic word.

What's wrong with most business plans? The answer is relatively straightforward. Most waste too much ink on numbers and devote too little to the information that really matters to intelligent investors. As every seasoned investor knows, financial projections for a new company—especially detailed, month-by-month projections that stretch out for more than a year—are an act of imagination. An entrepreneurial venture faces far too many unknowns to predict revenues, let alone profits. Moreover, few if any entrepreneurs correctly anticipate how much capital and time will be required to accomplish their objectives. Typically, they are wildly optimistic, padding their projections. Investors know about the padding effect and therefore discount the figures in business plans. These maneuvers create a vicious circle of inaccuracy that benefits no one.

Don't misunderstand me: business plans should include some numbers. But those numbers should appear mainly in the form of a business model that shows the entrepreneurial team has thought through the key drivers of the venture's success or failure. In manufacturing, such a driver might be the yield on a production process; in magazine publishing, the anticipated renewal rate; or in software, the impact of using various distribution channels. The model should also address the break-even issue: At what level of sales does the business begin to make a profit? And even more important, When does cash flow turn positive? Without a doubt, these questions deserve a few pages in any business plan. Near the back.

What goes at the front? What information does a good business plan contain?

If you want to speak the language of investors—and also make sure you have asked yourself the right questions before setting out on the most daunting journey of a businessperson's career—I recommend basing your business plan on the framework that follows. It does not provide the kind of "winning" formula touted by some current how-to books and software programs for entrepreneurs. Nor is it a guide to brain surgery. Rather, the framework systematically assesses the four interdependent factors critical to every new venture:

The People. The men and women starting and running the venture, as well as
the outside parties providing key services
or important resources for it, such as its
lawyers, accountants, and suppliers.

The Opportunity. A profile of the business itself—what it will sell and to whom,
whether the business can grow and how
fast, what its economics are, who and what
stand in the way of success.

The Context. The big picture—the regulatory environment, interest rates, demo-
graphic trends, inflation, and the like—
basically, factors that inevitably change
but cannot be controlled by the entrepreneur.

Risk and Reward. An assessment of everything that can go wrong and right, and a discussion of how the entrepreneurial team can respond.

The assumption behind the framework is that great businesses have attributes that are easy to identify but hard to assemble. They have an experienced, energetic managerial team from the top to the bottom. The team's members have skills and experiences directly relevant to the opportunity they are pursuing. Ideally, they will have worked successfully together in the past. The opportunity has an attractive, sustainable business model; it is possible to create a competitive edge and defend it. Many options exist for expanding the scale and scope of the business, and these options are unique to the enterprise and its team. Value can be extracted from the business in a number of ways either through a positive harvest event—a sale—or by scaling down or liquidating. The context is favorable with respect to both the regulatory and the macro-economic environments. Risk is understood, and the team has considered ways to mitigate the impact of difficult events. In short, great businesses have the four parts of the framework completely covered. If only reality were so neat.

THE PEOPLE

When I receive a business plan, I always read the résumé section first. Not because the people part of the new venture is the most important, but because without the right team, none of the other parts really matters.

I read the résumés of the venture's team with a list of questions in mind. (See "Who Are These People, Anyway?" at the end of this article.) All these questions get at the same three issues about the venture's team members: What do they know? Whom do they know? and How well are they known?

What and whom they know are matters of insight and experience. How familiar are the team members with industry players and dynamics? Investors, not surprisingly, value managers who have been around the block a few times. A business plan should candidly describe each team member's knowledge of the new venture's type of product or service;

{ 9 }

its production processes; and the market itself, from competitors to customers. It also helps to indicate whether the team members have worked together before. Not played—as in roomed together in college—but *worked*.

Investors also look favorably on a team that is known because the real world often prefers not to deal with start-ups. They're too unpredictable. That changes, however, when the new company is run by people well known to suppliers, customers, and employees. Their enterprise may be brand new, but they aren't. The surprise element of working with a start-up is somewhat ameliorated.

Finally, the people part of a business plan should receive special care because, simply stated, that's where most intelligent in-

vestors focus their attention. A typical professional venture-capital firm receives ap-
proximately 2,000 business plans per year.
These plans are filled with tantalizing ideas
for new products and services that will
change the world and reap billions in the
process—or so they say. But the fact is, most
venture capitalists believe that ideas are a
dime a dozen: only execution skills count. As
Arthur Rock, a venture capital legend associated with the formation of such companies as
Apple, Intel, and Teledyne, states, "I invest
in people, not ideas." Rock also has said, "If
you can find good people, if they're wrong
about the product, they'll make a switch, so
what good is it to understand the product
that they're talking about in the first place?"

Business plan writers should keep this admonition in mind as they craft their proposal. Talk about the people—exhaustively. And if there is nothing solid about their experience and abilities to herald, then the entrepreneurial team should think again about launching the venture.

THE OPPORTUNITY

When it comes to the opportunity itself, a good business plan begins by focusing on two questions: Is the total market for the venture's product or service large, rapidly growing, or both? Is the industry now, or can it become, structurally attractive? Entrepreneurs and investors look for large or rapidly growing markets mainly because it is often easier to obtain a share of a growing market than to fight with entrenched competitors for a share of a mature or stagnant market. Smart investors, in fact, try hard to identify high-growth-potential markets early in their evolution: that's where the big payoffs are. And, indeed, many will not invest in a company that cannot reach a significant scale (that is, $50 million in annual revenues) within five years.

As for attractiveness, investors are obviously looking for markets that actually allow businesses to make some money. But that's not the no-brainer it seems. In the late 1970s, the computer disk-drive business looked very attractive. The technology was new and exciting. Dozens of companies jumped into the fray, aided by an army of professional investors. Twenty years later, however, the thrill is gone for managers and investors alike. Disk drive companies must design products to meet the perceived needs of original equipment manufacturers (OEMs) and end users. Selling a product to OEMs is complicated. The customers are large relative to most of their suppliers. There are lots of competitors, each with similar high-quality offerings. Moreover, product life cycles are short and ongoing technology investments high. The industry is subject to major shifts in technology and customer needs. Intense rivalry leads to lower prices and, hence, lower margins. In short, the disk drive industry is simply not set up to make people a lot of money; it's a structural disaster area.

The information services industry, by contrast, is paradise. Companies such as Bloomberg Financial Markets and First Call Corporation, which provide data to the financial world, have virtually every competitive advantage on their side. First, they can assemble or create *proprietary* content—content that, by the way, is like life's blood to thousands of money managers and stock analysts around the world. And although it is often expensive to develop the service and to acquire initial customers, once up and running, these companies can deliver content to customers very cheaply. Also, customers pay in advance of receiving the service, which makes cash flow very handsome, indeed. In short, the structure of the information services industry is beyond attractive: it's gorgeous. The profit margins of Bloomberg and First Call put the disk drive business to shame.

Thus, the first step for entrepreneurs is to make sure they are entering an industry that is large and/or growing, and one that's structurally attractive. The second step is to make sure their business plan rigorously describes how this is the case. And if it isn't the case, their business plan needs to specify how the venture will still manage to make enough of a profit that investors (or potential employees or suppliers, for that matter) will want to participate.

Once it examines the new venture's industry, a business plan must describe in detail how the company will build and launch its product or service into the marketplace. Again, a series of questions should guide the discussion. (See "The Opportunity of a Lifetime—or Is It?" at the end of this article.)

Often the answers to these questions reveal a fatal flaw in the business. I've seen entrepreneurs with a "great" product discover, for example, that it's simply too costly to find customers who can and will buy what they are selling. Economically viable access to customers is the key to business, yet many entrepreneurs take the *Field of Dreams* approach to this notion: build it, and they will come. That strategy works in the movies but is not very sensible in the real world.

It is not always easy to answer questions about the likely consumer response to new products or services. The market is as fickle as it is unpredictable. (Who would have guessed that plug-in room deodorizers would sell?) One entrepreneur I know proposed to introduce an electronic news-clipping service. He made his pitch to a prospective venture-capital investor who rejected the plan, stating, "I just don't think the dogs will eat the dog food." Later, when the entrepreneur's company went public, he sent the venture capitalist an anonymous package containing an empty can of dog food and a copy of his prospectus. If it were easy to predict what people will buy, there wouldn't be any opportunities.

Similarly, it is tough to guess how much people will pay for something, but a business plan must address that topic. Sometimes, the dogs will eat the dog food, but only at a price less than cost. Investors always look for opportunities for value pricing—that is, markets in which the costs to produce the product are low, but consumers will still pay a lot for it. No one is dying to invest in a company when margins are skinny. Still, there is money to be made in inexpensive products and services—even in commodities. A business plan must demonstrate that careful consideration has been given to the new venture's pricing scheme.

The list of questions about the new venture's opportunity focuses on the direct revenues and the costs of producing and marketing a product. That's fine, as far as it goes. A sensible proposal, however, also involves assessing the business model from a perspective that takes into account the investment required—that is, the balance sheet side of the equation. The following questions should also be addressed so that investors can understand the cash flow implications of pursuing an opportunity:

- When does the business have to buy resources, such as supplies, raw materials, and people?

- When does the business have to pay for them?

- How long does it take to acquire a customer?

- How long before the customer sends the business a check?

- How much capital equipment is required to support a dollar of sales?

Investors, of course, are looking for businesses in which management can buy low, sell high, collect early, and pay late. The business plan needs to spell out how close to that ideal the new venture is expected to come. Even if the answer is "not very"—and it usually is—at least the truth is out there to discuss.

The opportunity section of a business plan must also bring a few other issues to the surface. First, it must demonstrate and analyze how an opportunity can grow—in other words, how the new venture can expand its range of products or services, customer base, or geographic scope. Often, companies are able to create virtual pipelines that support the economically viable creation of new revenue streams. In the publishing business, for example, *Inc.* magazine has expanded its product line to include seminars, books, and videos about entrepreneurship. Similarly, building on the success of its personal-finance software program Quicken, Intuit now sells software for electronic banking, small-business accounting, and tax preparation, as well as personal-printing supplies and on-line information services—to name just a few of its highly profitable ancillary spin-offs.

Now, lots of business plans runneth over on the subject of the new venture's potential for growth and expansion. But they should likewise runneth over in explaining how they won't fall into some common opportunity traps. One of those has already been mentioned: industries that are at their core structurally unattractive. But there are others. The world of invention, for example, is fraught with danger. Over the past 15 years, I have seen scores of individuals who have devised a better mousetrap—newfangled creations from inflatable pillows for use on airplanes to automated car-parking systems. Few of these idea-driven companies have really taken off, however. I'm not entirely sure why. Sometimes, the inventor refuses to spend the money required by or share the rewards sufficiently with the business side of the company. Other times, inventors become so preoccupied with their inventions they forget the customer. Whatever the reason, better-mousetrap businesses have an uncanny way of malfunctioning.

Another opportunity trap that business plans—and entrepreneurs in general—need to pay attention to is the tricky business of arbitrage. Basically, arbitrage ventures are created to take advantage of some pricing disparity in the marketplace. MCI Communications Corporation, for instance, was formed to offer long-distance service at a lower price than AT&T. Some of the industry consolidations going on today reflect a different kind of arbitrage—the ability to buy small businesses at a wholesale price, roll them up together into a larger package, and take them public at a retail price, all without necessarily adding value in the process.

Taking advantage of arbitrage opportunities is a viable and potentially profitable way to enter a business. In the final analysis, however, all arbitrage opportunities evaporate. It is not a question of whether, only when. The trick in these businesses is to use the arbitrage profits to build a more enduring business model, and business plans must explain how and when that will occur.

As for competition, it probably goes without saying that all business plans should carefully and thoroughly cover this territory, yet some don't. That is a glaring omission. For starters, every business plan should answer the following questions about the competition:

- Who are the new venture's current competitors?

- What resources do they control? What are their strengths and weaknesses?

- How will they respond to the new venture's decision to enter the business?

- How can the new venture respond to its competitors' response?

- Who else might be able to observe and exploit the same opportunity?

- Are there ways to co-opt potential or actual competitors by forming alliances?

Business is like chess: to be successful, you must anticipate several moves in advance. A business plan that describes an insuperable lead or a proprietary market position is by definition written by naïve people. That goes not just for the competition section of the business plan but for the entire discussion of the opportunity. All opportunities have promise; all have vulnerabilities. A good business plan doesn't whitewash the latter. Rather, it proves that the entrepreneurial team knows the good, the bad, and the ugly that the venture faces ahead.

THE CONTEXT

Opportunities exist in a context. At one level is the macroeconomic environment, including the level of economic activity, inflation, exchange rates, and interest rates. At another level are the wide range of government rules and regulations that affect the opportunity and how resources are marshaled to exploit it. Examples extend from tax policy to the rules about raising capital for a private or public company. And at yet another level are factors like technology that define the limits of what a business or its competitors can accomplish.

Context often has a tremendous impact on every aspect of the entrepreneurial process, from identification of opportunity to harvest. In some cases, changes in some contextual factor create opportunity. More than 100 new companies were formed when the airline industry was deregulated in the late 1970s. The context for financing was also favorable, enabling new entrants like People Express to go to the public market for capital even before starting operations.

Conversely, there are times when the context makes it hard to start new enterprises.

The recession of the early 1990s combined with a difficult financing environment for new companies: venture capital disbursements were low, as was the amount of capital raised in the public markets. (Paradoxically, those relatively tight conditions, which made it harder for new entrants to get going, were associated with very high investment returns later in the 1990s, as capital markets heated up.)

Sometimes, a shift in context turns an unattractive business into an attractive one, and vice versa. Consider the case of a packaging company some years ago that was performing so poorly it was about to be put on the block. Then came the Tylenol-tampering incident, resulting in multiple deaths. The packaging company happened to have an efficient mechanism for installing tamper-proof seals, and in a matter of weeks its financial performance could have been called spectacular. Conversely, U.S. tax reforms enacted in 1986 created havoc for companies in the real estate business, eliminating almost every positive incentive to invest. Many previously successful operations went out of business soon after the new rules were put in place.

Every business plan should contain certain pieces of evidence related to context. First, the entrepreneurs should show a heightened awareness of the new venture's context and how it helps or hinders their specific proposal. Second, and more important, they should demonstrate that they know the venture's context will inevitably change and describe how those changes might affect the business. Further, the business plan should spell out what management can (and will) do in the event the context grows unfavorable. Finally, the business plan should explain the ways (if any) in which management can affect context in a positive way. For example, management might be able to have an impact on regulations or on industry standards through lobbying efforts.

RISK AND REWARD

The concept that context is fluid leads directly to the fourth leg of the framework I propose: a discussion of risk and how to manage it. I've come to think of a good business plan as a snapshot of an event in the future. That's quite a feat to begin with—taking a picture of the unknown. But the best business plans go beyond that; they are like movies of the future. They show the people, the opportunity, and the context from multiple angles. They offer a plausible, coherent story of what lies ahead. They unfold possibilities of action and reaction.

Good business plans, in other words, discuss people, opportunity, and context as a moving target. All three factors (and the relationship among them) are likely to change over time as a company evolves from start-up to ongoing enterprise. Therefore, any business plan worth the time it takes to write or read needs to focus attention on the dynamic aspects of the entrepreneurial process.

Of course, the future is hard to predict. Still, it is possible to give potential investors a sense of the kind and class of risk and reward they are assuming with a new venture. All it takes is a pencil and two simple drawings. (See "Visualizing Risk and Reward" at the end of this article.) But even with these drawings, risk is, well, risky. In reality, there are no immutable distributions of outcomes. It is ultimately the responsibility of management to change the distribution, to increase the likelihood and consequences of success, and to decrease the likelihood and implications of problems.

One of the great myths about entre-preneurs is that they are risk seekers. All sane people want to avoid risk. As Harvard Business School professor (and venture capitalist) Howard Stevenson says, true entre-preneurs want to capture all the reward and give all the risk to others. The best business is a post office box to which people send cashier's checks. Yet risk is unavoidable. So what does that mean for a business plan?

It means that the plan must unflinchingly confront the risks ahead—in terms of people, opportunity, and context. What happens if one of the new venture's leaders leaves? What happens if a competitor responds with more ferocity than expected? What happens if there is a revolution in Namibia, the source of a key raw material? What will management actually *do*?

Those are hard questions for an entrepreneur to pose, especially when seeking capital. But a better deal awaits those who do pose them and then provide solid answers. A new venture, for example, might be highly leveraged and therefore very sensitive to interest rates. Its business plan would benefit enormously by stating that management intends to hedge its exposure through the financial-futures market by purchasing a contract that does well when interest rates go up. That is the equivalent of offering investors insurance. (It also makes sense for the business itself.)

Finally, one important area in the realm of risk/reward management relates to harvesting. Venture capitalists often ask if a company is "IPOable," by which they mean, Can the company be taken public at some point in the future? (See also "A Glossary of Business Plan Terms" at the end of this article.) Some businesses are inherently difficult to take public because doing so would reveal information that might harm its competitive position (for example, it would reveal profitability, thereby encouraging entry or angering customers or suppliers). Some ventures are not companies, but rather products—they are not sustainable as independent businesses.

Therefore, the business plan should talk candidly about the end of the process. How will the investor eventually get money out of the business, assuming it is successful, even if only marginally so? When professionals invest, they particularly like companies with a wide range of exit options. They like companies that work hard to preserve and enhance those options along the way, companies that don't, for example, unthinkingly form alliances with big corporations that could someday actually *buy* them. Investors feel a lot better about risk if the venture's endgame is discussed up front. There is an old saying, "If you don't know where you are going, any road will get you there." In crafting sensible entrepreneurial strategies, just the opposite is true: you had better know where you might end up and have a map for getting there. A business plan should be the place where that map is drawn, for, as every traveler knows, a journey is a lot less risky when you have directions.

THE DEAL AND BEYOND

Once a business plan is written, of course, the goal is to land a deal. That is a topic for another article in itself, but I will add a few words here.

When I talk to young (and old) entrepreneurs looking to finance their ventures, they obsess about the valuation and terms of the deal they will receive. Their explicit goal seems to be to minimize the dilution they will suffer in raising capital. Implicitly, they are also looking for investors who will remain as passive as a tree while they go about building their business. On the food chain of investors, it seems, doctors and dentists are best and venture capitalists are worst because of the degree to which the latter group demands control and a large share of the returns.

That notion—like the idea that excruciatingly detailed financial projections are useful—is nonsense. From whom you raise capital is often more important than the terms. New ventures are inherently risky, as I've noted; what can go wrong will. When that happens, unsophisticated investors panic, get angry, and often refuse to advance the company more money. Sophisticated investors, by contrast, roll up their sleeves and help the company solve its problems. Often, they've had lots of experience saving sinking ships. They are typically process literate. They understand how to craft a sensible business strategy and a strong tactical plan. They know how to recruit, compensate, and motivate team members. They are also familiar with the Byzantine ins and outs of going public—an event most entrepreneurs face but once in a lifetime. This kind of know-how is worth the money needed to buy it.

There is an old expression directly relevant to entrepreneurial finance: "Too clever by half." Often, deal makers get very creative, crafting all sorts of payoff and option schemes. That usually backfires. My experience has proven again and again that sensible deals have the following six characteristics:

- They are simple.

- They are fair.

- They emphasize trust rather than legal ties.

- They do not blow apart if actual differs slightly from plan.

- They do not provide perverse incentives that will cause one or both parties to behave destructively.

- They are written on a pile of papers no greater than one-quarter inch thick.

But even these six simple rules miss an important point. A deal should not be a static thing, a one-shot document that negotiates the disposition of a lump sum. Instead, it is incumbent upon entrepreneurs, before they go searching for funding, to think about capital acquisition as a dynamic process—to figure out how much money they will need and when they will need it.

How is that accomplished? The trick is for the entrepreneurial team to treat the new venture as a series of experiments. Before launching the whole show, launch a little piece of it. Convene a focus group to test the product, build a prototype and watch it perform, conduct a regional or local rollout of a service. Such an exercise reveals the true economics of the business and can help enormously in determining how much money the new venture actually requires and in what stages. Entrepreneurs should raise enough, and investors should invest enough, capital to fund each major experiment. Experiments, of course, can feel expensive and risky. But I've seen them prevent disasters and help create successes. I consider it a prerequisite of putting together a winning deal.

BEWARE THE ALBATROSS

Among the many sins committed by business plan writers is arrogance. In today's economy, few ideas are truly proprietary. Moreover, there has never been a time in recorded history when the supply of capital did not outrace the supply of opportunity. The true half-life of opportunity is decreasing with the passage of time.

A business plan must not be an albatross that hangs around the neck of the entrepreneurial team, dragging it into oblivion. Instead, a business plan must be a call for action, one that recognizes management's responsibility to fix what is broken proactively and in real time. Risk is inevitable, avoiding risk impossible. Risk management is the key, always tilting the venture in favor of reward and away from risk.

A plan must demonstrate mastery of the entire entrepreneurial process, from identification of opportunity to harvest. It is not a way to separate unsuspecting investors from their money by hiding the fatal flaw. For in the final analysis, the only one being fooled is the entrepreneur.

We live today in the golden age of entrepreneurship. Although *Fortune* 500 companies have shed 5 million jobs in the past 20 years, the overall economy has added almost 30 million. Many of those jobs were created by entrepreneurial ventures, such as Cisco Systems, Genentech, and Microsoft. Each of those companies started with a business plan. Is that why they succeeded? There is no knowing for sure. But there is little doubt that crafting a business plan so that it thoroughly and candidly addresses the ingredients of success—people, opportunity, context, and the risk/reward picture—is vitally important. In the absence of a crystal ball, in fact, a business plan built of the *right* information and analysis can only be called indispensable.

Business Plans: For Entrepreneurs Only?

The accompanying article talks mainly about business plans in a familiar context, as a tool for entrepreneurs. But quite often, start-ups are launched within established companies. Do those new ventures require business plans? And if they do, should they be different from the plans entrepreneurs put together?

The answer to the first question is an emphatic yes; the answer to the second, an equally emphatic no. All new ventures—whether they are funded by venture capitalists or, as is the case with intrapreneurial businesses, by shareholders—need to pass the same acid tests. After all, the marketplace does not differentiate between products or services based on who is pouring money into them behind the scenes.

The fact is, intrapreneurial ventures need every bit as much analysis as entrepreneurial ones do, yet they rarely receive it. Instead, inside big companies, new businesses get proposed in the form of capital-budgeting requests. These faceless documents are subject to detailed financial scrutiny and a consensus-building process, as the project wends its way through the chain of command, what I call the "neutron bomb" model of project governance. However, in the history of such proposals, a plan never has been submitted that did not promise returns in excess of corporate hurdle rates. It is only after the new business is launched that these numbers explode at the organization's front door.

That problem could be avoided in large part if intrapreneurial ventures followed the guidelines set out in the accompanying article. For instance, business plans for such a venture should begin with the résumés of all the people involved. What has the team done in the past that would suggest it would be successful in the future, and so on? In addition, the new venture's product or service should be fully analyzed in terms of its opportunity and context. Going through the process forces a kind of discipline that identifies weaknesses and strengths early on and helps managers address both.

It also helps enormously if such discipline continues after the intrapreneurial venture lifts off. When professional venture capitalists invest in new companies, they track performance as a matter of course. But in large companies, scrutiny of a new venture is often inconsistent. That shouldn't or needn't be the case. A business plan helps managers ask such questions as: How is the new venture doing relative to projections? What decisions has the team made in response to new information? Have changes in the context made additional funding necessary? How could the team have predicted those changes? Such questions not only keep a new venture running smoothly but also help an organization learn from its mistakes and triumphs.

Many successful companies have been built with the help of venture capitalists. Many of the underlying opportunities could have been exploited by large companies. Why weren't they? Perhaps useful lessons can be learned by studying the world of independent ventures, one lesson being: Write a great business plan.

Who Are These People, Anyway?

Fourteen "personal" questions every business plan should answer.

- Where are the founders from?
- Where have they been educated?
- Where have they worked—and for whom?
- What have they accomplished—professionally and personally—in the past?

- What is their reputation within the business community?

- What experience do they have that is directly relevant to the opportunity they are pursuing?

- What skills, abilities, and knowledge do they have?

- How realistic are they about the venture's chances for success and the tribulations it will face?

- Who else needs to be on the team?

- Are they prepared to recruit high-quality people?

- How will they respond to adversity?

- Do they have the mettle to make the inevitable hard choices that have to be made?

- How committed are they to this venture?

- What are their motivations?

The Opportunity of a Lifetime—or Is It?

Nine questions about the business every business plan should answer.

- Who is the new venture's customer?

- How does the customer make decisions about buying this product or service?

- To what degree is the product or service a compelling purchase for the customer?

- How will the product or service be priced?

- How will the venture reach all the identified customer segments?

- How much does it cost (in time and resources) to acquire a customer?

- How much does it cost to produce and deliver the product or service?

- How much does it cost to support a customer?

- How easy is it to retain a customer?

Visualizing Risk and Reward

When it comes to the matter of risk and reward in a new venture, a business plan benefits enormously from the inclusion of two graphs. Perhaps *graphs* is the wrong word; these are really just schematic pictures that illustrate the most likely relationship between risk and reward, that is, the relationship between the opportunity and its economics. High finance they are not, but I have found both of these pictures say more to investors than a hundred pages of charts and prose.

The first picture depicts the amount of money needed to launch the new venture, time to positive cash flow, and the expected magnitude of the payoff.

This image helps the investor understand the depth and duration of negative cash flow, as well as the relationship between the investment and the possible return. The ideal, needless to say, is to have cash flow early and often. But most investors are intrigued by the picture even when the cash

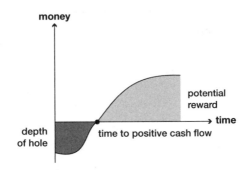

outflow is high and long—as long as the cash in-flow is more so.

Of course, since the world of new ventures is populated by wild-eyed optimists, you might expect the picture to display a shallower hole and a steeper reward slope than it should. It usually does. But to be honest, even that kind of picture belongs in the business plan because it is a fair warning to investors that the new venture's team is completely out of touch with reality and should be avoided at all costs.

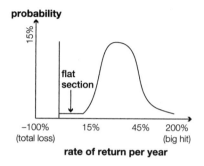

The second picture complements the first. It shows investors the range of possible returns and the likelihood of achieving them. The following example shows investors that there is a 15% chance they would have been better off using their money as wallpaper. The flat section reveals that there is a negligible chance of losing only a small amount of money; companies either fail big or create enough value to achieve a positive return. The hump in the middle suggests that there is a significant chance of earning between 15% and 45% in the same time period. And finally, there is a small chance that the initial outlay of cash will spawn a 200% internal rate of return, which might have occurred if you had happened to invest in Microsoft when it was a private company.

Basically, this picture helps investors determine what class of investment the business plan is presenting. Is the new venture drilling for North Sea oil—highly risky with potentially big payoffs—or is it digging development wells in Texas, which happens to be less of a geological gamble and probably less lucrative, too? This image answers that kind of question. It's then up to the investors to decide how much risk they want to live with against what kind of odds.

Again, the people who write business plans might be inclined to skew the picture to make it look as if the probability of a significant return is downright huge and the possibility of loss is negligible. And, again, I would say therein lies the picture's beauty. What it claims, checked against the investor's sense of reality and experience, should serve as a simple pictorial caveat emptor.

A Glossary of Business Plan Terms

What They Say...	and What They Really Mean
We conservatively project...	We read a book that said we had to be a $50 million company in five years, and we reverse-engineered the numbers.
We took our best guess and divided by 2.	We accidentally divided by 0.5.
We project a 10% margin.	We did not modify any of the assumptions in the business plan template

	that we downloaded from the Internet.
The project is 98% complete.	To complete the remaining 2% will take as long as it took to create the initial 98% but will cost twice as much.
Our business model is proven…	if you take the evidence from the past week for the best of our 50 locations and extrapolate it for all the others.
We have a six-month lead.	We tried not to find out how many other people have a six-month lead.
We only need a 10% market share.	So do the other 50 entrants getting funded.
Customers are clamoring for our product.	We have not yet asked them to pay for it. Also, all

	of our current customers are relatives.
We are the low-cost producer.	We have not produced anything yet, but we are confident that we will be able to.
We have no competition.	Only IBM, Microsoft, Netscape, and Sun have announced plans to enter the business.
Our management team has a great deal of experience . . .	consuming the product or service.
A select group of investors is considering the plan.	We mailed a copy of the plan to everyone in Pratt's Guide.
We seek a value-added investor.	We are looking for a passive, dumb-as-rocks investor.

If you invest on our terms, you will earn a 68% internal rate of return.

If everything that could ever conceivably go right does go right, you might get your money back.

ABOUT THE AUTHOR

William A. Sahlman is the Dimitri V. d'Arbeloff–Class of 1955 Professor of Business Administration at Harvard Business School. He has written numerous articles on topics including entrepreneurial management, venture capital and private equity, deal structuring, and the role of entrepreneurship in the global economy and has published over 150 case studies on entrepreneurial ventures around the world.

The most important management ideas all in one place.

We hope you enjoyed this book from *Harvard Business Review*. For the best ideas HBR has to offer turn to HBR's 10 Must Reads Boxed Set. From books on leadership and strategy to managing yourself and others, this 6-book collection delivers articles on the most essential business topics to help you succeed.

HBR's 10 Must Reads Series

The definitive collection of ideas and best practices on our most sought-after topics from the best minds in business.

- Change Management
- Collaboration
- Communication
- Emotional Intelligence
- Innovation
- Leadership
- Making Smart Decisions

- Managing Across Cultures
- Managing People
- Managing Yourself
- Strategic Marketing
- Strategy
- Teams
- The Essentials

hbr.org/mustreads

Buy for your team, clients, or event.
Visit hbr.org/bulksales for quantity discount rates.

Harvard
Business
Review
Press

DO YOU WANT TO KEEP YOUR CUSTOMERS FOREVER?

HARVARD BUSINESS REVIEW
CLASSICS

DO YOU WANT TO KEEP YOUR CUSTOMERS FOREVER?

B. Joseph Pine II, Don Peppers, and
Martha Rogers

Harvard Business Review Press
Boston, Massachusetts

Library-of-Congress cataloging information forthcoming

ISBN: 978-1-4221-4027-7

THE HARVARD BUSINESS
REVIEW CLASSICS SERIES

Since 1922, *Harvard Business Review* has
been a leading source of breakthrough ideas
in management practice—many of which still
speak to and influence us today. The HBR
Classics series now offers you the opportunity
to make these seminal pieces a part of your
permanent management library. Each volume
contains a groundbreaking idea that has
shaped best practices and inspired countless
managers around the world—and will change
how you think about the business world today.

DO YOU WANT TO KEEP YOUR CUSTOMERS FOREVER?

Customers, whether consumers or businesses, do not want more choices. They want exactly what they want—when, where, and how they want it—and technology now makes it possible for companies to give it to them. Interactive and database technology permits companies to amass huge amounts of data on individual customers' needs and preferences. And information technology and flexible manufacturing systems enable

{ 1 }

companies to customize large volumes of
goods or services for individual customers
at a relatively low cost. But few companies
are exploiting this potential. Most managers
continue to view the world through the twin
lenses of mass marketing and mass production. To handle their increasingly turbulent
and fragmented markets, they try to churn
out a greater variety of goods and services
and to target ever finer market segments with
more tailored advertising messages. But
these managers only end up bombarding
their customers with too many choices.

A company that aspires to give customers
exactly what they want must look at the world
through new lenses. It must use technology
to become two things: a *mass customizer* that

efficiently provides individually customized goods and services, and a *one-to-one marketer* that elicits information from each customer about his or her specific needs and preferences. The twin logic of mass customization and one-to-one marketing binds producer and consumer together in what we call a *learning relationship*—an ongoing connection that becomes smarter as the two interact with each other, collaborating to meet the consumer's needs over time.

In learning relationships, individual customers teach the company more and more about their preferences and needs, giving the company an immense competitive advantage. The more customers teach the company, the better it becomes at providing exactly what they want—exactly how they want it—and the more difficult it will be for a competitor to entice them away. Even if a competitor were to build the exact same capabilities, a customer already involved in a learning relationship with the company would have to spend an inordinate amount of time and energy teaching the competitor what the company already knows.

Because of this singularly powerful competitive advantage, a company that can cultivate learning relationships with its customers should be able to retain their business virtually forever—provided that it continues to supply high-quality customized products or services at reasonably competitive prices and does not miss the next technology wave. (Learning relationships would not have saved a buggy-whip manufacturer from the automobile.)

One company that excels at building learning relationships with its customers is named, appropriately enough, Individual, Inc. This Burlington, Massachusetts, company, which competes with wire, clipping, and information-retrieval services, provides published news stories selected to fit the specific, ever changing interests of each client. Instead of having to sort through a mountain of clippings or having to master the arcane commands needed to search databases, Individual's customers— which include such diverse companies as MCI Telecommunications, McKinsey &

Company, Avon Products, and Fidelity Investments—effortlessly receive timely, fresh, relevant articles delivered right to their desks by fax, groupware (such as Lotus Notes), online computer services, the Internet, or electronic mail.

When someone signs up for Individual's *First!* service, the company assigns an editorial manager to determine what sort of information the client wants. The editorial manager and the client reduce those requests to simple descriptions, such as articles about new uses of information technology in home health care or about new products developed by Japanese semiconductor companies. The editorial manager enters the requests into Individual's

SMART software system (for System for Manipulation and Retrieval of Text). Then SMART takes over. Every business day, the system searches 400 sources containing more than 12,000 articles for those pieces that will most likely fit the client's needs, and it delivers them by whatever method the client has chosen.

Every week, Individual asks a new client (by fax or computer) to rate each article as "not relevant," "somewhat relevant," or "very relevant." The responses are fed into the system, making SMART even smarter. In the first week of service, most customers find only 40% to 60% of the articles to be some-what or very relevant. By the fourth or fifth week, SMART has increased those ratings to a targeted 80% to 90%. Once it has achieved that level, Individual reduces the frequency of the ratings to once a month, which still enables it to keep abreast of customers' changing needs.

Individual also responds constantly to clients' requests for new sources and ways of receiving information. Sun Microsystems, for example, asked the company to place *First!* on its internal Internet server. Once Individual provided this service, it discovered that many other clients that also depended on the Internet for sending and sharing information wanted to receive the service in the same way. Such responsiveness is undoubtedly one reason why Individual, which has more than 30,000 users and more than 4,000 accounts, enjoys a customer-retention rate of 85% to 90%. But there is also another reason: because of the time and energy each client expends in teaching the company which articles are relevant and which are not, switching to a competitor would require the client to make that investment all over again.

FROM MASS PRODUCTION TO MASS CUSTOMIZATION

Although Individual uses information and interactive technology to its fullest, most managers fail to understand that variety is not the same thing as customization. Customization means manufacturing a product or delivering a service *in response* to a particular customer's needs, and mass customization means doing it in a cost-effective way. Mass customization calls for a customer-centered orientation in production and delivery processes, requiring the company to collaborate with individual customers to design each one's desired product or service, which is then constructed from a base of pre-engineered modules that can be assembled in myriad ways.

In contrast, product-centered mass production and mass marketing call for pushing options (and inventory) into distribution channels and hoping that each new option is embraced by enough customers to make its production worthwhile. It requires customers to hunt for the single product or service they want from among an ever growing array of alternatives.

Consider grocery stores. According to *New Products News*, the number of new products, including line extensions, introduced in grocery stores each year increased from less than 3,000 in 1980 to more than 10,000 in 1988 and more than 17,000 in 1993. And *Progressive Grocer* reports that the number of stock-keeping units in the average supermarket doubled to more than 30,000 between 1980 and 1994. The same trend can be seen in many service industries: witness the proliferation of affinity credit cards and the numerous options offered by telephone companies.

Companies are also deluging consumers with a wider variety of messages. And, of course, there is a greater array of media for carrying them: direct mail, telemarketing, special newspaper supplements, and a larger number of television channels, among others.

For example, the average newspaper weighs 55% more today than it did just ten years ago, mainly because of supplements designed to carry specially targeted advertising. The problem with such supplements is that they are distributed to every subscriber. Nongardeners still receive the gardening supplement, and people reading the paper before heading to the office still get the work-at-home supplement. So the supplements really aren't so special after all.

Mass marketers use information technology to define the most likely customers for the products they want to sell. For the most part, the information comes from simple transactional records (such as customer purchases and invoices) and public information (such as vehicle registrations, address-change forms, and census data) compiled by companies like R.L. Polk and Donnelley Marketing. From those data, the mass marketer generates a list of the most likely prospects and solicits them with offers or messages that the marketer has attempted to customize by guessing their tastes. By contrast, the one-to-one marketer conducts a dialogue with each customer—one at a time—and uses the increasingly more detailed feedback to find the best products or services for that customer. Although many companies are moving toward this model, few have fully implemented it yet or combined it with mass customization.

Take Hallmark Cards and American Greetings, the leaders of the variety-intensive greeting card industry. Both companies have installed electronic kiosks in stores and other public places to enable people to create their own greeting cards. Consumers can touch the screen of either company's kiosk, quickly select the type of card they need (for example, anniversary or birthday card), browse through a number of selections, and then modify them or compose their own wording to express exactly the right sentiment. The card is printed in a minute or so.

Both companies seem pleased with the performance of their mass customization businesses, but neither has fully exploited its potential. The graphics for the cards are all preset (so only the wording can be customized), and there is little organization (so browsing through the choices can be time consuming). The greatest weakness of the electronic kiosks, however, is the absence of a system for recording individual customers' preferences. Each time someone uses the system, he or she must start all over again.

If a greeting card company were to harness the full power of mass customization and one-to-one marketing, it would be able to remember the important occasions in your life and remind you to buy a card. It would make suggestions based on your past purchases. Its kiosk would display past selections, either to ensure that you don't commit the faux pas of sending the same card to the same person twice or to give you the option of sending the same funny card to another person—appropriately personalized, of course. Perhaps the company would mail your cards or ship them across the Internet for you so they would arrive at the appointed time. Maybe the company would be able to remind you to send a card, allow you to design it, and arrange for its delivery on your personal computer through an on-line service that would let you incorporate your own graphics or photographs. It might even find your design so good that it would ask your permission to add it to its inventory.

Certainly, not every customer would want to invest the time that such a relationship would require. Neither would every customer buy enough cards to make such a relationship worthwhile for the company. But the advantages to a greeting card company of establishing and cultivating a learning relationship with customers who buy cards frequently are immense. Because every card sold to those customers will be tailored precisely to their needs, the company will be able to charge them a premium and its profit margins will increase. And because the company will be equipped to ensure that the customer never forgets an occasion, it will sell more cards to that customer. The company's product development will become more effective because of the expanded ability to understand exactly who is buying what, when, and why—not to mention the ability to use new ideas that customers could provide.

But, most important of all, the company will retain more customers, especially the most valuable ones: frequent purchasers. The more customers teach the company about their individual tastes, celebration occasions, and card recipients (addresses, relationships, and so forth), the more reluctant they will be to repeat that process with another supplier. As long as the company fulfills its end of the bargain, a competitor should never be able to entice away its customers. The battle will be limited to attracting new ones.

WHEN ARE LEARNING
RELATIONSHIPS APPROPRIATE?

As compelling and powerful as the benefits of learning relationships are, this radically different business model cannot be applied in the same way by everyone. Companies such as home builders, real estate brokers, and appliance manufacturers—which do not interact frequently with end users—cannot learn enough to make a learning relationship with those customers work. But they might find it beneficial to develop such relationships with general contractors. Similarly, makers of products like paper clips, whose revenue or profit margin per customer is too low to justify building individual learning relationships with customers, might find it advantageous to cultivate learning relationships with office-supply chains, which interact directly with end users.

Even producers of commodities such as wheat or natural gas, which cannot be customized easily, and of commodity-like products bought mainly on the basis of price have much to gain from this approach. Learning relationships can enable such companies to design services that differentiate their offerings. This is the strategy that Bandag, which sells truck-tire retreads to more than 500 dealer-installers around the country, is pursuing.

Bandag's retreads are essentially a commodity because they are comparable in price and quality to those of competitors. To break out of the pack, Bandag is providing additional services. For example, it assists its dealers in filing and collecting on warranty claims from tire manufacturers and will soon begin offering comprehensive fleet-management services to its largest national accounts.

Bandag plans to embed computer chips in the rubber of newly retreaded tires to gauge each tire's pressure and temperature and to count its revolutions. That information will enable the company not only to tell each customer the optimal time to retread each tire (thus reducing downtime caused by blowouts) but also to help it improve its fleet's operations.

Because of the current high cost of building such capabilities, many manufacturers, service providers, and retailers may find, as Bandag did, that it pays to establish learning relationships only with their best customers. But as advances in information technology continue to drive down the cost of building learning relationships, they will make economic sense in many more businesses and for a wider spectrum of customers. Many types of industries are already ripe for revolution. They include the following.

Complex Products or Services

Most people do not want to work their way through hundreds or thousands of options, features, pricing structures, delivery methods, and networks to figure out which product or service is best for them. One solution is for companies to collaborate with customers in custom-designing the product, as Andersen Corporation, the window manufacturer based in Bayport, Minnesota, is doing. It resolved the information-overload problem for its customers (individual home owners and building contractors) by developing a multimedia system called the Window of Knowledge. A sales representative uses a workstation that features 50,000 possible window components to help customers design their own windows. The system automatically generates error-free quotations and manufacturing specifications, which can be saved for future use.

The resulting database of window configurations deepens Andersen's understanding of how its business is performing.

Big-Ticket Items

A company that succeeds in customizing all aspects of owning an expensive product or using a premium service stands to gain a competitive advantage over its rivals. Consider automobiles. A car buyer, over his or her lifetime, can generate hundreds of thousands of dollars' worth of business when financing, service, and referrals, as well as the original purchase, are taken into account. All together, they represent an enormous opportunity for companies that cater to customers' individual preferences.

The same opportunities apply to big-ticket commercial offerings, including machinery, information systems, outsourcing, and consulting. (See the box "How to Gain Customers Forever" at the end of the article.)

Digitizable Products and Services

Anything that can be digitized can be customized. If such products are purchased frequently, providing a discernible pattern of personal preferences, they may be ideally suited for one-to-one marketing as well. Obvious candidates include not only greeting cards but also software, periodicals, telecommunication services, and entertainment products such as movies, videos, games, and recorded music. Indeed, many companies in these businesses are working to develop learning relationships.

On-Line Services

Providers of on-line services already offer a broad spectrum of choices—including electronic shopping, special-interest forums, entertainment, news, and financial services—but few offer tailored convenience. Currently, the user must navigate through choice after choice. A competitor that learns a customer's wants and needs could navigate cyberspace on behalf of that customer and cull only the relevant choices.

Luxury and Specialty Products

Many businesses (such as apparel, perfume and cosmetics, athletic equipment, and fine wine) have customers with complex individual tastes. For example, people differ not only in their physical measurements but also in how they prefer their clothes to fit and look. Levi Strauss is capitalizing on these differences by mass-customizing blue jeans for women, using technology supplied by Custom Clothing Technology Corporation of Newton, Massachusetts. After a customer has her measurements taken in a store, she tries on a pair or two of jeans to determine her exact preference. The information is then sent to the factory for prompt production. Although Levi Strauss is currently limiting the program to one style of jeans, the approach offers the company tremendous opportunities for building learning relationships.

Retailing Services

In many industries, retailers have a big advantage over manufacturers in building learning relationships with end users, especially when customers want to touch, feel, and browse (clothing, shoes, and books) or when the product is immediately consumed (for example, in restaurants and bars). They also have the edge when individual customers do not buy a large amount of any one manufacturer's products (such as groceries and packaged goods). That is because the retailer is in a better position to see patterns in a customer's purchases and because it might be more expensive for the manufacturer to build learning relationships. Finally, many retailers offer consumers not products per se but service, and services can be mass-customized more readily than most products can. (See the box "How Peapod Is Customizing the Virtual Supermarket" at the end of the article)

VYING FOR THE END CUSTOMER

Retailers, insurance agents, distributors, interior decorators, building contractors, and others who deal face-to-face with the end customer can certainly make the case that they should be the ones who control the relationship with that customer. On the other hand, manufacturers and service providers have an advantage when a customer often buys the same type of product (toiletries, magazines, or office supplies); when products can be economically delivered to the home or office (personal computers, software, or services such as lawn care and plumbing); or when customers already value their relationship with the product or brand (as with premium Scotch, designer jeans, or luxury watches).

Obviously, those boundaries are permeable and constantly shifting: manufacturers and service providers can become retailers and vice versa. And advances in technology are making it increasingly easy for one member of the value chain to undermine another's natural advantages. Consider, for example, three basic reasons consumers go to retail stores: to obtain the information they need to make a purchasing decision, to pay for the product, and to take possession of it. Thanks to the same information-based technologies that make learning relationships possible, consumers increasingly will not have to visit stores for any of those reasons.

Today, consumers can get better information—information that is unbiased, comparative, accurate, and immediate— through on-line services, CD-ROM catalogs, and fax-response systems, and eventually they will be able to obtain it through interactive TV. As the continuing boom in catalog and home-TV shopping attests, consumers and organizations can buy goods and services over the phone and through dedicated on-line services as easily as, if not more easily than, in person, and security measures will almost certainly be in place soon that will make it possible to purchase products through the Internet. Finally, almost anything can be delivered direct to the home thanks to Federal Express, UPS, dedicated delivery services, and (for digitized products) fax and on-line services.

For retailers, the message is clear: if they want to maintain or increase their competitive advantage, they must begin establishing learning relationships with their best customers today. On the other hand, a manufacturer or a service company one or more links removed from the end user has a variety of options. It could build collaborative learning relationships with those occupying the next link, gaining knowledge about their wants, needs, and preferences over time, and mass-customizing products and services to meet their requirements. That is the approach ITT Hartford's Personal Lines business is taking with the independent agents who sell its automobile and home insurance. And it is also the direction in which Andersen—which realizes that individual home owners buy windows too infrequently to form a productive, long-term relationship with the company—is heading. Although Andersen plans to continue to mass-customize windows for consumers, it also intends to cultivate learning relationships with architects, home builders, and window distributors.

Another option for a manufacturer or a service company is to form tighter partnerships with retailers so that together they control the learning relationships with individual end customers. Such a partnership would require sharing information and knowledge (and maybe a common database), linking operations tightly so consumers' desires could be translated efficiently and quickly into tailored products and services, and possibly making joint investment and strategic decisions on how best to serve end customers over time. This option might make sense for companies such as automakers, which rely heavily on dealers to provide

the touch, feel, and test drive necessary for
consumers to make a buying decision.

HOW TO BUILD LEARNING RELATIONSHIPS

If managers decide that their company can
and should cultivate learning relationships
with customers, how do they go about it?
There are basically four components to think
about: an *information strategy* for initiating
dialogues with customers and remembering
their preferences; a *production/delivery
strategy* for fulfilling what the company
learns about individual customers; an
organizational strategy for managing both
customers and capabilities; and an

assessment strategy for evaluating performance.

The Information Strategy

Cultivating learning relationships depends on a company's ability to elicit and manage information about customers. The first step is to identify those individual customers with whom it pays to have a learning relationship. That is easy for businesses like hotels or airlines, whose customers make reservations in their own names and whose transactions and preferences are easy to track.

In industries whose customers are anonymous, such as retailing, a company may have to use one of two approaches to persuade them to identify and provide information

{ 36 }

about themselves: show them that it can serve them better if they do or give them something of value in return, such as a gift or a discount. For example, Waldenbooks offers a 10% discount on all purchases if customers identify themselves by becoming Preferred Readers. The program allows the company to track the purchases of those customers at any Waldenbooks store. Learning about customer preferences enables the bookseller to let a particular customer know when, for example, the next William Styron novel will be out or when an author whose work the customer has purchased will be in a local store, signing books.

Few companies will want to have such relationships with all customers. Waldenbooks' program, for example, is aimed at people who spend more than $100 a year at its stores. As a screening device, the company charges a $10 annual fee for Preferred Reader status.

As with any new program, it is often best to begin with a company's most valuable customers. When the company sees that the value of a learning relationship with them exceeds the costs, it can gradually expand the program to other customers.

Once a company has identified the customers with whom it wishes to have a learning relationship, there are a number of ways in which it can conduct a productive dialogue. A rapidly expanding array of interactive technologies—including electronic kiosks, on-line services, and database-driven mail—are making such dialogues easier and less costly. (See the box "How to Interact: A Sampler of Today's Technologies" at the end of the article.) Businesses that naturally involve personal contact with customers, either on the phone or in person, have golden opportunities to learn about them.

In conducting a dialogue with customers, it is important that the database "remember" not just preferences declared in past purchases but also the preferences that emerge from questions, complaints, suggestions, and actions.

The Ritz-Carlton hotel chain trains all its associates—from those on the front desk to those in maintenance and housekeeping—how to converse with customers and how to handle complaints immediately. In addition, it provides each associate with a "guest preference pad" for writing down every preference gleaned from conversations with and observations of customers. Every day, the company enters those preferences into a chainwide database that now contains profiles of nearly a half million patrons. Employees at any of the 28 Ritz-Carlton hotels worldwide can gain access to those profiles through the Covia travel-reservation system.

Say you stay at the Ritz-Carlton in Cancún, Mexico, call room service for dinner, and request an ice cube in your glass of white wine. Months later, when you stay at the Ritz-Carlton in Naples, Florida, and order a glass of white wine from room service, you will almost certainly be asked if you would like an ice cube in it. The same would be true if you asked for a window seat in a restaurant, a minibar with no liquor in your room, or a variety of other necessities or preferences that personalize your stay at the Ritz-Carlton.

By retaining such information, a company becomes better equipped to respond to suggestions, resolve complaints, and stay abreast of customers' changing needs. Many companies make the mistake of treating customers as if they were static entities rather than people whose preferences, lifestyles, and circumstances are constantly evolving and shifting.

Some managers may wonder whether customers will see requests for in-depth personal information as an invasion of privacy.

Most people don't mind divulging their shopping habits, measurements, and friends' names and addresses if they believe they're getting something of value in return. Consumers' fears also will be assuaged if a company states unequivocally that it will jealously guard personal information, which any company building learning relationships must do. Unlike mass marketers, who buy and sell customer data willy-nilly, companies seeking to build learning relationships realize that such information is a precious asset.

The Production/Delivery Strategy

Children can create an unlimited number of unique designs with Lego building blocks.

Service and manufacturing companies that
have successfully mass-customized employ
a similar approach: they create modules—
components or processes—that can be
assembled in a variety of ways to enable the
companies to tailor products or services
for specific customers at a relatively low
cost. (See B. Joseph Pine II, Bart Victor,
and Andrew C. Boynton, "Making Mass
Customization Work," HBR September–
October 1993.) Admittedly, there is more opportunity to adopt this approach in some
businesses than in others. For example, the
Ritz-Carlton is more of a customizer than a
mass customizer. If it could figure out how
to mass-customize its services, as Peapod
has done, it would be able to cater to the

preferences of more of its customers *and* increase its profits.

However, creating process or component modules is not enough. A company also needs a design tool that can take a customer's requirements and easily determine how to use its capabilities to fulfill them. Individual, Inc.'s SMART system and Andersen's Window of Knowledge system are examples of design tools that enable companies to be as effective as possible in ascertaining what customers need, as efficient as possible in production and delivery, and as effortless as possible in matching the two.

The Organizational Strategy

Traditional marketing organizations depend on product managers to push the product out the door, into the channels, and into customers' hands. Product managers are generally responsible for performing market research, specifying the requirements for a fairly standardized offering, and developing the marketing plan. And once the product is introduced, they are rewarded for selling as much of it as possible. While these techniques are ideally suited for mass marketing, they are ill suited for learning relationships in which the reverse is required: extracting a customer's wants and needs from a dialogue and creating the product or service that fulfills those requirements.

To build learning relationships, companies don't need product managers; they need *customer managers*. As the term implies, customer managers oversee the relationship with the customer. While they are responsible for a portfolio of customers with similar needs, they also are responsible for obtaining all the business possible from *each* customer, one at a time. To do this, customer managers must know their customers' preferences and be able to help them articulate their needs. They serve as gatekeepers within the company for all communication to and from each customer.

In addition, companies need *capability managers*, each of whom executes a distinct production or delivery process for fulfilling each customer's requirements. The head of each capability ensures that appropriate capacity exists and that the process can be executed reliably and efficiently.

Customer managers must know what capability managers can provide and must take the lead in determining when new capabilities may be required to meet customers' needs. For their part, capability managers must know what customer managers require and be able to figure out how to create it. For instance, when a Peapod customer informed his customer manager (a Membership Services representative) that he wanted to be able to order both ripe and unripe tomatoes, the company expanded the capabilities of its ordering software and created a new set of capability managers: produce specialists. These specialists have the skills and experience to squeeze tomatoes and thump melons, for example. Similarly, a customer manager at four year-old Individual asked the company's manager of information suppliers—the capability manager responsible for managing and acquiring new sources of information—to add the *New England Journal of Medicine* after learning that a client needed articles from the publication. Individual expands the number of its sources by 75 to 100 per year in this manner.

In contrast to the traditional product manager's role of finding customers for the company's products, the role of the customer manager is finding products for the company's customers. Often, a customer manager will learn of a need for some product or service component that the organization does not consider itself competent to produce or deliver. The capability manager might then arrange to obtain it from a strategic partner or a third-party vendor. For example, it would not pay for AT & T's computer hardware and software business, AT & T Global Information Solutions (formerly NCR), to write software for every conceivable customer need. When a customer-focused team (the unit's equivalent of customer managers) learns that a customer needs a particular application that is unavailable in-house, it often asks a capability-management team to acquire or license the software.

In all cases, however, the customer manager must be held accountable for satisfying the customer. At ITT Hartford's Personal

Lines business, every time a customer (an independent agent) makes a request, Personal Lines forms an instant team composed of people from whichever service modules (underwriting, claims payment, or servicing, for example) are needed to satisfy the request. But the customer manager is the one responsible for guaranteeing the promised customized service. He or she specifies the commitment to the agent at the beginning of each transaction, and a tracking system ensures that it is fulfilled.

The Assessment Strategy

Obviously, the value of a learning relationship to the company will vary from customer to customer. Some customers will be more willing than others to invest the time and effort. Those willing to participate are going to have a wide variety of demands or expectations, meaning that the company will have a varying ability to contribute to and profit from each relationship. Companies should therefore decide which potential learning relationships they will pursue.

The ideal way to approach this task is to think about a customer's lifetime value. Lifetime value is the sum of the future stream of profits and other benefits attributable to all purchases and transactions with an individual customer, discounted back to its present value. In their article "Zero Defections: Quality Comes to Services" (HBR September–October 1990), Frederick F. Reichheld and W. Earl Sasser, Jr., showed that the longer customers are retained by a company, the more profitable they become because of increased purchases, reduced operating costs, referrals, price premiums, and reduced customer acquisition costs. We would add one more element to the list: some customers will have higher lifetime values because the insights they provide to the company may result in new capabilities that can be applied to other customers. Although it is a daunting task, companies seeking to build learning relationships should therefore try to track as many of those elements as they can, using such information as transactional histories and customer feedback.

A company's *customer share*—its share of each customer's total patronage—is one of the most useful measures of success in building a learning relationship. To calculate customer share, a company must have some idea of what the customer is buying from the competition and what he or she might be willing to buy from the company. The best source of such information is the customer—another reason why dialogue is critical.

Yet another important performance measure is what we call *customer sacrifice*: the gap between what each customer truly wants and needs and what the company can supply. To understand individual customer sacrifice, companies building learning relationships must go beyond the aggregate customer-satisfaction figures that almost everyone collects today. That is why Peapod asks every customer at every shopping session how well it did on the last order. Understanding and tracking this gap will enable customer managers to demonstrate the need for new capabilities to deepen learning relationships and will give capability managers the information they need to decide how to expand or change their company's capabilities.

BECOMING A LEARNING BROKER

After a company becomes adept at cultivating learning relationships with its current customers, how might it expand?

Two choices are obvious: acquire new customers in the company's current markets or expand into new locations. But there is a third option: deliver *other* products to *current* customers and become a learning broker.

Because Peapod's customers already know how to interact with its on-line ordering system, the company could easily broker new product categories. For example, if Peapod could gain entry into a chain of home-improvement centers (meaning on-line access to the chain's computerized list of stock-keeping units and prices, and Peapod shoppers' access to the stores themselves), its knowledge about its customers and its customers' knowledge about it would immediately transfer to a whole new set of "virtual aisles." And once again, it would be Peapod—not the chains or the manufacturers that supply them—that would control the relationship with the customers. By arbitraging the information between customers and companies that supply products and services that they could potentially use, Peapod would have become a bona fide learning broker.

Discussions of what life will be like in the information-rich, interactive future often focus on personal electronic "agents" that will watch out for each individual's information and entertainment needs, sifting and sorting through the plethora of channels, messages, and offerings. But the dynamics of learning relationships are such that learning brokers can provide that service today in a wide variety of domains. They could provide individual customers with products and services beyond those that their companies have traditionally supplied. They also could advise their customers about other offerings and be on the lookout for items they might want.

One of the best examples of a company that already serves its customers in this fashion is the United Services Automobile Association. Seventy years ago, USAA began providing automobile insurance to military officers. It now supplies its customers—whom it still limits to current and former military officers and their families—with a wide variety of products and services. They include all types of insurance, full-service banking, investment brokerage, homes in retirement communities, and travel services. USAA also offers a buying service through which it purchases and delivers other companies' products, including automobiles, jewelry, major appliances, and consumer electronics. The relationship with the customer, however, remains the sole dominion of USAA.

USAA members have learned over the years that the company stands behind everything it sells and looks after their best interests. As more than one member has said, USAA could sell almost anything to them. More than nine of every ten active-duty and former military officers are members. And since opening up its services to members' adult children in the 1970s, USAA has been able to attract more than half of them, showing that learning relationships can even span generations.

The role of a learning broker clearly makes sense for distributors or agents such as Peapod and Individual, two companies that make no products themselves. Such companies are relatively free to go to whatever company can provide exactly what their customers want and need. Whether to take the path of a learning broker is a more complex decision for a manufacturer or a service company. But it is not out of the question. A company can become a hybrid like

USAA: it offers its members a wide variety of other companies' products, but, in its core business, financial services, it offers only its own products. While it may be difficult to imagine today, many companies could eventually decide that it pays to become a learning broker even of competitors' products. But adopting that strategy will make sense only if a company reaches the point where its knowledge of its customers and their trust in it yield a greater competitive advantage and greater profits than merely selling its own products can. When that happens, learning relationships with end customers will have become the company's primary competency.

How to Gain Customers Forever

Industrial companies that sell to other businesses can benefit just as much from learning relationships as companies that sell products or services to consumers. Consider the case of Ross Controls (formerly the Ross Operating Valve Company) of Troy, Michigan, a 70-year-old manufacturer of pneumatic valves and air-control systems. Through what it calls the ROSS/FLEX process, Ross learns about its customers' needs, collaborates with them to come up with designs precisely tailored to help them meet those needs, and quickly and efficiently makes the customized products. The process has enabled the medium-size manufacturer to forge learning relationships with such companies as General Motors, Knight Industries, Reynolds Aluminum, and Japan's Yamamura Glass.

For example, Ross is currently supplying GM's Metal Fabricating Division with 600 integrated-valve systems. Based on a common platform but individually customized for a particular stamping press, each integrated system performs better than the valves it is replacing at one-third the price.

Two elements have enabled Ross to transform itself from a sleepy industrial manufacturer into a dynamic organization that cultivates learning relationships with its customers.

A Desire to Listen to and Collaborate with Each Customer

This involves spending time on the phone, faxing ideas back and forth, and often visiting plants to see how pneumatic systems are to be used in the customer's manufacturing process. And once a system is designed to solve the customer's problem, Ross gets feedback from prototypes and encourages the customer to make continuous upgrades to its valve designs, yielding more precisely tailored designs over time. Ross then stores them in a library of design platforms, components, and computer instructions for its manufacturing equipment so it does not have to start from

scratch every time it works with a customer on a new project.

The Capability to Turn Complex Designs into Products

Through the effective use of computer-aided design (CAD) and computer numerically controlled (CNC) machines, Ross can electronically transmit tooling instructions directly from engineering workstations to multimillion-dollar production equipment, which can turn around new designs in as little as a day. But obviously, computer-aided-design and manufacturing equipment alone does not enable a company to mass-customize. Information about each customer's needs is also essential. To obtain such information, Ross created a crew of "integrators," each of whom is assigned to a given customer. The integrator talks with the customer, produces the valve designs, and determines the manufacturing specifications, including the instructions for the CNC machines. Using the CAD system, the integrator draws from the library's contents whenever possible to create a customized design and the computer coding required to make the product.

The ROSS/FLEX process has helped Ross boost the custom portion of its business from 5% to 20% of its revenues in the past four years. But the company is not yet satisfied with its ability to build learning relationships. It intends to add an interactive audio and video communications setup that will include a "what you see is what I see" CAD system so that an integrator and a customer do not have to be in the same place to collaborate on a design. And it plans to automate the access to its library so that integrators and customers—even on their own—can generate a wider range of designs and execute each one more quickly.

When Ross started down this road eight years ago, its primary goal was to gain customers for life by expanding the company's capabilities to meet each one's changing needs. It is clearly making a lot of progress. At a time when GM is reexamining virtually all its supplier relations, its Metal Fabricating Division won't go to any company but Ross for pneumatic valves and won't let its suppliers, either. Knight Industries, a supplier of ergonomic material-handling equipment, gives Ross 100% of its custom business and about 70% of its standard (catalog) business. When a competitor tried to woo Knight away, its president, James Zaguroli, Jr., responded, "Why would I switch to you? You're already five product generations behind where I am with Ross."

How Peapod Is Customizing the Virtual Supermarket

One company that is exploiting learning relationships in retailing services is Peapod, a grocery-shopping and delivery service based in Evanston, Illinois. Its customers—currently in Chicago and San Francisco—buy a software application for $29.95 that enables them to access Peapod's database through an online computer service. They then pay $4.95 per month for the service and a per-order charge of $5 plus 5% of the order amount. Peapod's back office is linked into the mainframe data-bases of the supermarkets at which it shops for its customers (Jewel in Chicago and Safe-way in San Francisco), allowing it to provide all the supermarkets' stock-keeping units and shelf prices electronically to its customers.

Rather than automating the trip to a retail store, as other on-line providers are doing, Peapod is using interactive technology to change the shopping experience altogether.

It lets each customer create the virtual super-market that best suits him or her. Using a personal computer, customers can shop in the way they prefer. They can request a list of items by category (snack foods), by item (potato chips), by brand (Frito-Lay), or even by what is on sale in the store on a given day. Within categories, they can choose to have the items arranged alphabetically by brand, by package size, by unit price, or even by nutritional value. Customers also can create and save for repeated use standard and special shopping lists (baby items, barbecue needs, and the like).

Peapod teaches its customers to shop so effectively in its virtual supermarket that most of them discover that—despite the company's rates—they *save* money because they use more coupons, do better comparison shopping, and buy fewer impulse items than they would if they shopped at a real supermarket. In addition, they save time and have more control over it because they can shop from home or work whenever they want.

Peapod has found that every interaction with a customer is an opportunity to learn. At the end of each shopping session, it asks the customer, "How did we do on the last order?" Peapod gets feedback on 35% of orders; most companies consider a 10% response rate to customer-satisfaction surveys to be good. And more than 80% of Peapod's customers have responded at one time or another. The feedback has prompted the company to institute a variety of changes and options, including providing nutritional information, making deliveries within a half-hour window (for an additional $4.95) rather than the usual 90-minute window, accepting detailed requests (such as three ripe and three unripe tomatoes), and delivering alcoholic beverages.

Peapod views delivery as another opportunity to learn about customers' preferences. It asks its deliverers to find out where customers would like the groceries left when they're not at home and anything else that will enhance the relationship. They fill out an "interaction record" for every delivery to track those preferences (as well as entering basic service metrics, such as the time of the delivery).

Even with the rates it charges, Peapod has to be efficient and effective to make money in what is a low-margin business. That is why it mass-customizes all shopping and delivery processes. Each order is filled by a generalist, who shops the aisles of the store, and as-needed specialists, who provide the produce, meats, deli, seafood, and bakery items to the generalist. The generalist pays for the groceries, often at special Peapod counters in the back of the store. The order is then taken to a holding area in the supermarket or in a trailer, where the appropriate items are kept cold or frozen until the deliverer picks up a set of orders and takes them to the customers. At each stage—ordering, shopping, holding, and delivery—the processes are modularized to provide personalized service at a relatively low cost.

If a customer has a problem, he or she can call Membership Services, and a service representative will try to resolve the matter. Peapod treats each call as yet another opportunity to learn (and remember) each customer's preferences and to figure out what the company can do to improve service for customers as a whole. For example, service representatives found that some customers were receiving five bags of grapefruits when they really wanted only five grapefruits. In response, Peapod now routinely asks customers to confirm orders in which quantities might be confused.

Peapod's results stand as a testament to the power of learning relationships. The four-year-old service, which has 7,500 customers and revenues of about $15 million, has a customer-retention rate of more than 80%. And the service accounts for an average of 15% of the sales volume of the 12 Jewel and Safeway stores where Peapod shops for its customers.

How to Interact: A Sampler of Today's Technologies

Interactive media that allow marketers to send specific messages to specific consumers and to conduct a dialogue with actual and potential customers already exist. One is the Internet, which now boasts more than 15 million users. Using it simply to prospect for customers remains problematic owing to the hostility of many users to commercial advertising on the Internet. But many companies have found the Internet to be a good way to obtain information from or about customers through bulletin boards, direct connections, and company-specific information services.

Other on-line services, such as those provided by Prodigy, America Online, and Compuserve, are much more advanced than the Internet in providing a full-fledged, structured medium through which customers and companies can interact. And several company-specific on-line services, such as grocery deliverer Peapod's, have proved useful for facilitating dialogues with customers.

Electronic kiosks have a wide variety of applications for interacting directly with customers. Some are purely informational—like those that provide directions to local spots from a hotel lobby. Others dispense coupons or gift certificates. And an increasing number are being used to dispense mass-customized products, including greeting cards, business cards, and sheet music.

A variety of interactive telephone services exists already. Seattle-based FreeFone Information Network offers one on the West Coast that enables marketers to find consumers willing to participate in a dialogue. When people sign up for the service, they fill out a questionnaire that is used to determine which advertiser's message is sent to which person. Each time a consumer makes a personal call and listens to a sponsored message while waiting for the call to connect, FreeFone credits the

household account a nickel. The household
gets a dime if the consumer requests more
information, a coupon, or a telephone connection to the advertiser. Companies that advertise through FreeFone, including TicketMaster,
the U.S. Postal Service, NBC, and the National
Association of Female Executives, can learn a
great deal about each household. But
FreeFone will not divulge a caller's identity to
an advertiser unless the caller chooses to
reveal it.

Cash-back telephone coupons provide a
similar way for companies and consumers to
learn about each other over the phone. These
services, offered by such companies as
Chicago-based Scherers Communications,
are essentially reverse 900 numbers. For

example, a car manufacturer might credit someone $5 for watching a videotape touting some particular models and calling in with the personal identification number contained on the tape.

Fax response is being used by many business-to-business organizations and a small but growing number of consumer-goods manufacturers to give customers up-to-the-minute price quotations and product options. Fax response provides the marketer with the telephone-number identity of the individual who requested the information, which can be linked with transactional data as well as with mailing information.

R.R. Donnelley & Sons' selective binding technology, which enables printers to put

different pages in different editions of a given
publication, has made it possible for publish-
ers to mass-customize periodicals. *Farm
Journal*, for example, assembles information
on individual subscribers—how many acres of
what particular crops they have planted, how
many head of cattle they own, and so on—and
then uses Donnelley's technology to tailor the
editorial content and the advertising of each
edition for the particular subscriber.

ABOUT THESE AUTHORS

B. Joseph Pine II is cofounder of Strategic Horizons in Aurora, Ohio.

Don Peppers and *Martha Rogers* are founders of the Peppers & Rogers Group, a consultancy headquartered in Norwalk, Connecticut, specializing in customer relationships. Rogers is also an adjunct professor at Duke University's Fuqua School of Business.

*Experience Economy: Work Is Theatre &
Every Business a Stage*
with James H. Gilmore

*Markets of One: Creating Customer-Unique
Value through Mass Customization*
with James H. Gilmore

*Mass Customization: The New Frontier in
Business Competition*

Don Peppers
Harvard Business Review Article
"*Is Your Company Ready for One-to-One
Marketing?*"
with Martha Rogers and Bob Dorf

Martha Rogers

Harvard Business Review Article

"*Is Your Company Ready for One-to-One Marketing?*"

with Don Peppers and Bob Dorf

The most important management ideas all in one place.

We hope you enjoyed this book from *Harvard Business Review*. For the best ideas HBR has to offer turn to HBR's 10 Must Reads Boxed Set. From books on leadership and strategy to managing yourself and others, this 6-book collection delivers articles on the most essential business topics to help you succeed.

HBR's 10 Must Reads Series

The definitive collection of ideas and best practices on our most sought-after topics from the best minds in business.

- Change Management
- Collaboration
- Communication
- Emotional Intelligence
- Innovation
- Leadership
- Making Smart Decisions

- Managing Across Cultures
- Managing People
- Managing Yourself
- Strategic Marketing
- Strategy
- Teams
- The Essentials

hbr.org/mustreads

MARKETING MYOPIA

HARVARD BUSINESS REVIEW
CLASSICS

MARKETING MYOPIA

Theodore Levitt

Harvard Business Review Press
Boston, Massachusetts

Library of Congress Cataloging-in-Publication Data
Levitt, Theodore, 1925-2006.
  Marketing myopia / Theodore Levitt.
    p. cm. – (Harvard business review classics)
  ISBN 978-1-4221-2601-1
1. Marketing. 2. Customer relations. I. Title.
HF5415.L4832 2008
658.8–dc22

                              2008005791

THE
HARVARD BUSINESS REVIEW
CLASSICS SERIES

Since 1922, *Harvard Business Review* has been a leading source of breakthrough ideas in management practice—many of which still speak to and influence us today. The HBR Classics series now offers you the opportunity to make these seminal pieces a part of your permanent management library. Each volume contains a groundbreaking idea that has shaped best practices and inspired countless managers around the world—and will change how you think about the business world today.

MARKETING
MYOPIA

Every major industry was once a growth industry. But some that are now riding a wave of growth enthusiasm are very much in the shadow of decline. Others that are thought of as seasoned growth industries have actually stopped growing. In every case, the reason growth is threatened, slowed, or stopped is *not* because the market is saturated. It is because there has been a failure of management.

FATEFUL PURPOSES

The failure is at the top. The executives responsible for it, in the last analysis, are those who deal with broad aims and policies. Thus:

- The railroads did not stop growing because the need for passenger and freight transportation declined. That grew. The railroads are in trouble today not because that need was filled by others (cars, trucks, airplanes, and even telephones) but because it was *not* filled by the railroads themselves. They let others take customers away from them because they assumed themselves to be in the railroad business rather than in the transportation business. The reason they defined their industry incorrectly was that they were railroad oriented instead of transportation oriented; they were product oriented instead of customer oriented.

- Hollywood barely escaped being totally ravished by television. Actually, all the established film companies went through drastic reorganizations. Some simply disappeared. All of them got into trouble not because of TV's inroads but because of their own myopia. As with the railroads, Hollywood defined its business incorrectly. It thought it was in the movie business when it was actually in the entertainment business. "Movies" implied a specific, limited product. This produced a fatuous contentment that from the beginning led producers to view TV as a threat. Hollywood scorned and rejected TV when it should have welcomed it as an opportunity—an opportunity to expand the entertainment business.

Today, TV is a bigger business than the old narrowly defined movie business ever was. Had Hollywood been customer oriented (providing entertainment) rather than product oriented (making movies), would it have gone through the fiscal purgatory that it did? I doubt it. What ultimately saved Hollywood and accounted for its resurgence was the wave of new young writers, producers, and directors whose previous successes in television had decimated the old movie companies and toppled the big movie moguls.

There are other, less obvious examples of industries that have been and are now endangering their futures by improperly defining their purposes. I shall discuss some of them in detail later and analyze the kind of policies that lead to trouble. Right now, it may help to show what a thoroughly customer-oriented management can do to keep a growth industry growing, even after the obvious opportunities have been exhausted, and here there are two examples that have been around for a long time. They are nylon and glass—specifically, E.I. du Pont de Nemours and Company and Corning Glass Works.

Both companies have great technical competence. Their product orientation is unquestioned. But this alone does not explain their success. After all, who was more pridefully product oriented and product conscious than the erstwhile New England textile companies that have been so thoroughly massacred? The DuPonts and the Cornings have succeeded not primarily because of their product or research orientation but because they have been thoroughly customer oriented also. It is constant watchfulness for opportunities to apply their technical know-how to the creation of customer-satisfying uses that accounts for their prodigious output of successful new products. Without a very sophisticated eye on the customer, most of their new products might have been wrong, their sales methods useless.

Aluminum has also continued to be a growth industry, thanks to the efforts of two wartime-created companies that deliberately set about inventing new customer-satisfying uses. Without Kaiser Aluminum & Chemical Corporation and Reynolds Metals Company, the total demand for aluminum today would be vastly less.

Error of Analysis

Some may argue that it is foolish to set the railroads off against aluminum or the movies off against glass. Are not aluminum and glass naturally so versatile that the industries are bound to have more growth opportunities than the railroads and the movies? This view commits precisely the error I have been talking about. It defines an industry or a product or a cluster of know-how so narrowly as to guarantee its premature senescence. When we mention "railroads," we should make sure we mean "transportation." As transporters, the railroads still have a good chance for very considerable growth. They are not limited to the railroad business as such (though in my opinion, rail transportation is potentially a much stronger transportation medium than is generally believed).

What the railroads lack is not opportunity but some of the managerial imaginativeness and audacity that made them great. Even an amateur like Jacques Barzun can see what is lacking when he says, "I grieve to see the most advanced physical and social organization of the last century go down in shabby disgrace for lack of the same comprehensive imagination that built it up. [What is lacking is] the will of the companies to survive and to satisfy the public by inventiveness and skill."[1]

SHADOW OF OBSOLESCENCE

It is impossible to mention a single major industry that did not at one time qualify for the magic appellation of "growth industry." In each case, the industry's assumed strength lay in the apparently unchallenged superiority of its product. There appeared to be no effective substitute for it. It was itself a runaway substitute for the product it so triumphantly replaced. Yet one after another of these celebrated industries has come under a shadow. Let us look briefly at a few more of them, this time taking examples that have so far received a little less attention.

Dry Cleaning

This was once a growth industry with lavish prospects. In an age of wool garments, imagine being finally able to get them clean safely and easily. The boom was on. Yet here we are 30 years after the boom started, and the industry is in trouble. Where has the competition come from? From a better way of cleaning? No. It has come from synthetic fibers and chemical additives that have cut the need for dry cleaning. But this is only the beginning. Lurking in the wings and ready to make chemical dry cleaning totally obsolete is that powerful magician, ultrasonics.

Electric Utilities

This is another one of those supposedly "no substitute" products that has been enthroned on a pedestal of invincible growth. When the incandescent lamp came along, kerosene lights were finished. Later, the waterwheel and the steam engine were cut to ribbons by the flexibility, reliability, simplicity, and just plain easy availability of electric motors. The prosperity of electric utilities continues to wax extravagant as the home is converted into a museum of electric gadgetry. How can anybody miss by investing in utilities, with no competition, nothing but growth ahead?

But a second look is not quite so comforting. A score of nonutility companies are well advanced toward developing a powerful chemical fuel cell, which could sit in some hidden closet of every home silently ticking off electric power. The electric lines that vulgarize so many neighborhoods would be eliminated. So would the endless demolition of streets and service interruptions during storms. Also on the horizon is solar energy, again pioneered by nonutility companies.

Who says that the utilities have no competition? They may be natural monopolies now,

but tomorrow they may be natural deaths.
To avoid this prospect, they too will have to
develop fuel cells, solar energy, and other
power sources. To survive, they themselves
will have to plot the obsolescence of what
now produces their livelihood.

Grocery Stores

Many people find it hard to realize that
there ever was a thriving establishment
known as the "corner store." The supermarket took over with a powerful effectiveness.
Yet the big food chains of the 1930s narrowly escaped being completely wiped out
by the aggressive expansion of independent
supermarkets. The first genuine supermarket was opened in 1930, in Jamaica, Long

Island. By 1933, supermarkets were thriving in California, Ohio, Pennsylvania, and elsewhere. Yet the established chains pompously ignored them. When they chose to notice them, it was with such derisive descriptions as "cheapy," "horse-and-buggy," "cracker-barrel storekeeping," and "unethical opportunists."

The executive of one big chain announced at the time that he found it "hard to believe that people will drive for miles to shop for foods and sacrifice the personal service chains have perfected and to which [the consumer] is accustomed."[2] As late as 1936, the National Wholesale Grocers convention and the New Jersey Retail Grocers Association said there was nothing to fear. They said that the supers' narrow appeal to the price buyer limited the size of their market. They had to draw from miles around. When imitators came, there would be wholesale liquidations as volume fell. The high sales of the supers were said to be partly due to their novelty. People wanted convenient neighborhood grocers. If the neighborhood stores would "cooperate with their suppliers, pay attention to their costs, and improve their service," they would be able to weather the competition until it blew over.[3]

It never blew over. The chains discovered that survival required going into the supermarket business. This meant the wholesale destruction of their huge investments in corner store sites and in established distribution and merchandising methods. The companies with "the courage of their convictions" resolutely stuck to the corner store philosophy. They kept their pride but lost their shirts.

A Self-Deceiving Cycle

But memories are short. For example, it is hard for people who today confidently hail the twin messiahs of electronics and chemicals to see how things could possibly go wrong with these galloping industries. They probably also cannot see how a reasonably sensible businessperson could have been as myopic as the famous Boston millionaire who early in the twentieth century unintentionally sentenced his heirs to poverty by stipulating that his entire estate be forever invested exclusively in electric streetcar securities. His posthumous declaration, "There will always be a big demand for efficient urban transportation," is no consolation to his heirs, who sustain life by pumping gasoline at automobile filling stations.

Yet, in a casual survey I took among a group of intelligent business executives, nearly half agreed that it would be hard to hurt their heirs by tying their estates forever to the electronics industry. When I then confronted them with the Boston streetcar example, they chorused unanimously, "That's different!" But is it? Is not the basic situation identical?

In truth, *there is no such thing as a growth industry*, I believe. There are only companies organized and operated to create and capitalize on growth opportunities. Industries that assume themselves to be riding some automatic growth escalator invariably descend into stagnation. The history of every dead and dying "growth" industry shows a self-deceiving cycle of bountiful expansion and undetected decay. There are four conditions that usually guarantee this cycle:

1. The belief that growth is assured by an expanding and more affluent population;

2. The belief that there is no competitive substitute for the industry's major product;

3. Too much faith in mass production and in the advantages of rapidly declining unit costs as output rises;

4. Preoccupation with a product that lends itself to carefully controlled scientific experimentation, improvement, and manufacturing cost reduction.

I should like now to examine each of these conditions in some detail. To build my case as boldly as possible, I shall illustrate the points with reference to three industries: petroleum, automobiles, and electronics. I'll focus on petroleum in particular, because it spans more years and more vicissitudes. Not only do these three industries have excellent reputations with the general public and also enjoy the confidence of sophisticated investors, but their managements have become known for progressive thinking in areas like financial control, product research, and management training. If obsolescence can cripple even these industries, it can happen anywhere.

POPULATION MYTH

The belief that profits are assured by an expanding and more affluent population is dear to the heart of every industry. It takes the edge off the apprehensions everybody understandably feels about the future. If consumers are multiplying and also buying more of your product or service, you can face the future with considerably more comfort than if the market were shrinking. An expanding market keeps the manufacturer from having to think very hard or imaginatively. If thinking is an intellectual response to a problem, then the absence of a problem leads to the absence of thinking. If your product has an automatically expanding market, then you will not give much thought to how to expand it.

One of the most interesting examples of this is provided by the petroleum industry. Probably our oldest growth industry, it has an enviable record. While there are some current concerns about its growth rate, the industry itself tends to be optimistic.

But I believe it can be demonstrated that it is undergoing a fundamental yet typical change. It is not only ceasing to be a growth industry but may actually be a declining one, relative to other businesses. Although there is widespread unawareness of this fact, it is conceivable that in time, the oil industry may find itself in much the same position of retrospective glory that the railroads are now in. Despite its pioneering work in developing and applying the present-value method of investment evaluation, in employee relations, and in working with developing countries, the petroleum business is a distressing example of how complacency and wrongheadedness can stubbornly convert opportunity into near disaster.

One of the characteristics of this and other industries that have believed very strongly in the beneficial consequences of an expanding population, while at the same time having a generic product for which there has appeared to be no competitive substitute, is that the individual companies have sought to outdo their competitors by improving on what they are already doing. This makes sense, of course, if one assumes that sales are tied to the country's population strings, because the customer can compare products only on a feature-by-feature basis. I believe it is significant, for example, that not since John D. Rockefeller sent free kerosene lamps to China has the oil industry done anything really outstanding to create a demand for its product. Not even in product improvement has it showered itself with eminence. The greatest single improvement—the development of tetraethyl lead—came from outside the industry, specifically from General Motors and DuPont. The big contributions made by the industry itself are confined to the technology of oil exploration, oil production, and oil refining.

Asking for Trouble

In other words, the petroleum industry's efforts have focused on improving the *efficiency* of getting and making its product, not really on improving the generic product or its marketing. Moreover, its chief product has continually been defined in the narrowest possible terms—namely, gasoline, not energy, fuel, or transportation. This attitude has helped assure that:

- Major improvements in gasoline quality tend not to originate in the oil industry. The development of superior alternative fuels also comes from outside the oil industry, as will be shown later.

• Major innovations in automobile fuel marketing come from small, new oil companies that are not primarily preoccupied with production or refining. These are the companies that have been responsible for the rapidly expanding multipump gasoline stations, with their successful emphasis on large and clean layouts, rapid and efficient driveway service, and quality gasoline at low prices.

Thus, the oil industry is asking for trouble from outsiders. Sooner or later, in this land of hungry investors and entrepreneurs, a threat is sure to come. The possibility of this will become more apparent when we turn to the next dangerous belief of many managements. For the sake of continuity, because this second belief is tied closely to the first, I shall continue with the same example.

The Idea of Indispensability

The petroleum industry is pretty much convinced that there is no competitive substitute for its major product, gasoline—or, if there is, that it will continue to be a derivative of crude oil, such as diesel fuel or kerosene jet fuel.

There is a lot of automatic wishful thinking in this assumption. The trouble is that most refining companies own huge amounts of crude oil reserves. These have value only if there is a market for products into which oil can be converted. Hence the tenacious belief in the continuing competitive superiority of automobile fuels made from crude oil.

This idea persists despite all historic evidence against it. The evidence not only shows that oil has never been a superior product for any purpose for very long but also that the oil industry has never really been a growth industry. Rather, it has been a succession of different businesses that have gone through the usual historic cycles of growth, maturity, and decay. The industry's overall survival is owed to a series of miraculous escapes from total obsolescence, of last-minute and unexpected reprieves from total disaster reminiscent of the perils of Pauline.

The Perils of Petroleum

To illustrate, I shall sketch in only the main episodes. First, crude oil was largely a patent medicine. But even before that fad ran out, demand was greatly expanded by the use of oil in kerosene lamps. The prospect of lighting the world's lamps gave rise to an extravagant promise of growth. The prospects were similar to those the industry now holds for gasoline in other parts of the world. It can hardly wait for the underdeveloped nations to get a car in every garage.

In the days of the kerosene lamp, the oil companies competed with each other and

against gaslight by trying to improve the illuminating characteristics of kerosene. Then
suddenly the impossible happened. Edison
invented a light that was totally nondepen-
dent on crude oil. Had it not been for the
growing use of kerosene in space heaters,
the incandescent lamp would have completely finished oil as a growth industry at
that time. Oil would have been good for little
else than axle grease.

Then disaster and reprieve struck again.
Two great innovations occurred, neither
originating in the oil industry. First, the successful development of coal-burning domestic central-heating systems made the space
heater obsolete. While the industry reeled,
along came its most magnificent boost yet:

the internal combustion engine, also invented by outsiders. Then, when the prodigious expansion for gasoline finally began to level off in the 1920s, along came the miraculous escape of the central oil heater. Once again, the escape was provided by an outsider's invention and development. And when that market weakened, wartime demand for aviation fuel came to the rescue. After the war, the expansion of civilian aviation, the dieselization of railroads, and the explosive demand for cars and trucks kept the industry's growth in high gear.

Meanwhile, centralized oil heating—whose boom potential had only recently been proclaimed—ran into severe competition from natural gas. While the oil companies themselves owned the gas that now competed with their oil, the industry did not originate the natural gas revolution, nor has it to this day greatly profited from its gas ownership. The gas revolution was made by newly formed transmission companies that marketed the product with an aggressive ardor. They started a magnificent new industry, first against the advice and then against the resistance of the oil companies.

By all the logic of the situation, the oil companies themselves should have made the gas revolution. They not only owned the gas, they also were the only people experienced in handling, scrubbing, and using it and the only people experienced in pipeline technology and transmission. They also understood heating problems. But, partly because they knew that natural gas would compete with their own sale of heating oil, the oil companies pooh-poohed the potential of gas. The revolution was finally started by oil pipeline executives who, unable to persuade their own companies to go into gas, quit and organized the spectacularly successful gas transmission companies. Even after their success became painfully evident to the oil companies, the latter did not go into gas transmission. The multibillion-dollar business that should have been theirs went to others. As in the past, the industry was blinded by its narrow preoccupation with a specific product and the value of its reserves. It paid little or no attention to its customers' basic needs and preferences.

The postwar years have not witnessed any change. Immediately after World War II, the oil industry was greatly encouraged about its future by the rapid increase in demand for its traditional line of products. In 1950, most companies projected annual rates of domestic expansion of around 6% through at least 1975. Though the ratio of crude oil reserves to demand in the free world was about 20 to 1, with 10 to 1 being usually considered a reasonable working ratio in the United States, booming demand sent oil explorers searching for more without sufficient regard to what the future really promised. In 1952, they "hit" in the Middle East; the ratio skyrocketed to 42 to 1. If gross additions to reserves continue at the average rate of the past five years (37 billion barrels annually),

then by 1970, the reserve ratio will be up to
45 to 1. This abundance of oil has weakened
crude and product prices all over the world.

An Uncertain Future

Management cannot find much consolation today in the rapidly expanding petrochemical industry, another oil-using idea
that did not originate in the leading firms.
The total U.S. production of petrochemicals
is equivalent to about 2% (by volume) of
the demand for all petroleum products. Although the petrochemical industry is now
expected to grow by about 10% per year, this
will not offset other drains on the growth of
crude oil consumption. Furthermore, while
petrochemical products are many and grow-

ing, it is important to remember that there are nonpetroleum sources of the basic raw material, such as coal. Besides, a lot of plastics can be produced with relatively little oil. A 50,000-barrel-per-day oil refinery is now considered the absolute minimum size for efficiency. But a 5,000-barrel-per-day chemical plant is a giant operation.

Oil has never been a continuously strong growth industry. It has grown by fits and starts, always miraculously saved by innovations and developments not of its own making. The reason it has not grown in a smooth progression is that each time it thought it had a superior product safe from the possibility of competitive substitutes, the product turned out to be inferior and notoriously subject to obsolescence. Until now, gasoline (for motor fuel, anyhow) has escaped this fate. But, as we shall see later, it too may be on its last legs.

The point of all this is that there is no guarantee against product obsolescence. If a company's own research does not make a product obsolete, another's will. Unless an industry is especially lucky, as oil has been until now, it can easily go down in a sea of red figures—just as the railroads have, as the buggy whip manufacturers have, as the corner grocery chains have, as most of the big movie companies have, and, indeed, as many other industries have.

The best way for a firm to be lucky is to make its own luck. That requires knowing what makes a business successful. One of the greatest enemies of this knowledge is mass production.

Production Pressures

Mass production industries are impelled by a great drive to produce all they can. The prospect of steeply declining unit costs as output rises is more than most companies can usually resist. The profit possibilities look spectacular. All effort focuses on production. The result is that marketing gets neglected.

John Kenneth Galbraith contends that just the opposite occurs.[4] Output is so prodigious that all effort concentrates on trying to get rid of it. He says this accounts for singing

commercials, the desecration of the countryside with advertising signs, and other waste-
ful and vulgar practices. Galbraith has a
finger on something real, but he misses the
strategic point. Mass production does indeed generate great pressure to "move" the
product. But what usually gets emphasized
is selling, not marketing. Marketing, a more
sophisticated and complex process, gets
ignored.

The difference between marketing and
selling is more than semantic. Selling focuses on the needs of the seller, marketing
on the needs of the buyer. Selling is preoccupied with the seller's need to convert the
product into cash, marketing with the idea
of satisfying the needs of the customer by

means of the product and the whole cluster of things associated with creating, delivering, and, finally, consuming it.

In some industries, the enticements of full mass production have been so powerful that top management in effect has told the sales department, "You get rid of it; we'll worry about profits." By contrast, a truly marketing-minded firm tries to create value-satisfying goods and services that consumers will want to buy. What it offers for sale includes not only the generic product or service but also how it is made available to the customer, in what form, when, under what conditions, and at what terms of trade. Most important, what it offers for sale is determined not by the seller but by the buyer. The seller takes cues from the buyer in such a way that the product becomes a consequence of the marketing effort, not vice versa.

A Lag in Detroit

This may sound like an elementary rule of business, but that does not keep it from being violated wholesale. It is certainly more violated than honored. Take the automobile industry.

Here mass production is most famous, most honored, and has the greatest impact on the entire society. The industry has hitched its fortune to the relentless requirements of the annual model change, a policy that makes customer orientation an especially urgent necessity. Consequently, the auto companies annually spend millions of dollars on consumer research. But the fact that the new compact cars are selling so well in their first year indicates that Detroit's vast researches have for a long time failed to reveal what customers really wanted. Detroit was not convinced that people wanted anything different from what they had been getting until it lost millions of customers to other small-car manufacturers.

How could this unbelievable lag behind consumer wants have been perpetuated for so long? Why did not research reveal consumer preferences before consumers' buying decisions themselves revealed the facts? Is that not what consumer research is for— to find out before the fact what is going to happen? The answer is that Detroit never really researched customers' wants. It only researched their preferences between the kinds of things it had already decided to offer them. For Detroit is mainly product oriented, not customer oriented. To the extent that the customer is recognized as having needs that the manufacturer should try to satisfy, Detroit usually acts as if the job can be done entirely by product changes. Occasionally, attention gets paid to financing, too, but that is done more in order to sell than to enable the customer to buy.

As for taking care of other customer needs, there is not enough being done to write about. The areas of the greatest unsatisfied needs are ignored or, at best, get stepchild attention. These are at the point of sale and

on the matter of automotive repair and maintenance. Detroit views these problem areas as
being of secondary importance. That is under-
scored by the fact that the retailing and servicing ends of this industry are neither owned and
operated nor controlled by the manufacturers.
Once the car is produced, things are pretty
much in the dealer's inadequate hands. Illus-
trative of Detroit's arms-length attitude is
the fact that, while servicing holds enormous
sales-stimulating, profit-building opportunities, only 57 of Chevrolet's 7,000 dealers
provide night maintenance service.

Motorists repeatedly express their dissatisfaction with servicing and their apprehensions about buying cars under the present
selling setup. The anxieties and problems
they encounter during the auto buying and

maintenance processes are probably more intense and widespread today than many years ago. Yet the automobile companies do not seem to listen to or take their cues from the anguished consumer. If they do listen, it must be through the filter of their own preoccupation with production. The marketing effort is still viewed as a necessary consequence of the product—not vice versa, as it should be. That is the legacy of mass production, with its parochial view that profit resides essentially in low-cost full production.

What Ford Put First

The profit lure of mass production obviously has a place in the plans and strategy of business management, but it must always *fol-*

low hard thinking about the customer. This is one of the most important lessons we can learn from the contradictory behavior of Henry Ford. In a sense, Ford was both the most brilliant and the most senseless marketer in American history. He was senseless because he refused to give the customer anything but a black car. He was brilliant because he fashioned a production system designed to fit market needs. We habitually celebrate him for the wrong reason: for his production genius. His real genius was marketing. We think he was able to cut his selling price and therefore sell millions of $500 cars because his invention of the assembly line had reduced the costs. Actually, he invented the assembly line because he had concluded that at $500 he could sell millions of cars. Mass production was the *result*, not the cause, of his low prices.

Ford emphasized this point repeatedly, but a nation of production-oriented business managers refuses to hear the great lesson he taught. Here is his operating philosophy as he expressed it succinctly:

> Our policy is to reduce the price, extend the operations, and improve the article. You will notice that the reduction of price comes first. We have never considered any costs as fixed. Therefore we first reduce the price to the point where we believe more sales will result. Then we go ahead and try to make the prices. We do not bother about the costs. The new price forces the costs down. The more usual way is to take the costs and then determine the price; and although that method may be scien-

tific in the narrow sense, it is not scientific in the broad sense, because what earthly use is it to know the cost if it tells you that you cannot manufacture at a price at which the article can be sold? But more to the point is the fact that, although one may calculate what a cost is, and of course all of our costs are carefully calculated, no one knows what a cost ought to be. One of the ways of discovering . . . is to name a price so low as to force everybody in the place to the highest point of efficiency. The low price makes everybody dig for profits. We make more discoveries concerning manufacturing and selling under this forced method than by any method of leisurely investigation. [5]

Product Provincialism

The tantalizing profit possibilities of low unit production costs may be the most seriously self-deceiving attitude that can afflict a company, particularly a "growth" company, where an apparently assured expansion of demand already tends to undermine a proper concern for the importance of marketing and the customer.

The usual result of this narrow preoccupation with so-called concrete matters is that instead of growing, the industry declines. It usually means that the product fails to adapt to the constantly changing patterns of consumer needs and tastes, to new and modified marketing institutions and practices, or to product developments in competing or complementary industries. The industry has its eyes so firmly on its own specific product that it does not see how it is being made obsolete.

The classic example of this is the buggy whip industry. No amount of product improvement could stave off its death sentence. But had the industry defined itself as being in the transportation business rather than in the buggy whip business, it might have survived. It would have done what survival always entails—that is, change. Even if it had only defined its business as providing a stimulant or catalyst to an energy source, it might have survived by becoming a manufacturer of, say, fan belts or air cleaners.

What may someday be a still more classic example is, again, the oil industry. Having let others steal marvelous opportunities from it (including natural gas, as already mentioned; missile fuels; and jet engine lubricants), one would expect it to have taken steps never to let that happen again. But this is not the case. We are now seeing extraordinary new developments in fuel systems specifically designed to power automobiles. Not only are these developments concentrated in firms outside the petroleum industry, but petroleum is almost systematically ignoring them, securely content in its wedded bliss to oil. It is the story of the kerosene lamp versus the incandescent lamp all over again. Oil is trying to improve hydrocarbon fuels rather than develop *any* fuels best suited to the needs of their users, whether or not made in different ways and with different raw materials from oil.

Here are some things that nonpetroleum companies are working on:

- More than a dozen such firms now have advanced working models of energy systems which, when perfected, will replace the internal combustion engine and eliminate the demand for gasoline. The superior merit of each of these systems is their elimination of frequent, time-consuming, and irritating refueling stops. Most of these systems are fuel cells designed to create electrical energy directly from chemicals without combustion. Most of them use chemicals that are not derived from oil—generally, hydrogen and oxygen.

- Several other companies have advanced models of electric storage batteries designed to power automobiles. One of these is an aircraft producer that is working jointly with several electric utility companies. The latter hope to use off-peak generating capacity to supply overnight plug-in battery regeneration. Another company, also using the battery approach, is a medium-sized electronics firm with extensive small-battery experience that it developed in connection with its work on hearing aids. It is collaborating with an automobile manufacturer. Recent improvements arising from the need for high-powered miniature power storage plants in rockets have put us within reach of a relatively small battery capable of withstanding great overloads or surges of power. Germanium diode applications and batteries using sintered plate and nickel cadmium techniques promise to make a revolution in our energy sources.

- Solar energy conversion systems are also getting increasing attention. One usually cautious Detroit auto executive recently ventured that solar-powered cars might be common by 1980.

As for the oil companies, they are more or less "watching developments," as one research director put it to me. A few are doing a bit of research on fuel cells, but this research is almost always confined to developing cells powered by hydrocarbon chemicals. None of them is enthusiastically researching fuel cells, batteries, or solar power plants. None of them is spending a fraction as much on research in these profoundly important areas as it is on the usual run-of-the-mill things like reducing combustion chamber deposits in gasoline engines. One major integrated petroleum company recently took a tentative look at the fuel cell and concluded that although "the companies actively working on it indicate a belief in ultimate success . . . the timing and magnitude of its impact are too remote to warrant recognition in our forecasts."

One might, of course, ask, Why should the oil companies do anything different?

Would not chemical fuel cells, batteries, or solar energy kill the present product lines? The answer is that they would indeed, and that is precisely the reason for the oil firms' having to develop these power units before their competitors do, so they will not be companies without an industry.

Management might be more likely to do what is needed for its own preservation if it thought of itself as being in the energy business. But even that will not be enough if it persists in imprisoning itself in the narrow grip of its tight product orientation. It has to think of itself as taking care of customer needs, not finding, refining, or even selling oil. Once it genuinely thinks of its business as taking care of people's transportation needs, nothing can stop it from creating its own extravagantly profitable growth.

Creative Destruction

Since words are cheap and deeds are dear, it may be appropriate to indicate what this kind of thinking involves and leads to. Let us start at the beginning: the customer. It can be shown that motorists strongly dislike the bother, delay, and experience of buying gasoline. People actually do not buy gasoline. They cannot see it, taste it, feel it, appreciate it, or really test it. What they buy is the right to continue driving their cars. The gas station is like a tax collector to whom people are compelled to pay a periodic toll as the price of using their cars. This makes the

gas station a basically unpopular institution.
It can never be made popular or pleasant,
only less unpopular, less unpleasant.

Reducing its unpopularity completely
means eliminating it. Nobody likes a tax collector, not even a pleasantly cheerful one.
Nobody likes to interrupt a trip to buy a
phantom product, not even from a handsome Adonis or a seductive Venus. Hence,
companies that are working on exotic fuel
substitutes that will eliminate the need for
frequent refueling are heading directly
into the outstretched arms of the irritated
motorist. They are riding a wave of inevitability, not because they are creating
something that is technologically superior
or more sophisticated but because they are

satisfying a powerful customer need. They are also eliminating noxious odors and air pollution.

Once the petroleum companies recognize the customer-satisfying logic of what another power system can do, they will see that they have no more choice about working on an efficient, long-lasting fuel (or some way of delivering present fuels without bothering the motorist) than the big food chains had a choice about going into the supermarket business or the vacuum tube companies had a choice about making semiconductors. For their own good, the oil firms will have to destroy their own highly profitable assets. No amount of wishful thinking can save them from the necessity of engaging in this form of "creative destruction."

I phrase the need as strongly as this because I think management must make quite an effort to break itself loose from conventional ways. It is all too easy in this day and age for a company or industry to let its sense of purpose become dominated by the economies of full production and to develop a dangerously lopsided product orientation. In short, if management lets itself drift, it invariably drifts in the direction of thinking of itself as producing goods and services, not customer satisfactions. While it probably will not descend to the depths of telling its salespeople, "You get rid of it; we'll worry about profits," it can, without knowing it, be practicing precisely that formula for withering decay. The historic fate of one growth industry after another has been its suicidal product provincialism.

DANGERS OF R&D

Another big danger to a firm's continued growth arises when top management is wholly transfixed by the profit possibilities of technical research and development. To illustrate, I shall turn first to a new industry—electronics—and then return once more to the oil companies. By comparing a fresh example with a familiar one, I hope to emphasize the prevalence and insidiousness of a hazardous way of thinking.

Marketing Shortchanged

In the case of electronics, the greatest danger that faces the glamorous new companies in this field is not that they do not pay enough attention to research and development but that they pay too much attention to it. And the fact that the fastest-growing electronics firms owe their eminence to their heavy emphasis on technical research is completely beside the point. They have vaulted to affluence on a sudden crest of unusually strong general receptiveness to new technical ideas. Also, their success has been shaped in the virtually guaranteed market of military subsidies and by military orders that in many cases actually preceded the existence of facilities to make the products. Their expansion has, in other words, been almost totally devoid of marketing effort.

Thus, they are growing up under conditions that come dangerously close to creating the illusion that a superior product will sell itself. It is not surprising that, having created a successful company by making a superior product, management continues to be oriented toward the product rather than the people who consume it. It develops the philosophy that continued growth is a matter of continued product innovation and improvement.

A number of other factors tend to strengthen and sustain this belief:

1. Because electronic products are highly complex and sophisticated, managements become top-heavy with engineers and scientists. This creates a selective bias in favor of research and production at the expense of market-

ing. The organization tends to view itself as making things rather than as satisfying customer needs. Marketing gets treated as a residual activity, "something else" that must be done once the vital job of product creation and production is completed.

2. To this bias in favor of product research, development, and production is added the bias in favor of dealing with controllable variables. Engineers and scientists are at home in the world of concrete things like machines, test tubes, production lines, and even balance sheets. The abstractions to which they feel kindly are those that are testable or manipulatable in the

laboratory or, if not testable, then functional, such as Euclid's axioms. In short, the managements of the new glamour-growth companies tend to favor business activities that lend themselves to careful study, experimentation, and control—the hard, practical realities of the lab, the shop, and the books.

What gets shortchanged are the realities of the *market*. Consumers are unpredictable, varied, fickle, stupid, shortsighted, stubborn, and generally bothersome. This is not what the engineer managers say, but deep down in their consciousness, it is what they believe. And this accounts for their concentration on what they know and what they can control—namely, product research, engineering, and production. The emphasis on production becomes particularly attractive when the product can be made at declining unit costs. There is no more inviting way of making money than by running the plant full blast.

The top-heavy science-engineering-production orientation of so many electronics companies works reasonably well today because they are pushing into new frontiers in which the armed services have pioneered virtually assured markets. The companies are in the felicitous position of having to fill, not find, markets, of not having to discover what the customer needs and wants but of having the customer voluntarily come forward with specific new product demands. If a team of consultants had been assigned specifically to design a business situation calculated to prevent the emergence and development of a customer-oriented marketing viewpoint, it could not have produced anything better than the conditions just described.

Stepchild Treatment

The oil industry is a stunning example of how science, technology, and mass production can divert an entire group of companies from their main task. To the extent the consumer is studied at all (which is not much), the focus is forever on getting information that is designed to help the oil companies improve what they are now doing. They try to discover more convincing advertising themes, more effective sales promotional drives, what the market shares of the various companies are, what people like or dislike about service station dealers and oil companies, and so forth. Nobody seems as interested in probing deeply into the basic human needs that the industry might be trying to satisfy as in probing into the basic properties of the raw material that the companies work with in trying to deliver customer satisfactions.

Basic questions about customers and markets seldom get asked. The latter occupy a stepchild status. They are recognized as existing, as having to be taken care of, but not worth very much real thought or dedicated attention. No oil company gets as excited about the customers in its own backyard as about the oil in the Sahara Desert. Nothing illustrates better the neglect of marketing than its treatment in the industry press.

The centennial issue of the *American Petroleum Institute Quarterly*, published in 1959 to celebrate the discovery of oil in Titusville, Pennsylvania, contained 21 feature articles proclaiming the industry's greatness. Only one of these talked about its achievements in marketing, and that was only a pictorial record of how service station architecture has changed. The issue also contained a special section on "New Horizons," which was devoted to showing the magnificent role oil would play in America's future. Every reference was ebulliently optimistic, never implying once that oil might have some hard competition. Even the reference to atomic energy was a cheerful catalog of how oil would help make atomic energy a success. There was not a single apprehension that the oil industry's affluence might be threatened or a suggestion that one "new horizon" might include new and better ways of serving oil's present customers.

But the most revealing example of the stepchild treatment that marketing gets is still another special series of short articles on "The Revolutionary Potential of Electronics." Under that heading, this list of articles appeared in the table of contents:

- "In the Search for Oil"

- "In Production Operations"

- "In Refinery Processes"

- "In Pipeline Operations"

Significantly, every one of the industry's major functional areas is listed, *except* marketing. Why? Either it is believed that electronics holds no revolutionary potential for petroleum marketing (which is palpably wrong), or the editors forgot to discuss marketing (which is more likely and illustrates its stepchild status).

The order in which the four functional areas are listed also betrays the alienation of the oil industry from the consumer. The industry is implicitly defined as beginning with the search for oil and ending with its distribution from the refinery. But the truth is, it seems to me, that the industry begins with the needs of the customer for its products. From that primal position its definition moves steadily back stream to areas of progressively lesser importance until it finally comes to rest at the search for oil.

The Beginning and End

The view that an industry is a customer-satisfying process, not a goods-producing process, is vital for all businesspeople to understand. An industry begins with the customer and his or her needs, not with a patent, a raw material, or a selling skill.

Given the customer's needs, the industry develops backwards, first concerning itself with the physical *delivery* of customer satisfactions. Then it moves back further to *creating* the things by which these satisfactions are in part achieved. How these materials are created is a matter of indifference to the customer, hence the particular form of manufacturing, processing, or what have you cannot be considered as a vital aspect of the industry. Finally, the industry moves back still further to *finding* the raw materials necessary for making its products.

The irony of some industries oriented toward technical research and development is that the scientists who occupy the high executive positions are totally unscientific when it comes to defining their companies' overall needs and purposes. They violate the first two rules of the scientific method: being aware of and defining their companies' problems and then developing testable hypotheses about solving them. They are scientific only about the convenient things, such as laboratory and product experiments.

The customer (and the satisfaction of his or her deepest needs) is not considered to be "the problem"—not because there is any certain belief that no such problem exists but because an organizational lifetime has conditioned management to look in the opposite direction. Marketing is a stepchild.

I do not mean that selling is ignored. Far from it. But selling, again, is not marketing.

As already pointed out, selling concerns itself with the tricks and techniques of getting people to exchange their cash for your product. It is not concerned with the values that the exchange is all about. And it does not, as marketing invariably does, view the entire business process as consisting of a tightly integrated effort to discover, create, arouse, and satisfy customer needs. The customer is somebody "out there" who, with proper cunning, can be separated from his or her loose change.

Actually, not even selling gets much attention in some technologically minded firms. Because there is a virtually guaranteed market for the abundant flow of their new products, they do not actually know what a real market is. It is as if they lived in a planned economy, moving their products routinely from factory to retail outlet. Their successful concentration on products tends to convince them of the soundness of what they have been doing, and they fail to see the gathering clouds over the market.

Less than 75 years ago, American railroads enjoyed a fierce loyalty among astute Wall Streeters. European monarchs invested in them heavily. Eternal wealth was thought to be the benediction for anybody who could scrape together a few thousand dollars to put into rail stocks. No other form of transportation could compete with the railroads in speed, flexibility, durability, economy, and growth potentials.

As Jacques Barzun put it, "By the turn of the century it was an institution, an image of man, a tradition, a code of honor, a source of poetry, a nursery of boyhood desires, a sublimest of toys, and the most solemn machine—next to the funeral hearse—that marks the epochs in man's life."[6]

Even after the advent of automobiles, trucks, and airplanes, the railroad tycoons remained imperturbably self-confident. If you had told them 60 years ago that in 30 years they would be flat on their backs, broke, and pleading for government subsidies, they would have thought you totally demented. Such a future was simply not considered possible. It was not even a discussable subject, or an askable question, or a matter that any sane person would consider worth speculating about. Yet a lot of "insane" notions now have matter-of-fact acceptance—for example, the idea of 100-ton tubes of metal moving smoothly through the air 20,000 feet above the earth, loaded with 100 sane and solid citizens casually drinking martinis—and they have dealt cruel blows to the railroads.

What specifically must other companies do to avoid this fate? What does customer orientation involve? These questions have in part been answered by the preceding examples and analysis. It would take another article to show in detail what is required for specific industries. In any case, it should be obvious that building an effective customer-oriented company involves far more than good intentions or promotional tricks; it involves profound matters of human organization and leadership. For the present, let me merely suggest what appear to be some general requirements.

The Visceral Feel of Greatness

Obviously, the company has to do what survival demands. It has to adapt to the requirements of the market, and it has to do it sooner rather than later. But mere survival is a so-so aspiration. Anybody can survive in some way or other, even the skid row bum. The trick is to survive gallantly, to feel the surging impulse of commercial mastery: not just to experience the sweet smell of success but to have the visceral feel of entrepreneurial greatness.

No organization can achieve greatness without a vigorous leader who is driven onward by a pulsating *will to succeed*. A leader has to have a vision of grandeur, a vision that can produce eager followers in vast numbers. In business, the followers are the customers.

In order to produce these customers, the entire corporation must be viewed as a customer-creating and customer-satisfying organism. Management must think of itself not as producing products but as providing customer-creating value satisfactions. It must push this idea (and everything it means and requires) into every nook and cranny of the organization. It has to do this continuously and with the kind of flair that excites and stimulates the people in it. Otherwise, the company will be merely a series of pigeon-holed parts, with no consolidating sense of purpose or direction.

In short, the organization must learn to think of itself not as producing goods or services but as *buying customers*, as doing the things that will make people *want* to do business with it. And the chief executive has the inescapable responsibility for creating this environment, this viewpoint, this attitude, this aspiration. The chief executive must set the company's style, its direction, and its goals. This means knowing precisely where he or she wants to go and making sure the whole organization is enthusiastically aware of where that is. This is a first requisite of leadership, for *unless a leader knows where he is going, any road will take him there.*

If any road is okay, the chief executive might as well pack his attaché case and go fishing. If an organization does not know or care where it is going, it does not need to advertise that fact with a ceremonial figurehead. Everybody will notice it soon enough.

NOTES

1. Jacques Barzun, "Trains and the Mind of Man," *Holiday*, February 1960.

2. For more details, see M.M. Zimmerman, *The Super Market: A Revolution in Distribution* (McGraw-Hill, 1955).

3. Ibid., pp. 45–47.

4. John Kenneth Galbraith, *The Affluent Society* (Houghton Mifflin, 1958).

5. Henry Ford, *My Life and Work* (Doubleday, 1923).

6. Barzun, "Trains and the Mind of Man."

ABOUT THE AUTHOR

Theodore Levitt was the Edward W. Carter Professor of Business Administration, Emeritus, at Harvard Business School. He was formerly a chairman of the Marketing Area at HBS and the Editor of *Harvard Business Review.* He is the author or coauthor of seven books and numerous award-winning articles on economic, political, management, and marketing subjects.

ALSO BY THIS AUTHOR

Harvard Business Press Books

Ted Levitt on Marketing

***Harvard Business Review* Articles**

"The Globalization of Markets"

"Exploit the Product Life Cycle"

"Marketing Success Through Differentiation—
of Anything"

"Production-Line Approach to Service"

"Marketing Intangible Products and Product Intangibles"

"After the Sale Is Over . . ."

"Creativity Is Not Enough"

"The Industrialization of Service"

Article Summary

The Idea in Brief

What business are you *really* in? A seemingly obvious question—but one we should all ask *before* demand for our companies' products or services dwindles.

The railroads failed to ask this same question—and stopped growing. Why? Not because people no longer needed transportation. And not because other innovations (cars, airplanes) filled transportation needs. Rather, railroads stopped growing because *railroads* didn't move to fill those needs. Their executives incorrectly thought that they were in the railroad business, not the transportation business. They viewed themselves as providing a product instead of serving customers. Too many other industries make the same mistake—putting themselves at risk of obsolescence.

How to ensure continued growth for your company? Concentrate on meeting customers' needs rather than selling products. Chemical powerhouse DuPont kept a close eye on its customers' most pressing concerns—and deployed its technical know-how to create an ever-expanding array of products that appealed to customers and continuously enlarged its market. If DuPont had merely found more uses for its flagship invention, nylon, it might not be around today.

The Idea in Practice

We put our businesses at risk of obsolescence when we accept any of the following myths:

Myth 1: An ever-expanding and more affluent population will ensure our growth. When markets are expanding, we often assume we don't have to think imaginatively about our businesses. Instead, we seek to outdo rivals simply by improving on what we're already doing. The consequence: We increase the efficiency of *making* our products, rather than boosting the *value* those products deliver to customers.

Myth 2: There is no competitive substitute for our industry's major product. Believing that our products have no rivals makes our companies vulnerable to dramatic innovations from outside our industries—often by smaller, newer companies that are focusing on customer needs rather than the products themselves.

Myth 3: We can protect ourselves through mass production. Few of us can resist the prospect of the increased profits that come with steeply declining unit costs. But focusing on mass production emphasizes our *company's* needs—when we should be emphasizing our *customers'*.

Myth 4: Technical research and development will ensure our growth. When R&D produces breakthrough products, we may be tempted to organize our companies around the technology rather than the consumer. Instead, we should remain focused on satisfying customer needs.

The most important management ideas all in one place.

We hope you enjoyed this book from *Harvard Business Review*. For the best ideas HBR has to offer turn to HBR's 10 Must Reads Boxed Set. From books on leadership and strategy to managing yourself and others, this 6-book collection delivers articles on the most essential business topics to help you succeed.

HBR's 10 Must Reads Series

The definitive collection of ideas and best practices on our most sought-after topics from the best minds in business.

- Change Management
- Collaboration
- Communication
- Emotional Intelligence
- Innovation
- Leadership
- Making Smart Decisions

- Managing Across Cultures
- Managing People
- Managing Yourself
- Strategic Marketing
- Strategy
- Teams
- The Essentials

hbr.org/mustreads

Buy for your team, clients, or event.
Visit hbr.org/bulksales for quantity discount rates.